MW00343582

MEDIEVAL CRUELTY

CHANGING
PERCEPTIONS,
LATE ANTIQUITY
TO THE EARLY
MODERN PERIOD

MEDIEVAL
CRUELTY

DANIEL BARAZ

Cornell University Press
Ithaca and London

Copyright © 2003 by Cornell University

All rights reserved. Except for brief quotations in a review, this book, or parts thereof, must not be reproduced in any form without permission in writing from the publisher. For information, address Cornell University Press, Sage House, 512 East State Street, Ithaca, New York 14850.

First published 2003 by Cornell University Press

Printed in the United States of America

Library of Congress Cataloging-in-Publication Data

Baraz, Daniel.
  Medieval cruelty : changing perceptions, late antiquity to the early modern period / Daniel Baraz.
        p. cm. -- (Conjunctions of religion & power in the medieval past)
Includes bibliographical references and index.
  ISBN 0-8014-3817-9 (cloth : alk. paper)
  1. Cruelty--History. 2. Civilization, Medieval. I. Title. II. Series.
  BJ1535.C7 B37 2003
  179'.09'02--dc21

                                                    2002154698

Cornell University Press strives to use environmentally responsible suppliers and materials to the fullest extent possible in the publishing of its books. Such materials include vegetable-based, low-VOC inks and acid-free papers that are recycled, totally chlorine-free, or partly composed of nonwood fibers. For further information, visit our website at www.cornellpress.cornell.edu.

Cloth printing   10 9 8 7 6 5 4 3 2 1

In memory of my father

CONTENTS

ACKNOWLEDGMENTS

I came to this project in a very roundabout way, for my first days as an undergraduate had little to do with either medieval history or with cruelty. During my first semester at Hebrew University, I majored in physics and computer science before switching to the humanities. I moved gradually from a literary to a historical focus, and by the time of my graduate studies, I had settled on medieval history. Even then, it was a while before I defined the contours of this project.

Many people influenced—directly and indirectly—my choices in the course of this long journey. Both my parents were deeply imbued in the classical humanistic tradition and spoke almost all European languages. My father was a true Renaissance man, who was equally comfortable with philosophy, literature, and intellectual history, but specialized in Renaissance French literature. His influence on my intellectual development cannot be overstated, and his untimely death in 1984, just before I started my undergraduate studies, freed me perhaps from the need to rebel against my humanistic tendencies.

Among my teachers at Hebrew University, it was Benjamin Kedar, my advisor, who introduced me to the field of medieval studies. His inductive, Socratic teaching method helped me discover my own interest. My work with him sparked my interest in comparative history, and it was he who raised the problem of "medieval cruelty" by referring me to Lucien Febvre's passionate article pleading for the writing of a "history of cruelty" among other "histories of sensibility." The result is less positivistic than Febvre had hoped for. It is also less empirical than Kedar thought it should be, but it is more so than I expected when I embarked on this project.

Many thanks are due to Patrick Geary for his comments as a reader of my dissertation on medieval perceptions of cruelty and for the suggestions he made during my stay as a visiting scholar at the Center for Medieval and Renaissance Studies at the University of California, Los Angeles. His initially intimidating advice—to change the focus and organizing principles and completely rewrite the manuscript—is in retrospect the best advice I received in forging the overall structure of the present book.

A great debt is owed also to Barbara Rosenwein. Her clear overall vision of the project, coupled with detailed, sometimes page-by-page comments, was the driving force behind the writing of the present version. Paul Freedman's insightful comments helped me rethink a central issue in my book: the construct of the "other" and its relation to cruelty. Ed Peters's original outlook on the subject of cruelty, which he shared with me during our conversations at the University of Pennsylvania, was indispensable to me in working out some of the finer points of my arguments. John Ackerman, director of Cornell University Press, read the whole manuscript, and his advice and encouragement were essential to the writing of the present version.

I benefited from the advice and interest of many people in the course of the project. My conversations with Sarah Stroumsa and Guy Stroumsa were extremely helpful in the initial stage of my research when I tried to chart the specific aspects of this vast topic that I would address. Esther Cohen read most of the initial dissertation manuscript and made invaluable comments and suggestions. The comparative analysis of Western and Islamic accounts of the Mongols, in many respects the center of this book, would not have been written without the guidance and support of the late Hava Lazarus-Yafeh, a great scholar of Islamic civilization and a friend. Reuven Amitai commented on my analysis of the Arabic sources dealing with the Mongols and shared with me his vast knowledge on the subject. Oren Falk served as my devil's advocate, pointing to the parts of my argument that seemed to him problematic or in need of further elaboration.

My wife Sonia Roccas, a social psychologist, and my childhood friend Amir Alexander, a historian of early modern science, provided the Archimedean point for this work. I subjected them to the cruelty of reading various drafts of this book, and their advice kept me from deviating into arcane arguments targeted at a handful of medievalists.

This work would not have been possible without the generous help of two institutions: the UCLA Center for Medieval and Renaissance Studies and the Penn Humanities Forum. I wrote the first draft of the manuscript during my stay as a visiting scholar at UCLA from 1998 to 1999. The finishing touches were added during my stay at Penn between 2000 and 2002, first as a Mellon postdoctoral fellow and later as a visiting scholar.

I consulted many other people on specific problems that I encountered in the course of my work: Natalie Davis, Susan Einbinder, Sidney Griffith, Maryanne Horowitz, Henry A. Kelly, Ora Limor, Elena Lourie, Michael Maas, William Miller, Aviezer Ravitzky, Boaz Shoshan, and Israel Y. Yuval. I am grateful for their interest and advice. Finally, I wish to thank Erica Nelson, my production editor, whose invaluable comments and patience made this a much better book.

ABBREVIATIONS

AASS	*Acta Sanctorum*
CCCM	*Corpus Christianorum Continuatio Mediaevalis*
CCSL	*Corpus Christianorum Series Latina*
CSEL	*Corpus Scriptorum Ecclesiasticorum Latinorum*
MGH AA	*Monumenta Germaniae historica. Auctores Antiquissimi*
MGH SS	*Monumenta Germaniae historica. Scriptores*
MGH SSRM	*Monumenta Germaniae historica. Scriptores Rerum Merovingicarum*
Musurillo	Musurillo, Herbert. *The Acts of the Christian Martyrs.* Oxford, 1979[1972].
PL	*Patrologia Latina*
RHC HOcc.	*Recueil des historiens des croisades. Historiens occidentaux*
RHC HOr.	*Recueil des historiens des croisades. Historiens orientaux*
RHGF	*Recueil des historiens des Gaules et de la France*
RS	*Rolls Series*
SBO	*Sancti Bernardi Opera*, ed. Jean Leclercq. Rome, 1957–1977.

MEDIEVAL CRUELTY

INTRODUCTION

In the winter of 1210, the crusaders advancing against the Albigensians captured the castle of Bram. The chronicler Peter of
Vaux-de-Cernay, who took part in this crusade, describes the fate
of its defenders: "As to the defenders of this place, more than a hundred, they
gouged out their eyes, and cut their noses, sparing one of them a single eye, so
that as a mockery of our enemies, he will lead all the others to [the castle of]
Cabaret."[1] Peter follows this description with a eulogy of Simon of Monfort,
the leader of the army who ordered the mutilation: Simon did not take pleasure in acts of cruelty or mutilation and did not enjoy the suffering of other
people; quite to the contrary, claims Peter, he was the most gentle of men.[2]

Accounts like Peter's, in which violent acts are presented without moral
censure, have been the building blocks of the image of the Middle Ages as a
"cruel period"—that is, a time when cruelty was a major aspect of everyday
life. This image—part of the anti-Catholic polemics of the Reformation—survived to the twentieth century in the writings of such scholars as Johan Huizinga and Norbert Elias. The latter, relying to a considerable degree on the
chronicle of Peter of Vaux-de-Cernay, concluded that "outbursts of cruelty did
not exclude one from social life. They were not outlawed. The pleasure in killing and torturing others was great, and it was a socially permitted pleasure. To
a certain extent, the social structure even pushed its members in this direction,
making it seem necessary and practically advantageous to behave in this way."[3]

This image of medieval civilization stands in marked contrast to another:
the image of Western medieval society as the Christian society par excel-

1. Petrus Vallium Sarnaii Monachus, *Hystoria Albigensis* 142, ed. Pascal Guébin and
Ernest Lyon (Paris, 1930), 1:148. All translations in the book are the author's own, unless
otherwise noted.
2. Hoc autem fecit fieri comes, non quia placeret ei tallis detruncatio membrorum
illata ... nunquam enim delectabatur nobilis comes aliqua crudelitate vel cruciatibus alie-
nis; omnium siquidem mitissimus erat (Petrus, *Hystoria Albigensis* 142, 1:148).
3. Norbert Elias, *The Civilizing Process*, trans. Edmund Jephcott (New York, 1978
[1939]), 194; Johan Huizinga, *The Autumn of the Middle Ages*, trans. Rodney J. Payton and
Ulrich Mammitzsch (Chicago, 1996[1924]).

lence. Indeed, this is much the way medieval society perceived itself, as a Christian society by definition opposed to any kind of violence. It is an image grounded in the words of Jesus himself: "All who take the sword shall perish by the sword."[4]

Attempting to decide which of these two images is more valid is all but pointless. The view that depicts the Middle Ages as a "cruel period" is unsustainable, but so for that matter is its direct opposite. This is not to say that the ideology of nonviolence was merely an empty rhetorical cover for a society in which cruelty and violence were the social norm. But neither was this ideology the sole guiding force of medieval society, and severe violence was indeed common in some places and in some periods.[5]

One problem that is immediately apparent in attempts to characterize an era is that modern notions of cruelty, or the lack thereof, are imposed on a remote historical period.[6] In addition, the characterization of a period as cruel is based on the mistaken assumption that cruelty is an objective category. Burning heretics at the stake seems cruel to our modern Western sensibilities, but the American prison system may seem equally cruel to observers from another culture. The debate as to whether the death penalty is a "cruel and unusual punishment" underscores the nature of the subjective concept. The manipulation of the issue of cruelty by both sides in the controversy over abortion shows that perceptions of cruelty are not only subjective but also shaped to a considerable degree by cultural factors.[7]

An individual's standpoint—as victim or perpetrator—in relation to a given act also influences his view of its cruelty. Jerome pointed to the rela-

4. Omnes enim qui acceperint gladium gladio peribunt (Matt. 26:52). Of relevance to this question are the essays in the first part of *The Final Argument: The Imprint of Violence on Society in Medieval and Early Modern Europe*, eds. Donald J. Kagay and L. J. Andrew Villalon (Rochester, N.Y., 1998). See also the remarks of Petit de Julleville on the reaction of medieval people to theatrical violence, cited in Jody Enders, *The Medieval Theater of Cruelty: Rhetoric, Memory, Violence* (Ithaca, 1999), 233.

5. On the contradiction between an ideology of nonviolence and actual violence, see the sociologic study of Buddhist violence against the Tamils in Sri Lanka, in Stanley J. Tambiah, *Buddhism Betrayed* (Chicago, 1992).

6. See Lucien P. Febvre, "La sensibilité et l'histoire: comment reconstituer la vie affective d'autrefois," *Annales d'histoire sociale* 3 (1941): 5–20; Febvre's plea for writing a "history of cruelty" was an important factor in leading me to investigate the subject.

7. For "pro-life" positions see Ohio Right to Life, *Abortion: Questions & Answers*. http://www.ohiolife.org/qa/qa26.htm (accessed 5/1/02); Al Lemmo, *War on the Unborn*, 1996. http://www.mich.com/~buffalo/alwar.html (accessed 5/1/02). For "pro-choice" positions see American Civil Liberties Union, *Colorado Prisoners Seek Abortion Rights*. http://www.aclu.org/news/wo82996a.html (accessed 5/1/02); National Abortion and Reproductive Rights Action League, *NARAL Names The Grinches Who Stole Choice*, 12/21/95. http://www.naral.org/publications/press/95dec/grinch2.html (accessed 5/1/02).

tivity of the concept in the fifth century, writing that "he who kills cruel [people] is not cruel . . . but the robber hanging from the gibbet thinks the judge cruel."[8] Thus one must bear in mind the role played by the individual who characterizes another as cruel and the interplay between his actual role and the role he may wish to project.

Returning to Peter of Vaux-de-Cernay, we see that he provides an apologia to justify the actions he has described. Yet there would be no need to vindicate such events—or their perpetrators—unless one suspected that others *would* interpret them as cruel. Consequently, even if we categorize these actions as objectively cruel, how do we square the traditional image of "the cruel Middle Ages" with Peter's determination to defend and justify these events before his audience?

My main objective in this book is to trace the treatment of cruelty as a cultural issue from late antiquity to the early modern period. Cultural references to cruelty vary considerably—both in their frequency and in their content—over this period. Thus, cruelty is an important issue in pagan late antiquity and ceases to be so with the transition to Christianity. This relative obscurity continues until the central Middle Ages, when the issue crops up in a variety of sources—philosophical texts, chronicles, and hagiography. Interest in the subject continues thereafter and reaches a peak in the sixteenth century.

Treatments of the subject also vary considerably. Thus, medieval and early modern philosophical discussions deal with different aspects of what their writers perceived as cruelty. The changes are most evident, however, in the analysis of the basic components of the concept, such as the types of cruelty attributed to the "other," which in the period treated here includes primarily such external invaders as the Vandals, Muslims, Vikings, and Mongols. In the early Middle Ages, for instance, chroniclers emphasize violence against clergy and Church property; in the late Middle Ages and the early modern period the focus is on sexual cruelty and cannibalism.

The oscillation in the fortunes of cruelty and its changing aspect—as a cultural issue—indicate that there is no *single* medieval perception of cruelty. There are instead multiple perceptions of cruelty that vary over time and depend on specific cultural, social, and political contexts. The objective of this book is to understand the factors that affect these changes. What, for instance, are the cultural processes that contribute to the renewed preoccu-

8. Jerome, *Commentarii in Isaiam*, 5.13.9, ed. Marc Adriaen, *CCSL* 73 (Turnhout, 1963), 162.

pation with cruelty in the thirteenth century? Why does cannibalism become a principal aspect of the cruelty of the "other" in the central and late Middle Ages?

But how can we reconstruct the medieval perceptions of a concept such as cruelty without imposing our own (modern) standards? Because cruelty is an abstract concept, the seemingly obvious way to start looking for an answer is to examine how medieval thinkers explicitly discuss and define it. Yet the fluctuations in the treatment of the subject over time accord these sources at best an auxiliary role; for there is no discussion of cruelty as a subject per se between the first and the thirteenth centuries.

The scarcity of texts obliges us to examine sources that represent cruelty but do not directly reflect on the concept. Two challenges confront us. First, how are we to identify explicit references to cruelty? Limiting the search to the occurrences for *crudelis*, the Latin word for cruel, and its derivatives gives us only a partial glimpse of medieval perceptions of cruelty. We must therefore reconstruct the conceptual framework—that is, the lexical field of the concept and the basic building blocks of its imagery. Yet expanding the lexical field from one to several words still reveals only part of the picture. The second and more difficult problem is that not all references to cruelty are explicit—that is, not all contain words from the relevant lexical field. But this brings us back to the initial question: How can we discern and interpret cruelty without imposing our own contemporary conceptual frame?

To reconstruct the basic conceptual framework of cruelty we must expand the lexical field from the word *cruel* to a whole set of words associated with the concept. This set of words enables us to grasp the ways in which "cruelty" was expressed and helps us to identify texts concerned with the concept. It is important to examine the biblical references to cruelty. They are an essential part of the conceptual framework, as they are the basis of cultural activity in the medieval West, and they point to the basic imagery associated with cruelty.

If in surveying lexical references to cruelty we follow the cross-references in some medieval dictionaries and glosses, we can begin to reconstruct the medieval concept. On the most basic and associative level, cruelty is linked with raw meat and blood, following the etymology of *crudelis* from *crudus* (raw). The lexical field of cruelty suggests two primary fields of references: Cruelty is related to a type of irrational and nonhuman violence that is associated with wild beasts or with demons, mainly through the nexus of lexical terms containing *crudelis*, *iratus* (wrathful), *saevus* (savage), *atrox* (fierce), and *ferox* (ferocious). Conversely, cruelty as a human quality is linked to judicial violence through terms such as *severitas* (severity), *austeritas* (rigor), and *integritas judicii* (integrity of judgment).[9]

The biblical references to cruelty complete this schematic conceptual framework. Cruelty as an animal or demonic quality figures prominently in the Scriptures, in both the Old and the New Testament. There are two contexts in which the Scriptures describe cruelty as a human trait: the passion of Christ and the violence of barbarian peoples. The image of the cruelty of the crucifixion, reinforced by accounts of the early martyrs for which it served as a model, is central to the study of medieval perceptions of cruelty. The Old Testament portrays violent heathens as agents of divine justice: God sends peoples—such as the Assyrians or the Babylonians—to murder, plunder, and rape as punishment for the sins of the people of Israel. These peoples, portrayed as morally and culturally inferior idolaters, combine in Western Christendom with the image of the barbarians of classical antiquity, such as the Scythians, to produce one of the most potent cultural constructs of cruelty, that of the "other."

In sum, this field of lexical and biblical references suggests that there were three principal contexts of cruelty: punishment by the law, martyrdom, and the violence of invading "others." These references present a blend—with the ratios changing over the centuries—of biblical and classical elements.

Having an idea of the lexical field and basic imagery of cruelty helps us locate the sources in which medieval writers refer to the concept explicitly. But how can we identify the sources that represent cruelty only implicitly— or not at all? The main difficulty is that of delineating the relation between violence and cruelty, which are similar but not identical concepts. The danger in linking them is, once more, that of an anachronistic blurring of categories. For example, the burning of heretics is a violent action, one that would be thought cruel by modern Western standards but not necessarily so by medieval ones.[10] Because explicit references to cruelty are rare through much of the period covered by this book, the concept of violence—and its relationship to cruelty—hovers constantly in the background. If we are to avoid conflating them, a few words on violence are in order.

The modern concept of violence is, to a considerable extent, objective and quantifiable. Violence can be defined as the application of physical force against an individual or against a group of people. It can be conceptualized according to standard, for the most part legal categories—such as

9. See Appendix 1 for a more detailed survey of the lexical and biblical references.

10. On medieval versus modern terminology, see Henry A. Kelly, "Meanings and Uses of *Raptus* in Chaucer's Time," *Studies in the Age of Chaucer* 20 (1998): 101–65.

murder, rape, assault, or robbery. Using these categories, one can compare, for example, the levels of violence in Los Angeles and Seattle or between high schools of the same neighborhood. Similarly, one can use these data for studying changes over time—that is, patterns of rise and fall in the levels of violence.

But these seemingly simple comparisons are often problematic. Thus, an increase in the number of court cases dealing with sexual harassment does not necessarily indicate an increase in the frequency of harassment itself but may indicate only that the attitudes to and awareness of such acts have changed. Comparisons across culture are even more problematic. The actual meanings of these categories may vary between cultures, as may the policies of law enforcement authorities in recording the various kinds of violence. Nevertheless, despite such caveats, these records provide a rough idea of the level of violence within a specific society or community.[11]

Difficulties multiply, almost exponentially, when we deal with violence in earlier periods.[12] Documentation is less comprehensive, and the sources may be more biased than their twentieth-century counterparts, as it was considered more acceptable during the Middle Ages to shape the description of the events to suit the purpose for which a source was composed. The challenges confronting the historian of the early Middle Ages are especially severe. The records for this period are scarce and, because they are mainly ecclesiastic, contain a built-in bias.[13]

The difficulty of identifying violence in historical sources is thus twofold: First, we must ask whether violence is itself an objective category (or can it, at least, be approximated as such)? If the reply to this question is positive, are the historical sources sufficient for reconstructing a reliable image of past violence? These issues render any positivistic reference to violence problematic, for it is always impressionistic to some degree, and its presence cannot be fully proved by the extant documentation.

In this book, I speak of violence in its modern sense, as a quantifiable and comparable category and, to the extent possible, one that is morally neu-

11. For a good survey, see Marshall H. Segall, Carol R. Ember, and Melvin Ember, "Aggression, Crime, and Warfare," in *Handbook of Cross-Cultural Psychology*, ed. John W. Berry, Marshall H. Segall, and Cigdem Kagitçibasi (Boston, 1997), 3:213–54.

12. See, for instance, J. S. Cockburn, "Patterns of Violence in English Society: Homicide in Kent 1560–1985," *Past and Present* 130 (1991): 70–106.

13. See Thomas N. Bisson, "The 'Feudal' Revolution," *Past and Present* 142 (1994): 6–42, and the ensuing debate over this article, with contributions by Dominique Barthélemy and Stephen D. White, *Past and Present* 152 (1996): 196–223, and Timothy Reuter, Chris Wickham, and Thomas N. Bisson, *Past and Present* 155 (1997): 177–225.

tral.[14] Yet the specific kinds of violence that are examined were chosen to coincide with actions that can be taken invariably to have been perceived as violent by medieval men and women. These include killing, especially mass killing by external invaders, rape, and destruction of property and shrines (churches, monasteries, and mosques).

With this checklist of violent actions, we can begin to talk in comparative terms about levels and perceptions of violence. In the early medieval period, for example, the types of violence listed above were practiced by external invaders—Muslims, Magyars, and Vikings—as well as by local knights and castellans. Because external invaders virtually disappear toward the turn of the twelfth century, we can conclude that there was less violence of this sort in the twelfth and thirteenth centuries than in the eleventh.[15]

What, however, is the relationship between violent acts and those that medieval people deemed cruel? In my view, this relationship is not unlike that between our contemporary concepts of violence and crime. The passage from violence to crime involves the application of moral judgment, and the point at which that judgment is made shows considerable variation across cultures. In some cultures, infanticide would not be classified as murder but instead regarded as an extension of late abortion.[16] In other cultural contexts, certain homicides related to adultery would be considered legitimate defenses of family honor. Similarly, homicide that is part of a religious ritual would not be categorized as murder.[17] The departures from the norm by which homicide equals morally unjustifiable violence bring into relief significant intercultural differences.

In a similar way, we apply a moral judgment when we deem a certain act of violence to be cruel. The perceptual shift from "mere" violence to cruelty obliges us consciously to define an action as cruel. In this respect, cruelty is a threshold concept. Violence that is deemed excessive—for a variety of reasons—is defined as cruelty. Thus, although most cultures allow for a controlled amount of violence in the penal system, excess of the prescribed measure is considered cruel. Based on this consideration, the Eighth Amendment to the U.S. Constitution was not innovative; it had its precursors in Seneca, Thomas Aquinas, and Montaigne. In many cases, then, cru-

14. One can speak of justified or unjustified violence with the underlying assumption that the same violent actions can acquire different meanings in different moral and cultural contexts.

15. Unless one posits a priori a zero-sum model of violence—that is, that when one kind of violence subsides (external) other types increase—a problematic assumption in itself.

16. Segall, Ember, and Ember, "Aggression, Crime, and Warfare," 220.

17. William Ian Miller, *Humiliation* (Ithaca, 1993), 82–83.

elty is defined in relation to a level of violence that is thought to be legitimate and is used as a baseline against which cruelty is measured.

By focusing on acts of violence committed by external invaders, we are better equipped to deal with the subjective and relative nature of the concept. In this book, we will examine a fixed group of violent acts—murder, rape, and destruction of property and shrines—committed by such invaders. Given the identity of the perpetrators, we can expect that their victims will agree in characterizing these acts as instances of cruelty. Although the victims' bias against the perpetrators may distort the factual representation of events, it actually helps in reconstructing how cruelty was perceived. Bias would, in these cases, always tend toward exaggerating the violence and maliciousness of the invaders, thereby throwing into high relief those qualities of individuals and acts that individual people perceived as cruel.

By concentrating on a fixed group of violent acts across the period considered here (late antiquity to the early modern period), we are able to trace fluctuations in the representation of cruelty between periods and across cultures. Thus we can determine when actions are represented explicitly as cruelty, when cruelty is only implied, and when there is no reference to it at all. As in the case of violence and crime, what is not defined as cruel is perhaps even more important for the understanding of cultural concepts than what is explicitly defined as such. The characterization of Simon of Monfort with which we began is a good case in point. When Peter of Vaux-de-Cernay supplies his apologetics for Simon of Monfort, claiming that the latter is not cruel, he is addressing himself to his audience's notion of cruelty. His justification of the crusaders' violence unwittingly reveals the notion of cruelty held by his "implied audience."[18]

These considerations will structure my approach to the medieval sources related to cruelty. I deal first with those sources that refer explicitly to cruelty. Understanding and mapping the contexts in which violence is most commonly defined as cruelty helps to identify and interpret implicit references to the issue. In this way, I hope to steer clear of two contrasting methodological pitfalls: the "literalistic" tendency to assume that cruelty does

18. The reconstruction of the audience of literary works is the focus of "reader response" criticism. Among the most important theoretical contributions in this field is the work of two German critics, Hans R. Jauss and Wolfgang Iser. Particularly important in the historical context is Jauss, "Literary History as a Challenge to Literary Theory," in *Toward an Aesthetic of Reception* (Minneapolis, 1982[1970]), 3–45 (esp. 22 ff.). Jauss discusses the relation between a literary work and what he terms the *horizon of expectations* of its audience. The term *implied reader* has been used by Iser, *The Implied Reader* (Baltimore, 1974). In a medieval context, "implied audience" seems more fit. For the application of these critical theories in the analysis of medieval texts, see Peter W. Travis, "Affective Criticism, the Pilgrimage of Reading, and Medieval English Literature" in *Medieval Texts and Contemporary Readers*, ed. Laurie A. Finke and Martin B. Shichtman (Ithaca, 1987), 201–33.

not exist where it is not mentioned and the anachronistic imposition of modern notions of cruelty in places where it does not exist.

The use of one component of this conceptual framework—the "other"—needs further elucidation. I refer primarily to one particular type of "other"—that of the invading archenemy, or the enemy whose violence is an imminent threat. This enemy is usually presented as culturally different (or as a complete opposite) to the civilization it invades, and extreme violence is one of its main attributes.

As Paul Freedman points out, the concept of the "other" is not static.[19] It changes over time, and different types and degrees of otherness are attributed to different people. The nature of this concept in relation to cruelty is perhaps best understood through a literary example. In George Orwell's *1984*, the fearsome Room 101 is the epitome of the repressive machine. When the protagonist Winston Smith is apprehended and interrogated, he asks his interrogator what is in Room 101, and the latter replies: "I told you that you knew the answer already. Everyone knows it. The thing that is in Room 101 is the worst thing in the world . . . [it] varies from individual to individual. It may be burial alive, or death by fire, or by drowning, or by impalement, or fifty other deaths."[20]

The peoples assigned the role of "other" change from late antiquity to the early modern period, and—as with Room 101—the kinds of terrorizing violence vary as well. But precisely because of these fluctuations, the changing references to this type of "other" are indicative of the changes in the representation of cruelty: In some periods, they are explicitly described as cruel, and in others their violence, or cruelty, is only implicitly represented. Because these descriptions are at least in part exaggerated imaginary projections of their authors' perception of the "worst cruelty," they are a good source for reconstructing perceptions of cruelty. The degree to which cruelty is attributed explicitly to these "others" is also indicative of the relative importance of this issue.

Our discussion suggests that cruelty is a primarily subjective concept that exists in the perceptions of the individuals touched by it. As a result, this book is concerned primarily with abstract entities—conceptions, representations, attitudes, and so on. Yet the conceptual realm is not divorced from reality. The circumstances of a historical study such as this one—unlike, perhaps, a philosophical treatise—resemble an inversion of the Platonic parable: The visible realm of ideas is the dim reflection of the historical reality. The con-

19. Paul Freedman, "The Medieval 'Other': The Middle Ages as 'Other,'" in *Marvels, Monsters, and Miracles: Studies in the Medieval and Early Modern Imagination*, ed. Timothy S. Jones and David A. Sprunger, (Kalamazoo, Mich., 1999), 1-24.

20. George Orwell, *1984* (New York, 1949), 286.

nection between the two is more discernible in certain periods, less so in others. Thus, for example, there is a parallel between the increasing severity of judicial violence from the late Middle Ages to the early modern period and the development and parallel thickening of the discourse of cruelty.[21]

But the role of cruelty as a cultural issue in medieval civilization is not merely a reflection of historical reality. The relation between culture and reality was at times inverse, with cultural images of cruelty influencing historical reality. As with modern representations of violence—movies and video games—medieval cultural images may have influenced patterns of actual violence. Thus, for example, images of cruelty revived from pagan antiquity may account in part for the types of violence practiced in the course of the Jacquerie.

The theoretical issue of cruelty intersected with reality in other ways as well. The close link between cruelty and tyranny rendered cruelty a political tool. In conjunction with the theoretical discussions of tyrannicide, the accusation of cruelty was used to imply that a ruler was a tyrant and hence an illegitimate ruler. The practical implications of the cultural preoccupation with cruelty are also reflected in the evolution of complex mechanisms for justifying violence. From the thirteenth century onward, cruelty serves as a label to delegitimize minority groups and to justify violence against them.

To understand the significant fluctuations in the treatment of the concept of cruelty in the medieval West, we must adopt a broad comparative approach, one that is both chronological and cross-cultural. By exploring the reasons for increased interest in the issue in late antiquity and the early modern period, for example, we may better understand the factors behind the medieval reluctance to deal with this issue. Similarly, an examination of the ways in which violence is described outside the medieval West brings into higher relief what is particular to the Western concept.

The focus of this cross-cultural inquiry is the Mongol conquests of the thirteenth century. These conquests coincide with the reawakening of Western interest in the issue of cruelty, and the accounts relating to them reflect the ensuing changes in its representation. In addition, the Mongol conquests affected a multitude of peoples, from the Chinese to Central Europeans, and

21. A similar relation existed in the first centuries A.D., when the cultural preoccupation with cruelty was related to the increasing severity of punishments in the Empire. See Jean-Pierre Callu, "Le jardin des supplices au Bas-Empire," in *Du châtiment dans la cité* (Rome, 1984), 336; Piero Fiorelli, *La tortura giudiziaria nel diritto comune* (Milan, 1953–54), 1:39–43; and K. M. Coleman, "Fatal Charades: Roman Executions Staged as Mythological Enactments," *Journal of Roman Studies* 80 (1990): 44–73, esp. 55.

thus one can compare a wide range of reports from different cultures. I compare the Western accounts concerning the Mongols with Eastern ones—Islamic and Christian—written in regions that suffered much greater devastation than Western Europe. The extreme violence that was almost invariably practiced by the Mongols can lead to the expectation that their actions would be characterized as cruelty. Failure of some of the sources to do so would be significant with regard to the role of cruelty in a specific cultural context.

The book is divided into six chapters. In the first, I trace the changing conceptions of cruelty expressed by Western thinkers, starting with Seneca and ending with Montaigne. Because theoretical discussions of cruelty are the most direct way of dealing with the subject, tracing their existence and comprehensiveness serves as a convenient baseline for measuring the level of attention paid to the issue over time. Moreover, this mode of addressing the subject—by its self-conscious nature—also illuminates some of the factors that affect how a society distinguishes a cruel act from one that is not and how cruelty is represented.

In the subsequent chapters, I address representations and perceptions of cruelty from late antiquity to the early modern period. Chapter 2 deals with the foundations of the Western representations of cruelty laid in the first centuries A.D.: the early martyrdom accounts and the descriptions of the barbarian "others" surrounding and invading the Roman Empire.

In Chapter 3, I trace the transition into the medieval period and the changes in the treatment of cruelty that accompanied it. The primary characteristic of this transition is the almost complete disappearance of explicit references to cruelty despite historical circumstances that included severe internal violence and incursions from the outside by Muslims, Magyars, and Vikings. This lack of references to cruelty in the contemporary sources describing these events poses the problem of implicit representation of cruelty: Is this silence an indication that these events were not perceived as cruel, or can one account for it in other ways?

In chapters 4 and 5, I explore the "Renaissance of cruelty" of the central Middle Ages and the intensifying cultural preoccupation with this issue in the late medieval period. The reappearance of cruelty as a subject for theoretical speculation in the thirteenth century marks a distinct change in the status of our topic, one that is evident in most aspects of medieval culture. Representations of cruelty in chronicles, martyrdom accounts, and dramas become more explicit, detailed, and affective. In addition, works from pagan classical antiquity related to cruelty become increasingly popular, both in the form of theoretical treatises, such as Seneca's moral essays, and literary works, such as Ovid's *Metamorphoses* and Seneca's plays.

Directly related to this rise in the status of cruelty as a cultural issue is its increasingly manipulative use. This process becomes noticeable around the turn of the thirteenth century but develops mainly in the late medieval period, in the fourteenth and fifteenth centuries. In other words, the greater cultural sensitivity to the issue was accompanied by the development of mechanisms that would justify violence. Both sides in the Jacquerie justified their violence by very elaborate efforts to highlight the cruelty of their opponents. In the political realm, cruelty functioned as a delegitimizing label. Portraying a ruler as cruel signified that he was a tyrant, with all the accompanying implications. This issue was raised in relation to some of the more unlucky rulers of the central and late Middle Ages: John of England and Pedro I of Castile, who entered history as Pedro "the Cruel."

Chapter 6 addresses the explosive growth of the cultural role of cruelty in the early modern period. The sheer amount and variety of references to the subject are unprecedented. Moreover, some of the approaches to the issue present a break with medieval modes of addressing it. Thus, cruelty appears for the first time as a dramatic character in the anonymous sixteenth-century English play, *New Custom* (1573). Jean de Léry (1534–1613) is even more innovative in his *Histoire d'un voyage en terre de Brésil*, first published in 1578. The preoccupation with the issue of cruelty increases gradually in subsequent editions of this work, and Léry appended to the fourth edition a separate treatise comparing the cruelty of the natives of the New World with that of the Turks and the Spaniards.

The sixteenth century is a good place to end our survey, not only because later periods are much beyond the scope of a study that focuses on the medieval period, but also because the century seems to have been the peak of preoccupation with this subject in Western culture. Notable references to cruelty exist in later centuries as well: Hogarth's (1697–1764) *Four Stages of Cruelty* was influential and elicited written comments and elaborations in the eighteenth century.[22] Also in the eighteenth century, the Marquis de Sade penned his elaborate depictions of sexual violence.[23] In the nineteenth century, Nietzsche contributed his insights on this subject, but on the whole, the issue seems less central than it was in the sixteenth century. Moreover—and this point applies to much that was written on the subject in the twentieth century as well—little was added to the conceptual tools developed in the sixteenth century for dealing with the subject: Classic, medieval, and early modern categories were either borrowed, inverted, or expanded.[24]

22. Paul A. Oppé, *The Drawings of William Hogarth* (London, 1948), plates 68–71. See also John Trusler, *Hogarth Moralized* (London, no date [18th century]), 132–44.

23. See James A. Steintrager, "Perfectly Inhuman: Moral Monstrosity in Eighteenth-Century Discourse," *Eighteenth-Century Life* 21.2 (1997): 114–32.

24. See Appendix 2.

CHAPTER ONE
SPECULATING ON CRUELTY, FROM SENECA TO MONTAIGNE

ruelty is mentioned explicitly in descriptions of violent events, but these references only label particular actions as cruel, and this label does not require a full conceptual construct of cruelty. In contrast, a theoretical discussion of cruelty does require such a construct, so the presence or absence of these discussions in different historical periods is indicative of the level of cultural preoccupation with cruelty. Thus, a review of the theoretical discussions of cruelty provides a baseline for the assessment of the role of cruelty in Western culture rather than being a merely arbitrary review of references to cruelty in a specific genre.

In this chapter, I examine theoretical discussions of cruelty from late antiquity to the early modern period. There appears to be great variability in the level of preoccupation with the subject. Seneca dealt with it in the first century, and his writings on cruelty have a dominant influence on the few instances in which it was discussed before the sixteenth century. Christian thinkers of late antiquity did not deal with the issue of cruelty as a subject per se, and this attitude continued throughout the early Middle Ages. The first medieval discussion appeared in Thomas Aquinas's *Summa theologiae*, but even after this, cruelty did not become a popular topic. Aquinas's discussion is not taken up by other medieval scholars until the fifteenth century, when Antoninus of Florence reconsiders it and elaborates it. Cruelty does become an important issue in the early modern period, however, and this new attitude is reflected in Montaigne's writings.

I review the writings of these thinkers and attempt to identify the factors that affected their choices in addressing cruelty: Why is cruelty in general ignored in some periods and discussed in others? And why do certain aspects of the issue feature prominently in some discussions but are absent in others?

---

1. I have treated in more detail some of the issues discussed in this chapter in Daniel Baraz, "Seneca, Ethics, and the Body—The Treatment of Cruelty in Medieval Thought," *Journal of the History of Ideas* 59:2 (1998): 195–215.

Seneca is the first thinker to deal with cruelty as a subject per se, yet ancient Greek culture also has some important antecedents to the treatment of cruelty in the medieval West. Herodotus did not discuss cruelty, but he did create one of the most potent images of cruelty in Western civilization: the Scythians as the embodiment of the cruel "other."[2] Aristotle dealt with various kinds of extremely violent behavior in *Nicomachean Ethics*. He distinguished between human behavior that falls under the category of wickedness and nonhuman behavior characterized as "brutish" or "morbid" (that is, originating in illness, usually mental). Aristotle's discussion deals with concepts related to cruelty but not with cruelty itself. Nevertheless, his examples contain some of the images, such as cannibalism and the figure of Phalaris, that appear in later discussions of cruelty.

Seneca's intellectual preoccupation with cruelty was not divorced from historical circumstances; he lived during the reigns of Caligula, Claudius, and Nero. As the writings of first-century Roman authors show, these three rulers were perceived as excessively violent and were explicitly portrayed as cruel.[3] Seneca was Nero's teacher, and it is likely that his intimate acquaintance with his young pupil triggered him to write on cruelty.

Seneca discusses cruelty in a systematic manner in his essay *De clementia*, which was written at the beginning of Nero's reign and is addressed to the young emperor. The concept of *clementia* describes a quality of political men, and it acquired political significance during the times of Caesar and Augustus.[4] In the second book of *De clementia*, Seneca draws the following scheme for evaluating the morality of the exercise of judiciary power:

$$misericordia \leftarrow clementia—severitas \rightarrow crudelitas$$
$$\text{(compassion} \leftarrow \text{mercy—severity} \rightarrow \text{cruelty)}$$

Virtuous behavior is a continuum that extends from *clementia* to *severitas*. Following the Aristotelian model of virtues and vices, virtue can turn into two contrasting vices: *misericordia*, the irrational mitigation of punishment, and *crudelitas*, the irrational exaggeration of punishment.

Seneca, then, discusses cruelty as a quality opposite *clementia*. In this legal context, *cruelty* is defined as "brutality of mind in exacting punishment" [atrocitas animi in exigendis poenis]. Seneca emphasizes the function of

---

2. See François Hartog, *The Mirror of Herodotus: The Representation of the Other in the Writing of History*, trans. Janet Lloyd (Berkeley, Calif., 1988[1980]).

3. See Chapter 2, 30.

4. Miriam T. Griffin, *Seneca—A Philosopher in Politics* (Oxford, 1976), 149.

rationality when he repeats that the definition refers to the "mind's intemperance in exacting punishment" [in poenis exigendis intemperantiam animi]. This definition is restrictive, and Seneca explicitly rejects any attempt to widen its scope. Thus, he states that enjoying the suffering of others and inflicting violence without any cause or purpose is not cruelty—which is a human behavior—but rather ferocity (*feritas, ferocitas*) or savagery (*saevitia*), which are irrational and nonhuman.

When dealing with cruelty, Seneca adopts an intermediate position between two ethical stances. One can distinguish between two types of ethics: ethics of intention, which pertain to the intentions of the actor, and ethics of action, which pertain to the morality of the actions regardless of the actor's intentions. Throughout his discussion, Seneca associates the abstract qualities (*crudelitas, clementia*, and others) with the mind (*animus*).[5] Nevertheless, his definitions refer to actual, rational, and objective criteria, which are external to the actor. In this context, therefore, the actions of the tyrant Phalaris are classified as *crudelitas* rather than as *feritas* or *saevitia*: Phalaris burned his victims inside an iron bull, but they were not innocent and did deserve *some* punishment.[6]

Although the second book of *De clementia* contains Seneca's only systematic discussion of cruelty, he refers to this subject elsewhere in his writings, and in those instances, he does not follow the strict definition he offers in the second book of *De clementia*. *Crudelitas, saevitia*, and *feritas* are used as synonyms, and cruelty is primarily defined as pleasure in inflicting suffering on others.

Christian thinkers of late antiquity did not discuss cruelty as a subject per se, yet they did refer to it in passing. The influence of figures such as Augustine or Jerome on Western medieval culture cannot be overestimated. The attitude to the issue undertaken by these thinkers was in itself self-perpetuating in terms of both influencing the attitude of later thinkers and accounting for the existence or absence of such systematic discussions. Early Christian thinkers' references to cruelty and the attitudes they reflect help us understand the passing references to the subject by other thinkers, and their reluctance to deal with cruelty in a systematic manner was in itself influential in discouraging subsequent medieval thinkers to address

---

5. Seneca's distinction between king and tyrant (*De clementia* [hereafter *DC*], 1.11.4–1.12.2) reflects this middle position: kings are cruel out of necessity, whereas tyrants do so for their pleasure (in voluptatem saeviunt). Yet Seneca immediately emphasizes that the difference is in deeds as well, and not only in intentions (tyrannus autem a rege factis distat).

6. *DC* 2.4.3.

the issue. But beyond that, the content of their references brings into relief the ideological factors behind the repulsion for this subject until the thirteenth century.

Cruelty figures only marginally in Augustine's writings, but when he addresses it, he does so in a context that differs entirely from Seneca's. Augustine's passing remarks on the subject indicate that, for him, cruelty is primarily spiritual, not physical. Physical cruelty is natural to man in his fallen state[7]; the sons of Adam are born with it after the Fall.[8] In contrast to cruelty, compassion is not innate but is instead a trait acquired from kinship in suffering.[9] Thus, physical cruelty is the natural state of those who do not enjoy grace: pagans, Manicheans, and Jews.[10]

Augustine's references to nonphysical cruelty derive from his anthropological outlook. More specifically, they demonstrate his perception of the relation between body and soul: To what extent is this relation perceived as dichotomic, and what is the relative importance of each of the two components in this composite? Augustine, in line with the Platonic tradition, accords the soul a privileged position, as reflected in his construct of reflexive spiritual cruelty. Cruelty, for Augustine, consists of actions that harm the soul and impair its prospects for salvation. This type of cruelty is reflexive because it is committed by a person against his own soul; it is not related to interpersonal violence.

The transposition of cruelty from its predominantly physical and interpersonal context (as evident also from the etymology of the word *crudelitas* from *crudus* [raw]) to a spiritual and reflexive context is much more than a mere rhetorical device or metaphor. In a system in which the body is subordinate to the soul, the body or physical images are not entities unto themselves but images or reflections of the soul. For example, physical illnesses or defects could be considered consequences of sin.[11] Bodily images for

7. On the centrality of the concept of grace in Augustine's thought, see Gillian R. Evans, *Augustine on Evil* (Cambridge, 1991[1982]). On the inaccessibility of virtue to the pagans, see James Wetzel, *Augustine and the Limits of Virtue* (Cambridge, 1992).

8. *De civitate Dei* (hereafter *CD*) 22:22.

9. Augustine, *Sermo* 259, PL 38:1199. Augustine adopts here a wider definition of cruelty, which includes passive indifference to the suffering of others.

10. Augustine presents the rape of the Sabine women as a constitutive event of Roman history (*CD* 3:13). On pagan cruelty, see also *CD* 2:18, 2:22, 3:17, 3:24–29, 5:19, 7:26. On cruel practices of the Manicheans, see *De moribus ecclesiae catholicae et Manichaeorum* 2, PL 32:1367–75; on the Jews' cruelty in crucifying Christ, see *CD* 3:15.

11. Caesarius of Arles preached that those who had intercourse on Sundays and other days of abstinence would beget lepers, epileptics, or possessed children (*Sermo* 44.7; Césaire d'Arles, *Sermons au peuple*, ed. and trans. Germain Morin [*Sources chrétiennes* 243] [Paris, 1971], 2:338–40; cited in Peter Brown, *The Body and Society* [New York, 1988], 439).

spiritual ideas or entities are used also in the concept of the Church as body, of which the believers are the members.[12]

The notion that physical cruelty was negligible compared with cruelty sustained by the soul had other implications as well, especially in the context of martyrdom during the great persecutions of the third century. The "medical metaphor" is the more common theological formulation of the link between the cruelty (real or apparent) of the physical act of martyrdom and its spiritual end. The metaphor was tersely formulated by Tertullian, who compared the apparent cruelty of martyrdom to the apparent, but misleading, cruelty of medical operations:

> And the healing art has manifestly an apparent cruelty [*saevitia*], by reason of the lancet, and of the burning iron . . . yet to be cut and burned, and pulled and bitten, is not on that account evil, for it occasions helpful pains . . . The fruit excuses the horror of the work. . . . Thus martyrdoms also rage savagely, but for salvation. God also will be at liberty to heal for everlasting life by means of fires and swords, and all that is painful.[13]

Jerome took over this idea but transposed it to another plane, creating one of the most potent apologies for violence during the Middle Ages. In the original version of this metaphor, both body and soul—as in the passage from Tertullian—referred to the same individual. Jerome changed this reference by playing with the ambiguity of the concept of the body: the physical body of an individual and the Church as the body of believers. Just as ailing members of the individual body have to be amputated at times, so do ailing members of the Church. Cruelty to these members is only apparent cruelty—just as the surgeons' cruelty is apparent—because the amputation contributes to the overall health of the Church's body. Thus, instead of leaving both sides of the equation on the individual level, namely that the individual suffers in his body

---

12. Guy G. Stroumsa, "Caro salutis cardo," in Guy G. Stroumsa, *Savoir et salut* (Paris, 1992), 209. It must be noted that to avoid the dualist repugnance from the physical aspects of existence, Augustine carefully warns against the other extreme of negating the body by various means of self-inflicted physical cruelty or suicide. See *In Iohannis euangelium tractatus*, 51:10 on a cruel mode of committing suicide; *CD* 2:7 on practices such as self-castration, performed by the devotees of Cybele.

13. Tertullian, *Scorpiace*, V, 6–8, ed. August Reifferscheid and Georg Wissowa (*Corpus Christianorum Series Latina* 2) (Turnhout, 1954), 1077–78; trans. S. Thelwall (*Ante-Nicene Fathers* 3) (Grand Rapids, Mich., 1978), 637–38 (the translation was modified). There is no agreement as to whether this work belongs to Tertullian's "Catholic" period or to his "Montanist" period (see William H. C. Frend, *The Rise of Christianity* [London, 1984], 348); however, this particular issue seems unimportant because similar ideas were expressed by Catholic writers.

for the sake of his own soul, in Jerome's formulation the individual may be made to suffer for the well-being of the Church.[14]

Replying to a question of pastoral care brought to him by Amandus the Presbyter, Jerome urged him not to hesitate to take harsh measures and concluded the letter with the following sentence: "Rotten flesh requires iron or cauterization; and it is not the fault of medicine but of the wound when, with clement cruelty [*cum crudelitate clementi*], the doctor does not spare in order to be sparing, and is cruel [*saevit*] in order to be compassionate."[15]

Jerome's notion of the medical metaphor circulated widely. Alvar of Cordova called this kind of cruelty *sancta crudelitas* at the time of the Cordovan martyr movement in the middle of the ninth century.[16] Gratian also made use of Jerome's negative definition of cruelty, that is, his clarification of what is *not* to be characterized as cruelty.[17] In this manner, the notion of spiritual cruelty was reversed from being mainly a speculative issue for theologians and philosophers to becoming fraught with practical physical implications.

Although no thinker of the early medieval period addressed the issue of cruelty or was as influential as Augustine or Jerome, one can see that both pagan and Christian notions of cruelty from late antiquity did circulate. Thus, in 869 Hincmar of Laon placed the diocese of Laon under interdict after a long dispute with King Charles the Bald over what he perceived as the infringement of ecclesiastical rights. His uncle and superior, Archbishop Hincmar of Reims, opposed this step and in a letter to his nephew accused him of cruelty. In defining this action as cruelty, Archbishop Hincmar referred to the excessiveness of the measure and to the fact that it did not conform to the requirements of justice: that unbaptized children who die will be punished for another's sin.[18] In this regard, Hincmar of Reims's reference is externally similar, although not identical, to the pagan classical notion of cruelty as excess. But in its content, cruelty conforms to the Augustinian model. He accuses Hincmar of Laon of being crueler than the

14. See for instance Jerome, *Epistulae*, 40:1, ed. Isidor Hilberg (*CSEL* 54) (Leipzig, 1910), 309.

15. Ibid., 495. The same metaphor is repeated in a milder, educational context in the *Tractatus in psalmos* 51, in which reluctance to correct or reprove is compared to a doctor who sees infected tissue but would not remove it. Jerome says that this is cruelty, whereas the removal of the tissue constitutes compassionate behavior.

16. Alvar, *Indiculus luminosus*, PL 115:526–27.

17. Gratian, *Decretum*, C XXIII. q. 5.28, ed. Emil A. Friedberg (Leipzig, 1879). The more general context of *causa* 23 is the combating of heresy by the Church.

18. Sed et illae non minores grandium animulae parvulorum, qui non suo sed alieno peccato obnoxiae liberari potuerunt, nisi tua crudelitate et furore ac indignatione animi forent perditae, et clamabunt adversum te? (*PL* 126:518–19). See Peter R. McKeon, *Hincmar of Laon and Carolingian Politics* (Urbana, Ill., 1978).

pagan persecutors because they killed the body, whereas Hincmar of Laon killed souls by preventing salvation.[19]

The pagan notion of cruelty in a legal context also appears in the writings of Peter Damian (1007–1072). In a fragment from a sermon, we find a brief remark that echoes Seneca's definition: "Crudelitas dignae ultionis mensuram excedat [Cruelty exceeds the measure of the fitting punishment]."[20] Elsewhere, Damian mentions the bull of Phalaris as an example of legal punishment perverted into cruelty. The prominence of this context is reflected in Damian's use of *crudelitas* to describe God's final judgment, evidently using the term as a synonym for severity in judgment, and not in a negative sense.[21]

Yet cruelty is a marginal issue for early medieval thinkers and theologians, even more so than for Augustine or Jerome. Remarks regarding cruelty are brief and few in number. Evidence of the continuity in the early medieval period with pagan and Christian writings of late antiquity only emphasizes this point: The cultural traditions regarding cruelty were not lost during the early Middle Ages but were neglected as a matter of choice by the authors of this period.

The twelfth century did not bring breakthroughs with respect to the treatment of cruelty as it did for other matters. Central thinkers, such as Bernard of Clairvaux or Abelard, did not take up cruelty in their writings as a subject per se. Yet considering Bernard's representation of the mainstream intellectual and political activity of his time and the great influence of his writings, his references to cruelty deserve special attention. Bernard acknowledges the basic physical nature of cruelty and enumerates it as one of the vices of the body. But he refers to this aspect of cruelty only rarely.[22] Most of Ber-

19. Et plerumque contingit ut hunc judicii locum teneat, cui ad locum vita minime concordat: ac saepe agitur ut vel damnet immeritos, vel alios ipse ligatus solvat. Igitur, quantum ex te est, haec crudelitas tua omnem crudelitatem omnium paganorum, et omnes persecutiones omnium persecutorum, quae Christianis illatae fuerunt, excedunt, dicente Domino: "Nolite timere eos qui occiderunt corpus, animam autem non possunt occidere" (Matt. X) (*PL* 126:518).

20. *PL* 144:924.

21. Tunc ille misericors oculus non parcet . . . sed percutiet et occidet . . . plenus crudelitate (*PL* 144:818). On Phalaris see *De bono suffragiorum et variis miraculis, c.* 1, *PL* 145:561–62.

22. Bernard draws in two places a schematic typology of vices in which *superbia, vana gloria,* and *invidia* are vices of the soul, whereas *curiositas, loquacitas, crudelitas,* and *voluptas* are vices of the body: *Sermones de diversis, sermo* 74 (commentary on Psalms 13:1), in *Sancti Bernardi Opera* (hereafter *SBO*), ed. Jean Leclercq (Rome, 1957–1977), 6a:312–13; *Sententiae,* 3:9 (commentary on Amos 2:4) *SBO* 6b:70 (a similar scheme can be found in Peter Damian, *Sermo* 61; *PL* 144:843). In the second place, Bernard also characterizes cruelty as a beastly quality.

nard's remarks consist of a more elaborate and extreme formulation of Augustine's construct of spiritual and reflexive cruelty.

Bernard pushes the Augustinian dichotomy between body and soul further, making them almost autonomous entities. Thus, an individual can be cruel to his own soul. "Good mercy is to take mercy on your soul," says Bernard. Anything else "is not mercy . . . but cruelty; it is not charity, but iniquity."[23] Nevertheless, Bernard is careful not to fall into the dualist trap when defining the relation between body and soul. In fact, most of his references to reflexive spiritual cruelty deal with exaggerated asceticism, not with the indulgence of bodily appetites. Bernard realized that exaggerated asceticism, even if it aims at achieving a higher spirituality, paradoxically accords too much importance to the body, which is detrimental to the soul and hence a form of cruelty.[24] The process of waging war against the body necessarily ends in an alliance with it, and this is one of the traps used by the devil to ensnare monks.[25] Even an overly strict observance of the Rule may be cruel. Bernard ridicules the opinion that it is possible to refrain completely from sin or from violating the Rule by calling such a belief "credulity, or rather cruelty [*credulitas, vel potius crudelitas*]."[26] In sum, Bernard's scope of cruelty is very wide, and the concept may refer to anything that hinders the salvation of the soul.[27]

THE RE-EMERGENCE OF CRUELTY: THOMAS AQUINAS

The turning point for the attitude toward cruelty comes in the thirteenth century. Thomas Aquinas is the first medieval thinker to devote a separate discussion to cruelty. His discussion provides some insights into the factors that shape his perception and affect attitudes to the subject in preceding centuries. In the section on temperance in his *Summa theologiae*, Aquinas

23. *Apologia ad Guillelmum abbatem* 8(16–17), SBO 3:95–96.

24. This paradox was concisely formulated seven centuries later by Jorge L. Borges: "In spite of religions, this conviction [that one is immortal] is very rare. Israelites, Christians and Moslems profess immortality, but the veneration they render this world proves they believe only in it, since they destine all other worlds, in infinite number, to be its reward or punishment" ("The Immortal," trans. James E. Irby in Jorge L. Borges, *Labyrinths* [Harmondsworth, 1978(1964)], 144).

25. *Sermo super Cantica Canticorum* 33:10, SBO 2:240; see also *Liber de gradibus humilitatis et superbiae* 14(42), SBO 3:49.

26. *Liber de praecepto et dispensatione* 33–34, SBO 3:276–77.

27. His attack on the cruelty of the Cathars may be interpreted in this context as well, to the effect that they are leading souls to perdition (*Sermo super Cantica Canticorum* 66:1, SBO 2:178). Establishing the cruelty of the Cathars was a necessary step for the application of violence against them. See Chapter 4, 85 ff.

includes a question entitled *De crudelitate*.[28] Aquinas bases his analysis almost exclusively on Seneca's systematic discussion in the second book of *De clementia*, and he quotes extensively from his source. Similar to Seneca, he restricts the scope of cruelty to a legal context and distinguishes between this concept and irrational cruelty, which is labeled *saevitia* and *feritas*.

Aquinas, however, shifts the context of the discussion radically, from the legal-political sphere to the psychological one. Seneca was concerned with excessive punishment, which could be appraised according to external standards of judiciary procedure. Aquinas, conversely, is concerned only with the subjective psychology of the topic. The external action belongs to a different category altogether, and he explicitly declines to deal with it in the context of his discussion of cruelty: "excess in punishing, as regards the external action, belongs to injustice [*injustitia*]; but as regards the harshness of mind [*austeritas animi*], which makes one ready to increase punishment, belongs to cruelty [*crudelitas*]."

The most obvious influence on Aquinas's discussion—and by extension his treatment of cruelty in general—is Seneca. Aquinas's use of Seneca as his main authority reflects an increase in Seneca's influence and in the diffusion of his works. Many of Seneca's philosophical works, including *De beneficiis*, *De clementia*, and the *Dialogues*, became popular in the thirteenth century.[29] Thus, the rise of cruelty as a subject per se and the way in which it is discussed are related to the Senecan revival of that time.

But given the extent of Seneca's influence, how is one to account for the transformation of his discussion of cruelty to another context? This change was the result of two other cultural developments. The first is Aquinas's new—and from a certain perspective revolutionary—definition of the relation between body and soul. The second process, the importance of which

28. *Summa theologiae* 2-2-159; English translation: St. Thomas Aquinas, *Summa Theologica*, trans. The Fathers of the English Dominican Province (Westminster, Md., 1981[1920]), 4:1838–39.

29. For a survey on the transmission and reception of Seneca's writings from the central Middle Ages to the early modern period, see Baraz, "Seneca, Ethics, and the Body," 209–11. Also see Richard H. Rouse, "The *A* Text of Seneca's Tragedies in the Thirteenth Century," *Revue d'histoire des textes* 1 (1971): 93–121; Richard H. Rouse, "New Light on the Circulation of the *A* Text of Seneca's Tragedies," *Journal of the Warburg and Courtauld Institute* 40 (1977): 283–86; Otto Zwierlein, "Spuren der Tragoedien Senecas bei Bernardus Silvestris, Petrus Pictor und Marbod von Rennes," *Mittellateinisches Jahrbuch* 22 for 1987(1989): 171–96. For the transmission of the Dialogues, see Leighton D. Reynolds, "The Medieval Tradition of Seneca's Dialogues," *Classical Quarterly* 18:2 (1968): 355–72; see also Birger Munk Olsen, *L'étude des auteurs classiques latins aux XIe et XIIe siècles* (Paris, 1985), 2:395, 412, 414, 415, 417, 426, 455.

increased steadily throughout the twelfth century, is the emergence of an ethical system based almost exclusively on intentions.

The reappearance of cruelty in the writings of Thomas Aquinas corresponds, as does the re-emergence of Senecan influence, to a significant redefinition of the relation between body and soul. Aquinas encapsulated this new relation in the formula "the soul is the form of the body," which indicates that body and soul are perceived as an inseparable unity.[30] Aquinas does not accept any dichotomy between them, nor does he accept the Augustinian (or Platonic) conception of the soul "using a body."[31] Aquinas is not entirely free of the hierarchic conception of the two entities, and he does not place them on the same plane, but his position does consist of a move in this direction. The distance between the Augustinian position and the Thomistic one, however, is such that the magnitude of the quantitative difference turns it into a qualitative difference as well.[32] The Augustinian soul-centered view of the relation between body and soul is one of the reasons cruelty was regarded as irrelevant or unworthy for discussion by Christian thinkers before the time of Aquinas. The diminishing dominance of the Augustinian paradigm of the relation between body and soul and the appearance of the Thomistic formulation correspond to the re-emergence of cruelty as a topic for speculation in the thirteenth century.

The circulation of Seneca's works and the perceived relation between body and soul were not only crucial factors in determining whether cruelty was discussed as a subject per se, but they also affected the content of the discussion—that is, *how* cruelty was discussed. In the latter respect, however, there was an even more influential factor: the relative weight accorded to actions and intentions in the dominant ethical systems. Aquinas deals exclusively with intentions, which differs from Seneca's

30. Thomas Aquinas, *Summa contra gentiles*, II:67–72, esp. II:71: "ostensum est enim (cf. capp. 68, 70) quod anima unitur corpori ut forma eius." See also Aquinas, *Summa theologiae* 1-76 (De unione animae ad corpus) "anima intellectiva est forma corpori" (1-76-1, co.); "Sed si posamus animam corpori uniri sicut formam" (1-76-3, co.).

31. See Brian Davies, *The Thought of Thomas Aquinas* (Oxford, 1992), 210–11. The question of the relation between body and soul is treated extensively in the *Summa contra gentiles*, II:56–82. In these chapters, Aquinas refutes a number of other opinions concerning this relation. The Platonic conception is refuted in II:57. A similar refutation can be found in the *Summa theologiae* 1-76-3, co.

32. Etienne Gilson terms Aquinas's new conception of the soul "the Thomistic reformation" (Etienne Gilson, *The History of Christian Philosophy in the Middle Ages* [New York, 1955], 361–62). On the Thomistic conception of body and soul and its consequences, see also Etienne Gilson, *The Philosophy of St. Thomas Aquinas*, trans. Edward Bullough (New York, 1929[1924]), 204–20; Davies, *Thought of Thomas Aquinas*, 207–226; Anthony Kenny, *Aquinas on Mind* (London, 1993), 145–59.

intermediate position.[33] Aquinas's definition of cruelty refers solely to the psychology of its perpetrator. He explicitly refuses to deal with the actual actions and their consequences, which he relegates to another conceptual category.

In his choice of ethical framework for the discussion of cruelty, Aquinas is in line with the mainstream of central medieval ethics. His position is related to a more general concern with ethics and the sometimes controversial rise of a radical "ethics of intention" in the twelfth century. The most extreme formulation of this ethical position came from the pen of Abelard, who claimed that actions are morally neutral.[34] On the basis of such premises, he argued, for instance, that the persecutors of Christ did not sin because they really believed him to be a criminal.[35] Although Abelard's extreme positions aroused antagonism and were not adopted, they formed part of a wider process of the interiorization of ethics that was shared by other theologians and had lasting effects.[36] Thus, Aquinas's pivotal discussion of cruelty is the intersection of three processes: the growing circulation of Seneca's works, the redefinition of the relation between body and soul, and the rise of an ethical system focused on intentions.

Even after Aquinas, however, cruelty did not become an important cultural issue. Two full centuries passed before Antoninus of Florence (1389–1459), a Dominican as was Aquinas, took up this subject again in his *Summa theologica*. Antoninus explicitly acknowledges the relation to his predecessor, quoting verbatim from Aquinas's *Summa*. Following Aquinas, Antoninus makes the distinction between *crudelitas* on the one hand and *feritas* and *saevitia* on the other. Similar to Aquinas and Seneca, he opposes *crudelitas* to *clementia*.

33. See earlier, 15.

34. Opera quippe quae, ut prediximus, eque reprobis ut electis communia sunt, omnia in se indifferentia sunt nec nisi pro intentione agentis bona uel mala dicenda sunt (Peter Abelard, *Ethics*, ed. and trans. David E. Luscombe (Oxford, 1979[1971]), 44–45). Gillian R. Evans relegates the debate between the position that actions are important and the position that emphasizes faith alone to the fifteenth century. Abelard's writings indicate that the controversy already existed in the twelfth century, although Evans is correct in pointing out that the St. Bernard's mainstream position does not concur with Abelard (Gillian R. Evans, *Bernard of Clairvaux* [Oxford, 2000], 132.)

35. Abelard, *Ethics*, 66–67.

36. Robert Blomme, *La doctrine du péché dans les écoles théologiques de la première moitié du XIIe siècle* (Louvain, 1958). Roger Bacon, for instance, refers to adultery and quotes Seneca to the effect that "if a man has intercourse with his own wife under the impression that she is the wife of another, he will be an adulterer, although she will not be an adulteress" (*Opus majus*, 7.3.11, ed. John H. Bridges [Oxford, 1896], 2:306; trans. Robert B. Burke [New York, 1962], 2:719).

Nevertheless, Antoninus's entry is different in some essential aspects from Aquinas's. Its scope is encyclopedic, unlike Aquinas's limited and focused question in the *Summa*. Antoninus deals with cruelty in the political context of tyranny; with justified cruelty, according to Jerome's version of the "medical metaphor"; and with the cruelty of the Jews against Christ, and this list is not exhaustive. The range of Antoninus's discussion renders it a comprehensive summary of medieval attitudes toward the subject, but it also makes it less focused and more inconsistent compared to its main source: Aquinas's discussion. Thus, in contrast to Aquinas and Seneca, Antoninus defines *clementia* as the moderation of exterior punishment (and not as a reference to the actor's inner intentions).[37]

Antoninus's entry, however, is not only a compendium of earlier medieval references to cruelty; it also points to his transitory position from the medieval to the early modern mode of reference to cruelty. Antoninus's entry is entitled "On taking pleasure in the afflictions of one's neighbor" [De exsultatione in adversis proximi], and not "On Cruelty" (*De crudelitate*) as in Aquinas's *Summa*. This title points to the irrational aspect of cruelty—pleasure derived from the suffering of others—which was explicitly rejected by Aquinas and Seneca in their systematic discussions of cruelty.[38] Irrational cruelty shall be a key aspect in the early modern treatment of the subject.

THE EARLY MODERN PERIOD

The most radical shift in the philosophical treatment of cruelty occurs in the early modern period and is manifested in Montaigne's essay "On Cruelty" [De la cruauté]. The enhanced importance accorded to the subject is reflected in the appearance, for the first time, of a separate work devoted to it. Moreover, in an unprecedented manner, cruelty is termed the "ultimate vice [l'extreme de tous les vices]."

Unlike Seneca or Thomas Aquinas, Montaigne does not provide a rigid theoretical definition of cruelty but works inductively through a set of examples that involve personal experience. Thus, Montaigne's main concern is the type of irrational cruelty he had ample opportunity to witness during the wars of religion:

37. Differunt autem ab invicem, in quantum clementia est moderativa exterioris punitionis. Mansuetudo autem proprie diminuit passionem irae (*Summa theologica* 4-4-3 [Graz, 1959] [a reprint of the 1740 Verona edition], 4:122). In the chapter on *clementia*, Antoninus mentions once more that *clementia* is opposed to *crudelitas* (4-4-9; 4:161–62).

38. This aspect of cruelty did feature in some of their passing remarks on the subject.

If I had not seen it I could hardly have made myself believe that you could find souls so monstrous that they would commit murder for the sheer fun of it; would hack at another man's limbs and lop them off and cudgel their brains to invent unusual tortures and new forms of murder, not from hatred or for gain but for the one sole purpose of enjoying the pleasant spectacle of pitiful gestures and twitchings of a man in agony, while hearing his screams and groans. For there you have the farthest point that cruelty [*cruauté*] can reach: "(C) Ut homo hominem, non iratus, non timens, tantum spectaturus occidat" [quoting Seneca: that man should kill not in anger or in fear but merely for the spectacle].[39]

The reference to Seneca emphasizes the selective nature of cultural influences. Aquinas did not wish to deal with irrational cruelty and therefore used only Seneca's discussion in the second book of *De clementia*. Montaigne, however, concentrates on the irrational aspect of cruelty and uses Seneca's passing remarks in his other writings on this type of cruelty, which better fit his purpose.

Montaigne's emphasis on the irrational aspect of cruelty points to a change in the ethical framework that shaped the medieval references of Aquinas and Antoninus to the subject. Montaigne occupies an intermediate position between ethics of action and ethics of intention. The intentions of the actor are highly relevant to his discussion but are not the sole factor determining the cruelty of an action. The implications of this shift with regard to the conception of cruelty are particularly noticeable in the legal context, in which they can be compared to Aquinas's treatment of the issue. According to Montaigne, in the context of punishment there are actions that are cruel in themselves, even if "pure" justice would have allowed them (that is, the punished person is culpable, and the intention of the person inflicting the punishment remains uncontaminated). The limit is the death penalty: "Even in the case of justice itself, anything beyond the straightforward death penalty seems pure cruelty."[40] Thus, the exclusive focus on intentions that characterized Aquinas's discussion precluded the discussion of irrational cruelty; the disappearance of this focus in the writings of Montaigne moves this aspect of cruelty to the center.

The importance of cruelty as a cultural issue in the early modern period is linked to other changes in the factors that affected the medieval treatment of the subject. It is linked to the Renaissance emphasis on the body and the physical aspects of existence, which stand in contrast to the Chris-

39. Montaigne, *Essais*, 2:11, ed. Albert Thibaudet (Paris, 1950), 476–77; English translation: Michel de Montaigne, *Essays of Michel de Montaigne*, trans. Michael A. Screech (Harmondsworth, 1991[1987]), 484 (references to the translation will be given hereafter according to the translator's name).

40. *Essais*, 2:11, 475; Screech, 482. This statement is repeated verbatim in the essay "Couardise mère de la cruauté," *Essais*, 2:27, 785; Screech, 794.

tian-Augustinian tradition of disparaging the body and emphasizing the soul. Montaigne emphasizes the harmony between body and soul and between physical and spiritual existence. The unity of body and soul also has less pleasant aspects, such as pain. The body is no longer an inferior element, and Montaigne reflects this in his style, which abounds with physical and body-related imagery, even that referring to the "ugly aspects of the bodily existence."[41] Such a view of the relation between body and soul makes cruelty an important issue within Montaigne's thought.

The peak in the cultural preoccupation with cruelty is related to another factor that influenced the rise of the issue in the central Middle Ages: the circulation of Seneca's writings. Interest in his works increased steadily from the thirteenth century; starting in the 1470s, editions and translations of his works became increasingly numerous.[42] The extent of their circulation in the sixteenth century was unparalleled. The identity of the editors and commentators is also revealing. For instance, in 1529 Erasmus published his edition of Seneca's works, and in 1532 Calvin published his commentary on De clementia.[43] Seneca's tragedies were no less influential than his philosophical works, and they had great impact on Renaissance literature, especially on the English genre of "revenge tragedy."[44] The relation between the renewed interest in cruelty and the reception of Seneca is not a one-way influence; it is a dynamic relation between two processes, one fueling the other.

Legal sources are ostensibly absent from this survey of theoretical approaches to cruelty because cruelty is almost never an issue in legal sources. Throughout the Middle Ages, both secular and canon law, with few exceptions, do not

41. See Michaël Baraz, L'être et la connaissance selon Montaigne (Paris, 1968), 81, 194–98. The increased interest in the human body and the physical is one of the basic features of the Renaissance [see Jacob Burckhardt, The Civilization of the Renaissance in Italy, trans. S. G. C. Middlemore (New York, 1965[1860]), 2:338–43, 510–16]. See also Mikhail Bakhtin, Rabelais and His World, trans. Hélène Iswolsky (Bloomington, Ind., 1984[1965]), 368–436. Montaigne's references to pain are related to the Epicurean outlook on sense perception. See Diogenes Laertius 10 (Epicurus) 63ff; and Hugo Friedrich, Montaigne, trans. Dawn Eng (Berkeley, Calif., 1991[1967,1949]), 322–23. Indicative of the new attitude toward cruelty is a letter of Ficino, in which he sets crudelitas as the opposite of humanitas, presents the possibility that cruelty may be attributed to physical (not just mental) causes, and links cruelty to madness [Ficino, Epistolae 1:55 (Turin, 1962 [repr. of Basel, 1576]), 635].

42. The first complete edition (of the philosophical works) is that of Moravus (Naples, 1475).

43. Calvin's Commentary on Seneca's De Clementia, ed. and trans. Ford L. Battles and Andre M. Hugo (Leiden, 1969).

44. See Baraz, "Seneca, Ethics, and the Body," 209–11.

refer to cruelty.[45] The disregard for cruelty in legal discourse is not surprising because legal violence is never perceived as cruel from within the system. In Jerome's formulation, "he who kills cruel [people] is not cruel ... But the robber hanging from the gibbet thinks the judge cruel."[46] Thus, references to cruelty in legal sources are rare in the early medieval period.

The rise of legal studies in the central Middle Ages did not change this situation. In his discussion of the legal means of combating heresy, Gratian repeats Jerome's aforementioned saying as his authority in sanctioning the use of violence against heretics. Nicolaus Eymeric's manual for inquisitors does not refer to torture as problematic or as related to cruelty. Canon lawyers, such as Bartolus of Saxoferrato (1313–1357), do not refer to cruelty in the chapters *De quaestionibus* [On Investigations] and *De poenis* [On Punishments].[47] In treatises dealing specifically with torture, the situation is much the same. The thirteenth-century *Tractatus de tormentis* [*Treatise on Torments*] attributed to Guido de Suzzara deals only with the avoidance of *excessive* torture and with the judge's liability if he fails to observe this limit. Later works, up to the fifteenth century, based on the *Tractatus* do not expand much beyond that.[48] The situation changes only slightly in the early modern period, when inquisitors, such as Francisco Peña and André Morellet, refer to cruelty in their apologetic efforts to present the inquisitorial practices, particularly torture, as *not* cruel.[49]

45. The *Codex Justinianus* and the *Codex Theodosianus* do not refer to cruelty in the sections on torture and on punishments. One exception is the Visigothic law, which explicitly prohibits the unchecked killing or dismemberment of slaves, defining it explicitly as cruelty (*Lex Visigothorum* VI, 5, 13, *MGH Leges nationum Germanicarum* 1:274, 278–79).

46. Jerome, *Commentarii in Isaiam* 5.13.9, ed. Marc Adriaen (*CCSL* 73) (Turnhout, 1963), 162. This comment has been quoted extensively from the twelfth century onward for justifying various penalties, especially against heretics. (See Gratian, *Decretum*, C 23.5.28, ed. Emil A. Friedberg [Graz, 1959], 1:938.)

47. The only place where Bartolus seems to stress the need for moderation more than his sources is in his commentary on *Digesta*, 48.18.7, in which he specifies that the judge is legally liable if he applied excessive torture (si iudex excessit modum consuetum, & modum qui debeat adhiberi secundum qualitatem personæ tortae).

48. Guido de Suzzara's treatise and those following it were published in *Tractatus de indiciis homicidii* (Venice, 1549). For the relevant passages, see 68r; 83r-v; Baldo de' Perigli of Perugia (thirteenth century), *Tractatus de indiciis homicidii*, 99r; Francesco Bruni (fifteenth century), *Tractatus de indiciis homicidii*, 37v–41r; Marc'Antonio Bianchi (1498–1548), *Tractatus de indiciis homicidii*, 7r.

49. Nicolás Eymerich, Francisco Peña, *Directorium Inquisitorum*, trans. Maria J. L. da Silva (Rio de Janeiro, 1993), 209–13; André Morellet, *Abrégé du Manuel des Inquisiteurs*, ed. Jean-Pierre Guicciardi (Grenoble, 1990), 134.

The early modern period is the culmination of the process that started in the thirteenth century. Thomas Aquinas's philosophical innovations and the cultural trends he was part of rendered cruelty a legitimate subject for speculation, but they did not make cruelty an important issue. This status of the topic continued, without significant changes, until the end of the medieval period. In the sixteenth century, cruelty emerges—for the first time since Seneca—as an important philosophical topic. But for all these fluctuations, the same factors affect the philosophical treatment of cruelty from the first century to the sixteenth. It is affected by changes in the following factors: the perceived relation between body and soul, the diffusion of the Latin classical heritage, and the relative weight of actions and intentions in the ethical systems dominant in a particular cultural context. A debasing attitude to the body and to the pagan classical heritage leads to the decline of interest in cruelty with the transition to Christianity in late antiquity. Conversely, Montaigne's essay on cruelty brings together a new positive attitude toward the body, an ethical conception that gives equal weight to actions and intentions, and the wide diffusion and prestige of Seneca's works.

CHAPTER TWO
LATE ANTIQUITY—THE
BUILDING BLOCKS OF
A DISCOURSE

T he first centuries A.D. were a crucial phase in the shaping of medieval perceptions of cruelty. Several factors contributed to making this period so significant with respect to the issue of cruelty until the modern period. Cruelty was an important cultural issue in the first century—as reflected in Seneca's writings—mainly because actual violence was pervasive in Rome, the cultural center of the Empire. Some of the emperors of the first century were particularly notorious for their violence. Nero's actions had a direct impact on Seneca's writings, and his persecution of Christianity made him an enduring symbol of cruelty from his own time to the end of the Middle Ages. In addition, Rome suffered increasingly from external violence perpetrated by "barbarian" peoples within and outside the Empire. Thus, in pagan writings there are two primary contexts of cruelty: the political sphere in which cruelty is perceived as an aspect of tyranny, and the violence of the barbarian "other," which is a cultural topic that goes back to the *Histories* of Herodotus.

Attitudes toward cruelty changed with the transition to a Christian context. In comparison with pagan writers, Christian thinkers, who did not deal with cruelty per se, viewed cruelty less urgently as a cultural issue. Nevertheless, cruelty was still represented in early Christian culture; the Christian representations of cruelty were linked to the pagan tradition but displayed different emphases. The new and most important context in which Christians dealt with cruelty was martyrdom. The persecutions against Christians may have been less significant in the overall contemporary balance of violence in the Empire, but they were constitutive events in forging the Christian outlook on violence and, by extension, on cruelty. The Christian outlook on the issue moved into dominance with the Christianization of the Empire in the fourth century, and it influenced medieval attitudes to cruelty until the central Middle Ages.

In this chapter, I review briefly the ways in which pagan writers of the first centuries A.D. represent cruelty, because these are the foundations on which later Western constructs of cruelty are built. I then examine how the transition to Christianity modifies the pagan attitudes to the subject by following Christian representations of the violence of the barbarian peoples and comparing them with pagan ones. The focus of the discussion, however, is the representation of cruelty in martyrdom accounts, which is the main context in which cruelty is represented by Christian writers. The modes of representing cruelty change over time as well as geographically between Latin and Greek zones of influence. They are indicative of significant differences in the perception of cruelty and point to the factors influencing the treatment of the subject.

PAGAN WRITERS

Pagan writers, such as Seneca, Tacitus, Suetonius, and Valerius Maximus, leave us a very unflattering account of some of the Roman leaders and emperors of the first century A.D. Suetonius provides numerous examples of Caligula's "innate cruelty" (*saevitiam ingenii*). According to him, Caligula, who reigned between 37 and 41 A.D., liked to attend sessions of torture and execution and insisted on slow and painful executions so that the condemned would be made "to feel that [they] were dying." Suetonius also describes how he fed human beings to animals. Claudius, despite his popularity in modern times, shared some of Caligula's tastes. Likewise, Suetonius provides numerous instances of Nero's cruelty, such as rape, murder, torture, and dismemberment.[1] These actions are explicitly characterized by Suetonius as cruelty.[2] Tacitus also refers explicitly to instances of cruelty committed by the emperors. In a famous passage, Tacitus characterizes as cruelty Nero's persecution of the Christians after the burning of Rome. However, his criticism is aimed primarily at Nero's mode of administering the punishment, which gives the impression that the Christians were executed as a consequence of a tyrannical whim, not on account of Tacitus's opinion as to their innocence.

The second focus for the representation of cruelty is the barbarian "others." The model for this type of representation has been set by Herodotus, whose portrayal of the Scythians became the most enduring image of the cruel "other" in Western historiography until the sixteenth century. Their violence is extraordinary because they are characterized as cannibals. Moreover, violence

1. Suetonius, *De vita Caesarum*, IV.11, 27–32, 36 [Caligula]; V.34 [Claudius]; VI.27–38 [Nero], ed. John C. Rolfe (Cambridge, Mass., 1997–98[1913–14]), 1:430–33, 458–69, 472–73; 2:62–65, 124–51.

2. *Saevitia* (and derivatives) is the term most commonly used by Suetonius in this context. *Crudelitas*, however, is used as well (*Nero* 27).

in itself is valued by them, as reflected in the central place of the god of war, Ares, in their pantheon. They are systematically differentiated from the "civilized" Greeks and in many respects presented as the Greeks' mirror image.[3]

Both of these focuses are present in Valerius Maximus's *Facta et dicta memorabilia*, a collection of historical examples of various virtues and vices. It devotes a short chapter to cruelty (*crudelitas*), reflecting the two principal contexts of Roman preoccupation with the subject: cruelty in the legal-political context and the cruelty of the barbarians. As a matter of procedure, Valerius Maximus divides his examples of virtues and vices into two groups—of the Romans (*Romanorum*) and of non-Romans (*externorum*). The Roman examples refer mainly to extreme brutality of the conventional kind: murders and massacres in the contexts of war—primarily civil war—and tyranny. In contrast, many of the non-Roman examples, although no less brutal than their Roman counterparts, are characterized by inventiveness in devising new and more painful modes of torture and execution.[4]

The Roman preoccupation with the cruelty of the barbarians increased as their attacks became more frequent and dangerous. Ammianus Marcellinus died not long before barbarian attacks culminated in the sack of Rome in 410. He left relatively detailed descriptions of several barbarian peoples, such as the Goths and the Huns, that leave no doubt that he conceived them as "other." Ammianus linked cruelty and savagery to irrationality and consequently related it to madness and beastly behavior.[5] This characterization is reflected in the bestialized portraits of the barbarians in general as well as in the terms used to describe their violence. Ammianus uses such terms as *saevus* (and *saevire*), *trux*, and *truculentus* for both Romans and barbarians. Yet the terms *ferus* and *feritas*, animal characteristics, are used almost exclusively for barbarians.[6] Thus, he describes the Huns as two-footed animals and comments that they "exceed every mode of ferocity

3. On Herodotus's portrayal of the Scythians and on the concept of systematic differentiation in the representation of the "other," see François Hartog, *The Mirror of Herodotus: The Representation of the Other in the Writing of History*, trans. Janet Lloyd (Berkeley, Calif., 1988[1980]), 8:188–92. A similar technique is used by Syed M. Islam for analyzing Marco Polo's narrative ("Marco Polo: Order/Disorder in the Discourse of the Other," *Literature and History*, ser. 3, 2:1 [1993]: 1–22).

4. Valerius Maximus, *Facta et dicta memorabilia* 9.2, ed. John Briscoe (Stuttgart, 1998), 2:778–81. On Valerius Maximus, see W. Martin Bloomer, *Valerius Maximus & the Rhetoric of the New Nobility* (Chapel Hill, N.C., 1992).

5. I am indebted to Robin Seager's meticulous study of Ammianus's terminology. Seager comments that "for Ammianus savagery and madness are also common symptoms of excessive behavior and extremes of vice" (Robin Seager, *Ammianus Marcellinus* [Columbia, Mo., 1986], 54).

6. Seager, *Ammianus Marcellinus*, 54–58.

[*ferocitas*]." Although having the outward "figure of man," their whole mode of life suggests that they are not: They do not cook their meat; they do not live in buildings but in mountains and woods; they look as if glued to their horses (that is, united with their animals); they do not have any political system, they do not engage in agricultural activities, and, most important, like animals, they have no moral consciousness and no religion.[7]

The ominous atmosphere of imminent violence in the first centuries A.D. was not reflected only in historical accounts of the actions of the emperor or in descriptions of external attacks by barbarians. It comes forth from Apuleius's fictional account of his travel through the Empire in the *Golden Ass*. It is aestheticized in Ovid's *Metamorphoses* with various stories of murder, rape, mutilation, and cannibalism. Seneca's plays, especially *Thyestes*, also contain motifs of rape, murder, and cannibalism. Ovid's story of Procne is telling in this respect: Procne was the wife of Tereus, king of Thracia, who used to feed his horses with human flesh. Tereus raped Procne's sister, Philomela, and cut out her tongue so that she would be unable to reveal his crime. But Philomela did manage to convey to her sister what happened, and Procne, burning with desire for revenge, killed her son, cooked his flesh, and served the dish to Tereus.[8] Only after the meal did she tell him that he ate his own son.

THE TRANSITION TO CHRISTIANITY

The cultural role of cruelty changes significantly with the transition to a Christian context. As mentioned, cruelty is no longer a subject for theoretical discussion or speculation. Unlike Seneca or Valerius Maximus, Christian thinkers such as Augustine or Jerome did not deal with cruelty as a subject per se. But cruelty is still represented (rather than discussed) by Christian authors. These representations present continuity and, at the same time, a break away from the pagan mode of dealing with the subject. Christian historiography displays preoccupation with the two main contexts of cruelty addressed by pagans: tyranny and the cruelty of the "other." However, the main context in which Christians represent cruelty is martyrdom, and this particular perspective on the subject is essentially new.

Christian historians' writings about the barbarians show—perhaps surprisingly so for a community persecuted by the imperial authorities—a high

---

7. Ammianus Marcellinus, *Rerum gestarum libri* 31.2.1–12, ed. and trans. John C. Rolfe (Cambridge, Mass., 1950–52[1936–39]) 3:381–87. Ammianus names another Asiatic people as *Anthropophagi*, mentioning that they are nomads and feed on human flesh (31.2.15, 3:388–89); the Anthropophagi are mentioned also (23.6.66, 2:384–85).

8. See *Metamorphoses* 6:533–34, 652 for explicit references to cruelty.

degree of identification with Roman culture. Similar to pagan Romans, they see cruelty as the outstanding quality of the barbarians and regard this trait as essentially un-Roman. Lactantius, for instance, describes Diocletian's cruelty as being alien to Roman mores.[9] Victor of Vita, writing in the fifth century, deals with the Vandal occupation of North Africa. As Lactantius before him, Victor perceives cruelty as an inherent quality of the barbarians, which is essentially un-Roman: Victor maintains that for him *barbarian* is synonymous with *cruelty*.[10]

Victor is much more explicit and outspoken than pagan writers such as Ammianus in attributing cruelty to the barbarians. He sets the tone in the opening sentence of the first chapter of his *History of the Persecution of the Province of Africa*: "It is evident that this is now the sixtieth year since the cruel and savage [*crudelis ac saevus*] people of the Vandal race set foot on the territory of wretched Africa."[11] He describes in detail the atrocities committed by the persecuting Vandals and inserts numerous explicit references to cruelty into his narration. He tells of people tormented to death so that they would bring forth their money and valuables. He complains that the Vandals had no regard for the aged or for women and dwells on instances of infants snatched from their mothers' breasts and dashed to the ground or cut into two by the Vandals.[12]

For all their similarity to pagan accounts of the "other," however, the shift to Christianity entails some changes. For example, sexual cruelty is much less dominant in the writings of Christian historians compared with those of pagan historians. In addition, a new category of cruelty emerges: Violence against religious officeholders and against Church property is explicitly labeled as cruelty. Another conceptual change evident in Victor's chronicle is the fusion of cruelty and tyranny. These concepts overlapped considerably in Latin pagan culture but were not identical: The cruelty of

9. "Inerat huic bestiae naturalis barbaries, efferitas a Romano sanguine aliena: non mirum, cum mater eius Transdanuuiana infestantibus Carpis in Daciam nouam transiecto amne confugerat" (*De mortibus persecutorum* 9.2, ed. Joseph Moreau [*Sources Chrétiennes* 39] [Paris, 1954], 1:87).

10. "Numquid alio proprio nomine vocitari poterant nisi ut barbari dicerentur, ferocitatis utique, crudelitatis et terroris vocabulum possidentes?" (Victor Vitensis, *Historia persecvtionis Africanae provinciae temporibus Geiserici et Hvnirici regvm Wandalorum* 3.62, ed. C. Halm, *MGH AA* 3:56; English trans. *Victor of Vita: History of the Vandal Persecution*, trans. John Moorhead [Liverpool, 1992], 89 [the translation of this sentence has been modified]. The translation will be referenced hereafter as *Moorhead*).

11. Victor Vitensis, *Historia persecvtionis* 1.1, 2; *Moorhead*, 3.

12. See Victor Vitensis, *Historia persecvtionis* 1.6-7, 3; and *Moorhead*, 4–5. The affective narration of these passages is interspersed with numerous explicit references related to cruelty (*crudelibus, crudelia, sine misericordia, crudeles*, and *barbarus furor*).

tyranny was not perceived as identical to the cruelty of the barbarian "others."[13] In Victor's chronicle, the two terms are used synonymously. Victor writes that Catholic churches were Arianized with tyrannical presumption (*licentia tyrannica*).[14] He refers to Huniric as *tyrannus* when he tells of his edict that all officeholders should be Arian and of the torture of Catholic bishops or lay believers.[15] The term is not reserved for the king alone; it is used as a generic term for persecuting Vandal officers.[16] The conflation of the terms is evident in the instances in which the narrow political meaning of tyranny does not fit the context, and it is clear that the writer uses it as a synonym for cruelty.

Christian attitudes toward cruelty reflect a complex relation to the pagan references to the issue. Despite some shifts of emphasis, Christian historiography presents a continuity with pagan historiography. Historiography is an exception, however; in other areas, the changes with respect to the pagan attitudes are significant. These changes are marked by the disappearance of some modes of reference to cruelty and the appearance of others. Thus, speculative discussions of cruelty disappear in Christian ambience, while a new, fully Christian mode of reference to cruelty emerges in the context of martyrdom and its celebration.

The pagan and the Christian outlooks overlap partially. Christians executed by the pagan emperors could still be seen as victims of tyranny, but their primary characterization was that of martyrs. Pagan writers who wrote about cruelty as an attribute of the tyrant were mainly concerned with the ruler's violence reflecting the abuse of power and the breakdown of political structure. Christian writers were concerned primarily with the persecution of their religion, and martyrdom was the event in which this cruelty was enacted. Christians killed by the Huns or the Vandals were perceived as victims of barbarian cruelty in accordance with the pagan view, but they, too, were in many cases primarily martyrs.

There were also links between the Christian concept of martyrdom and pagan culture. Glen Bowersock points out that the Roman legacy glorified voluntary death (for example, Lucretia, Dido, and Cleopatra), thus creating a favorable attitude toward martyrdom. Ian Donaldson shows how Christian writers and thinkers before Augustine accepted Lucretia as a symbol of

13. Ammianus Marcellinus, for instance, distinguished between the two types of cruelty even in the terminology he used: The terms *crudelis* and *crudelitas* were used almost exclusively for cruelty in the context of tyranny.

14. Victor Vitensis, *Historia persecvtionis* 1.9, 3; *Moorhead*, 6.

15. Victor Vitensis, *Historia persecvtionis* 2.23, 2.27, 3.32, 18, 19, 42; *Moorhead*, 32, 33, 77.

16. *Violentia tyrannorum* (Victor Vitensis, *Historia persecvtionis* 3.47, 52; *Moorhead*, 83).

martyrdom.[17] Likewise, Jerome presents Seneca as a martyr.[18] In some of the accounts of female martyrs, one can also identify traces of the pagan preoccupation with sexual violence.[19]

Nevertheless, martyrdom is primarily a Christian, not pagan, approach to violence and cruelty because it is a systematic effort to organize violence, suffering, and cruelty into a theologically meaningful structure.[20] Christian thinkers had a complex attitude toward violence and suffering. They saw suffering as a response to what they considered the natural and innate violence of pagan culture, epitomized for Augustine in the gladiatorial games. Conversely, suffering, as demonstrated by Christ's example, is essential for salvation. Thus the participants in martyrdom are divided into two opposing and morally distinct groups: The suffering martyr is virtuous, and the persecutor who inflicts the physical tortures is wicked. Moreover, martyrdom is not a story about individuals; it represents a conflict between much larger entities. On the earthly level, martyrdom represents the conflict of Christianity versus paganism. On the metaphysical level, martyrdom is a conflict between God and the Devil.

The way in which martyrdom is represented changes considerably in antiquity from the early contemporary accounts to those written in the post-Constantinian period. In many of the early accounts—the "historical" *passiones*[21]—cruelty is represented only implicitly. The detailed descriptions of the tortures inflicted on the martyrs are linked to one of the traditional contexts associated explicitly with cruelty in other sources: excess of punishment in the legal context, tyranny in the political sphere, pleasure derived from the suffering of others, and nonhuman (that is, irrational) violence (the last two associated primarily with the "other"). As I show later, in some of the early accounts, the martyrs' ordeals are associated with these traditional contexts of cruelty. The references to issues such as judicial violence and tyranny suggest that these reports of the suffering of the martyrs are, indeed, representations of cruelty, even when explicit references to cruelty are lacking.

17. Glen W. Bowersock, *Martyrdom and Rome* (Cambridge, 1995), 63–64; and Ian Donaldson, *The Rapes of Lucretia* (Oxford, 1982), 25–28.

18. Jerome, *De viris inlustribus* 12, ed. Carl Albrecht Bernoulli (Freiburg, 1895), 15.

19. See Brent D. Shaw, "The Passion of Perpetua," *Past and Present* 139 (1993): 3–45.

20. Stoicism also touches on those issues, but it was an elitist approach with limited appeal. Christianity dealt with these issues in a way that had a wide appeal. See also *Acta Alexandrinorum—The Acts of the Pagan Martyrs*, ed. Herbert A. Musurillo (Oxford, 1954).

21. The dating of martyrdom accounts is one of the most problematic and contested issues. When dealing with the early, nearly contemporary accounts I refer to the texts in Herbert Musurillo's collection [*Acts of the Christian Martyrs* (Oxford, 1979[1972])], hereafter cited as *Musurillo*]. Musurillo's collection is almost identical to Hippolyte Delehaye's list of "historical" martyrdoms [*Les passions des martyres et les genres littéraires* (Brussels, 1966[1921])].

A number of the early *passiones* refer to the legal context of cruelty—that is, cruelty as the excessive application of judicial violence. Thus, they point to perceptions of cruelty that were shared by pagans and Christians.[22] In the *Passio Sanctorum Mariani et Iacobi*, it is implied that the persecutors' cruelty consists of excessive torture and the invention of new methods of torture rather than the act of torture per se.[23] In the *Martyrdom of Saint Conon*, the prefect threatens Conon: "If our tortures have no power over you, I shall devise even more painful ones for you." True to his word, he "ordered spikes to be driven under [Conon's] ankles, and thus he made the martyr run ahead of his chariot with his feet pierced" and had him "driven on by two men with whips."[24] In the *Letter of Phileas*, it is also implied that the cruelty of the prefect is the invention of new modes of torture.[25]

Characterizing the violence of the persecutor as tyranny is another way of portraying him as cruel. The close association between the two concepts is revealed in instances in which tyranny is dislocated from a political context and used as a pointer to cruelty. Thus, in the *Letter of the Churches of Lyons and Vienne*, the persecutor is called tyrant and so is the prefect who persecuted Conon.[26]

Other modes of representing cruelty in the context of martyrdom are drawn from the characteristics of the barbarians' cruelty: The violence of the pagan persecutors is rendered exceptional by making it nonhuman, and it is presented either as diabolical or as bestial. In the martyrdom of Polycarp, a clear simile is drawn between the wild beasts with which the martyr is threatened and the mob at the amphitheater. Other accounts present the persecutor as the devil's servant, and some even present the devil himself participating in the action. Thus, a day before her martyrdom, Perpetua has a vision that makes her realize that she is not going to fight against wild animals but against the devil.[27] In the *Passio Sanctorum Montani et Lucii*, the arrest is presented as an intermediate victory over the devil.[28] The execu-

22. See Andrew Lintott, "Cruelty in the Political Life of the Ancient World," in *Crudelitas: The Politics of Cruelty in the Ancient and Medieval World*, ed. Toivo Viljamaa, Asko Timonen, and Christian Krötzl (Krems, 1992), 9–27.

23. Quaenam illa tormenta, quam noua, quam diaboli uenenato sensu et deiciendi artibus exquisita supplicia (*Passio Sanctorum Mariani et Iacobi*, in *Musurillo*, 200–1).

24. Ibid., 191.

25. *The Letter of Phileas*, in *Musurillo*, 323.

26. *Musurillo*, 70–71, 190–91, respectively. Both of these accounts are in Greek. On tyranny as the primary context of cruelty in the Greek world, see Lintott, "Cruelty in the Political Life."

27. *Passio Sanctarum Perpetuae et Felicitatis*, in *Musurillo*, 118.

28. Unde prostrato diabolo uictores sumus in carcerem reuersi et ad alteram uictoriam reseruati (*Passio Sanctorum Montani et Lucii*, in *Musurillo*, 218–19).

tioners are called *ministri diaboli* (assistants of the devil) both in the *Passio Iuli Veterani* and in the martyrdom of the Bishop Carpus, the Deacon Pamfilus, and Agathonicê.[29]

Thus, although the violence of the pagan persecutors is clearly presented as cruelty in these early accounts, cruelty is not mentioned explicitly. What are the reasons for this omission in view of the explicit references to cruelty in other sources of late antiquity? Why do the writers of these texts refrain from referring directly to this issue?

The absence seems to be the result of a combination of social and ideological factors. On the most basic level, it has to do with the fact that the martyrs, the persecutors, the authors of the accounts, and the immediate audience of these texts were part of the same community. Because of this cohabitation, members of the community had nontextual knowledge of the events—they had either witnessed them themselves or had heard stories from eyewitnesses. The audience's knowledge bound the authors, for reasons of credibility, to relate the facts of the case accurately and prevented them from overdemonizing the persecutors, their pagan neighbors. The absence of this constraint in later adaptations of the account led, as we shall see, to a significantly greater emphasis on cruelty.

The day-to-day interaction between pagans and Christians and the partially overlapping cultural perceptions of cruelty mitigated the representation of pagan cruelty in other ways as well. In some accounts, the martyrs, or the authors of the accounts, perceive the pagan officials as performing, sometimes unwillingly, their legal duty. The imperial decrees concerning the Christians are evidently seen as unjust, but the pagan officials themselves do not exceed their legal duty, and, consequently, according to the notion that only *exaggerated* judicial violence is cruelty, these officials are not cruel. The absence of explicit references to cruelty in these cases is due to the incongruity arising from the perception of the event itself as unjust and violent and the difficulty of characterizing its perpetrators as cruel. These cases are a minority, but they are a significant one: Phileas, Cyprian of Carthage, Irenaeus, and Flavian all have to urge reluctant prefects to fulfill their duty and execute them.[30] This attitude suggests—as in the percep-

---

29. *Musurillo*, 264, 32, respectively.

30. The phrases used by the martyrs are similar in most cases. Phileas: "quod iussum tibi est fac" (*Musurillo*, 350–51; the Greek version is similar, 340–41); Cyprian: "fac quod tibi praeceptum est" (*Musurillo*, 172); Irenaeus: "Fac quod iussum est" (*Musurillo*, 296–97). Flavian knowingly forces a reluctant prefect to execute him: "sed magis ipse habebat in animo certum quod et fides propria et petitio antecessorum suorum extorqueret praesidi uel inuitam, licet populo reclamante, sententiam" (*Musurillo*, 230–31).

tion of the barbarian "others"—that notions of cruelty in the legal context were shared by pagans and Christians even in times of persecution.

Ideological factors were even more influential in pushing cruelty to the background or even suppressing it. The portrayal of the martyr's suffering was related both to the image of God as Christians perceived him and to the image of him they wished to project to the pagans. Internally, the suffering of the martyrs raised the question of theodicy: How does God permit the just to suffer so much?[31] Externally, images of suffering Christians might have projected an image of a weak Christian God who cannot protect his believers. The difficulties posed by these issues are reflected in accounts that ignore or even deny the martyrs' suffering. Thus, the account relating the martyrdom of Pionius refers to the actual act of martyrdom in less than one paragraph out of twenty-three:

> And so they raised him up on the gibbet . . . After they brought the firewood and piled up the logs . . . . Pionius shut his eyes so that the crowd thought he was dead. But he was praying in secret. . . . The flames were just beginning to rise as he pronounced his last Amen with a joyful countenance and said: "Lord, receive my soul." Then peacefully and painlessly as though belching he breathed his last and gave his soul in trust to the Father.[32]

Ideological motivations were also intermingled with literary and stylistic issues in determining the representation of cruelty in martyrdom. Reference or nonreference to the suffering of the martyr and the degree of affectivity of the narration were influenced by considerations of the expected effect on the audience. Christian authors preferred a muted, toned down representation, seeing it as more austere and dignified and more similar to the understatement characterizing the biblical style.[33] The choice of the implicit narrative mode can be better understood if one bears in mind the only partial overlap between the audience of the actual spectacle of martyrdom and the implied audience of the texts (and their respective "horizons of expectations").[34] The spectacle of martyrdom was addressed both to fellow Christians and to pagans. The texts, however, were written primarily for

31. One way of dealing with this problem was through the "medical metaphor," which has been discussed in Chapter 1, 17.

32. *The Martyrdom of Pionius the Presbyter and his Companions*, in *Musurillo*, 165.

33. See Erich Auerbach, *Literary Language and its Public in Late Latin Antiquity and in the Middle Ages* (London, 1965[1958]), chap. 1, esp. 60–66 on the *Passio SS. Perpetuae et Felicitatis*.

34. This term is borrowed from the "reader response" school of literary criticism; the term *implied audience* is a medievalization of the term *implied reader*. See the Introduction, 8.

Christians and could therefore take into account a shared ideological background of author and audience. Thus, the author could assume that the persecutor would be considered cruel and that the martyr would be understood to have suffered greatly, even if this was not stated explicitly.

Whatever the reservations in earlier periods concerning the explicit reference to cruelty and their motivations, they seem to fade away in the Latin West in the course of the fourth century. Cruelty moves more and more to the foreground. The chronicle of Victor of Vita, which has been mentioned in relation to the pagan representations of the "other," belongs to this period. But whereas it could be seen in terms of continuity with the pagan mode of reference to cruelty, martyrdom accounts from this period present significant changes compared with earlier ones.

Thus the *Passio Sanctorum Mariani et Iacobi*, probably written at the beginning of the fourth century, refers extensively to the cruelty of the pagans, using the whole lexical field of reference to this issue.[35] The irrational aspect of the behavior of the persecutors is emphasized by repeated references to their *furor* and to their blindness. In the second paragraph, the author uses the expressions "with blind fury [*caeco furore*]," "the devil's wrath [*rabies diaboli*]," "raged with fury [*fureret*]," and "the blood-shedding and blind fury of the governor [*cruenti et caecati praesidis furor*]." A concluding sentence ties up all the elements:

> The madness [*insania*] of his cruelty [*crudelitas*] was exercised not only against those who were living freely for God and had remained undisturbed by the earlier persecutions; but the devil stretched forth his insatiate hand as well against those who, though earlier driven out into exile, the insanity [*amentia*] of the ferocious [*ferox*] prefect had crowned as martyrs in spirit, though not yet in blood.[36]

The tortures suffered by the martyrs are described in detail, and their definition as cruel is explicit.[37]

This trend of increasingly explicit references to cruelty stands out even more visibly in "second-generation" accounts produced in this period.

35. Derivatives of *crudelitas*, *saevitia*, and *ferocitas*. For the dating of this *passio*, see *Musurillo*, xxxiv.

36. *Musurillo*, 196–97 (translation modified).

37. "Adhibitis in auxilium crudelitatis eius centurione," "uicta denique feritate torquentium" (*Musurillo*, 198–201).

These accounts were composed on the basis of earlier texts (and not according to eyewitness testimonies). Thus, they supply a "running commentary"
on the earlier texts they use by stressing certain ideological points or cor-
recting questionable issues in the early accounts. Consequently, whereas the
early versions provide a more accurate picture of the actual chain of events,
the second-generation accounts provide a clearer picture of the issues their
writers perceived as ideologically important in the context of martyrdom,
including the more prominent role of cruelty.

The *Peristephanon* of Prudentius (348–ca. 410) is one of the earliest and
more influential of such second-generation retellings in the West. It demonstrates effectively the change in presentation from the early "historical"
accounts. If in factual details Prudentius's narrations are close to the earlier accounts, in spirit they are far removed, particularly in their representations of cruelty. The most apparent difference, which is not only
external, is that Prudentius's accounts are in verse and not in prose. They
are, in fact, a more stylistically and ideologically elaborate "second
thought" on the events, the aim of which is to distill the ideological message of the texts.

The *Peristephanon* emphasizes the theological function of the martyr's
suffering, not just the readiness to die, in the scheme of salvation.[38] It also
brings into relief the Roman prefect's irrational fury and cruelty. These
characteristics stand out when Prudentius's text is compared with its earlier
sources. Such is the case, for instance, with his rendering of the martyrdom
of Fructuosus and his companions.[39] The lifelike quality of the original *passio* is due to the inclusion of mundane details, such as Fructuosus's conversa-
tion with the arresting soldiers, in which he asks permission to put on his
sandals.[40] Such details are absent from the *Peristephanon*, and its narration of
the events preceding the saint's condemnation is filled instead with passionate eulogies of the saint, abuse of the governor, and a heroic speech that
Fructuosus delivers to his companions.

The actual arrest in Prudentius's text is made by a "blood-fed execu-
tioner" [*pastus sanguine carnifex*], an expression that evokes the context of

38. See, for instance, "Scripta sunt caelo duorum martyrum vocabula, / aureis quae
Christus illic adnotavit litteris, / sanguinis notis eadem scripta terris tradidit" [Pruden-
tius, *Peristephanon liber* I, ll. 1–3, in *Prudentius*, ed. and trans. Henry J. Thomson (Cambridge, Mass., 1961[1953]), 2:98–99]. The same idea is formulated more crudely in the
martyrdom of Marian and James, another post-Constantinian text: "Ii sunt . . . qui quod
difficilius et tardius uincunt, gloriosius coronantur" (*Musurillo*, 206).

39. See the Introduction in *Musurillo*, xxxii.

40. The motif of the sandals reappears once more at the scene of Fructuosus's execution, when he takes them off before being burnt, symbolically recalling Moses before the
burning bush.

cannibalism and hence of cruelty.[41] The prefect is characterized as a "fierce (or cruel [*atrox*]), violent, arrogant, unholy man," and he "orders [Fructuosus and his companions] to worship at the 'devilish altars.'"[42] The prefect's diabolically macabre wit, which is only implicit in the *passio*, is made explicit by Prudentius.[43]

The saints' entrance into the amphitheater is a truly infernal scene in Prudentius's rendering:

> By this time they were entering a place enclosed by tiers of seats in a circle, where frenzied crowds attend and are drunk with much blood of wild beasts, when the din rises from the bloody shows, and as the gladiator, whose life is held cheap, falls under the stroke of the stark sword there is a roar of delight. Here a black officer, bidden to make ready the fiery torture on a blazing pyre.[44]

The wrath (*furor*) of the governor and audience is contrasted throughout with the calm and quiet speech of the saint. The allusion to the drinking of blood is, once more, not merely an allusion to cruelty but also to its barbarian and cannibalistic nature.[45] In contrast, the *passio* tells that the audience "began to sympathize with him, for he was much beloved of pagans and Christians alike."[46] It relates that many of the audience, without specifying their religious identity, offered him some wine to relieve his suffering, which the martyr refused. This incident is omitted by Prudentius.[47]

The *Peristephanon* thus reveals a tendency to emphasize the cruelty of the persecutors more than did the original *passiones*, primarily by representing the persecutors' violence in terms of the cruelty of the "other." As in Valerius Maximus's examples of non-Roman cruelty, the persecutors are shown enjoying the torture of the martyrs and attempting to be inventive in their tortures. The association with the "other" is made as well through the beastly imagery used to depict the persecutors and through implicit and explicit references to cannibalism. The demonization of the persecu-

---

41. *Prudentius*, VI, l. 17, 2:204–5. Later in the martyrdom, Prudentius uses the same metaphor for the crowd in the theater: madens ferarum multo sanguine (VI, ll. 62–63, 2:206–7). On cannibalism as representative of the cruelty of the "other," see above, 30.

42. *Peristephanon* VI, l. 36, 204–5.

43. *Peristephanon* VI, ll. 61–68 in *Prudentius*, 2:206; for the corresponding scene in the *passio*, see *Musurillo*, 178–79.

44. *Peristephanon* VI, ll. 61–68, 206–7.

45. As in the case of the Mongols, see Chapter 4, 98–100 *passim*.

46. *Musurillo*, 178–79.

47. The black officer has no parallel in the *passio* and seems to be added by Prudentius to heighten the diabolical character of the scene.

tors—that is, presenting them as the devil's subordinates—is also part of the same process.

An additional way of pointing to the persecutors' cruelty is Prudentius's representation of them as tyrants, a characterization that appears more systematically than in the early *passiones*. The term *tyrant* is at times accompanied by other words from the semantic field of cruelty, such as *trux tyrannus*; by references to acknowledged symbols of cruelty, such as the Babylonians; or by actions that would be unequivocally interpreted as cruelty, such as the amputation of the martyr's tongue. The word *tyrannus* (and derivatives) in reference to the persecutor is used sixteen times, more than the word *crudelis* (and derivatives), which appears seven times.[48]

The common denominator of all these tendencies is the ideological filter through which the early versions were passed. The variations from the sources in Prudentius's poems can be accounted for, in part, by the theological refinement imposed on the earlier text, evident especially in the presentation of martyrdom as a struggle with the devil. The more rigid theological framework is constructed also from the greater density of scriptural images and analogies (as the reference to the books of Maccabees for prefigurations of martyrdom). This phenomenon recalls Jonathan Riley-Smith's observation of the theological framework imposed on the second-generation Crusade chronicles of Guibert of Nogent, Baldric of Bourgueil, and Robert the Monk.[49] These tendencies of fourth-century accounts indicate that cruelty became an important issue in the theology of martyrdom in the West. This development is significant and is not "natural" or self-evident. As we have seen, in the earlier accounts martyrdom could be represented with no explicit—and at times with no implicit—reference to cruelty.

48. Roy J. Deferrari and James M. Campbell, *A Concordance of Prudentius* (Hildesheim, 1966[1932]).

49. A significant amount of his observations is relevant to the martyrdom accounts: "But most of the clergy with [the crusaders] were not of a high intellectual caliber and the resulting ideas, as they appeared in the eyewitness accounts, were awkward and unsophisticated. Urban's message has been distorted and popularized, and also greatly developed, in the traumas of the crusade, but the result was too rough to be of much use to the Church without some theological restatement. . . . It was later writers, especially Robert the Monk, Guibert of Nogent and Baldric of Bourgueil, who provided a *modus vivendi* for both theologians and the general public . . . Robert, Guibert and Baldric put the miraculous nature of the crusade into the framework of providential history." Jonathan Riley-Smith, *The First Crusade and the Idea of Crusading* (London, 1986), 154.

The later, second-generation accounts have been termed *epic martyrdoms* by Hippolyte Delehaye, and they were set apart from the earlier *historical martyrdoms*. Yet the distinction between epic and historical is somewhat misleading. When we possess both the historical account and a later version of it, the basic facts are often identical; what changes most is the mood of the narration. Delehaye noted the excessive cruelty of the torments in the epic martyrdoms, especially in the long lists of tortures the martyrs undergo.[50] Yet he fails to note that in many instances of what he repeatedly terms as cruelty, the texts do not define the action as such—even those epic texts in which such reference to cruelty could be expected.

What then determines the presence or absence of cruelty as an explicit issue in the text? The literary, or epic, character of the text and its being a later adaptation are evidently only partial answers to this question. Another element in this puzzle seems to be the cultural ambience in which the accounts were written. Martyrdom accounts circulated throughout the Roman Empire in late antiquity regardless of the geographical identity of the martyr or the language of the original *acta*. Accounts were translated at an early stage from Greek to Latin and vice versa. Yet nevertheless, cruelty is an explicit issue mainly in accounts produced in the Latin part of the Empire, not in those produced in the Greek cultural sphere. A difference between East and West regarding the cultural treatment of cruelty is already visible toward the end of the fourth century.

The most prominent example of the differentiated attitudes toward cruelty according to cultural ambience is Eusebius's (ca. 260–before 341) *Historia ecclesiastica*, written in Greek, and its Latin translation made by Rufinus (ca. 345–410). The *Historia ecclesiastica* was written with the purpose of telling the history of the Church from the beginning until the conversion of Constantine. As such, it is a summary of the persecutions suffered by early Christians. It is the most ambitious compilation of its kind to the date of its composition, and it became a canonical text throughout the Empire. In the Latin West, it was perhaps the single most influential martyrological text throughout the medieval period.

The persecutions and the texts commemorating them were shared by the Greek and Latin Christians of the Empire, which would lead us to expect a common outlook on martyrdom and consequently on the issue of cruelty in this context. Yet a close examination of the representation of cruelty in parallel accounts reveals that, as in many other cases, there is no such thing as a "translation." Eusebius's work underwent a process of inter-

50. Delehaye, *Les passions des martyres*, 197–207.

pretation and adaptation to the Latin world, and concerning the issue of cruelty, it reveals, perhaps for the first time with such clarity, "a parting of the ways" between East and West.[51] Rufinus consistently adds explicit references to cruelty that are absent in the Greek text. Whereas Eusebius is content to represent cruelty by *showing*, Rufinus not only describes cruelty and tags the action as such but also talks *about* cruelty—that is, he combines *telling* and *showing*. A parallel reading of a section of the *Historia ecclesiastica* (presented in Appendix 3) reflects these additions. It also shows that the Latin text of Rufinus has a more affective character. Rufinus adds rhetorical interjections referring to the limited linguistic capacity to describe the tormentors' cruelty.[52] These additions sometimes come at the expense of the actual details of the martyrs' torments, which are related more minutely in the Greek text.

Beyond this marked difference in the character of the two texts, there are other, more nuanced, variations in their representation of cruelty. In the Latin text, cruelty is linked much more explicitly to the tormentors' inventiveness in applying a wide range of tortures and devising new ones (paragraphs 2, 4, and 5 in Appendix 3). Another distinctive angle is the legalistic view of cruelty, which is reflected in the Latin version. Twice in this rather brief passage, the Latin text adds remarks that point to the illegality of the tortures: "*contra ius fasque*" (against the law and divine law) and "*contra praeceptum Caesaris*" (against the precepts of the emperor [paragraphs 3 and 9]). As shown in the previous chapter, the legal point of view is the starting point and a prominent aspect of the more important discussions of cruelty in Latin culture, from Seneca to the early modern period.

Another passage links Rufinus's version even more closely to the Latin perceptions of cruelty and of martyrdom. In the *Historia ecclesiastica* 8.14, Eusebius describes acts of sexual violence committed by Maxentius and Maximin against Christians and non-Christians. Sophronia was one of two Christian women who dared refuse the tyrants and committed suicide to prevent being raped. For Eusebius, these actions fall mainly under the category of tyranny. In contrast, Rufinus refers explicitly to cruelty and links together tyranny, sexual violence, and cruelty. These

51. The phrase is borrowed from the title of an article by Peter Brown ("Eastern and Western Christendom in Late Antiquity. Parting of the Ways," in *Orthodox Churches and the West*, ed. Derek Baker [*Studies in Church History* 113] [Oxford, 1976], 1–24) with no relation to its content.

52. Such as "saevitiae eius species singulas nemo possit exponere" or "si quid ultra posset inferre humana crudelitas etiam in eos" (paragraphs 2 and 12, respectively, in Appendix 3).

additions stand out because Rufinus follows Eusebius rather closely for most of the chapter. Only in this particular instance does he expand considerably, adding these references to cruelty and to sexual violence.[53] These additions make Rufinus's version almost double the length of Eusebius's, and they become the center of the chapter.[54] Rufinus is influenced here not only by the generally more explicit Latin mode of reference to cruelty. His representation of Sophronia is evidently influenced by the more sexually explicit Latin Roman tradition, going back to the image of Lucretia and to Ovid's stories.

The tendencies of these writers seem to demonstrate the cultural differences between the Greek and Latin cultures of the Empire, both Christian and pagan. As mentioned above, the Latin classical tradition had a favorable view of martyrdom and joined together sexual cruelty, tyranny, and martyrdom.[55] Conversely, the Greek tradition shunned violent death, especially when it was self-inflicted. Glen Bowersock identifies these two distinct attitudes when confronting Christian thinkers from Latin and Greek zones of influence (such as Tertullian compared with Clement of Alexandria).[56] Likewise, Andrew Lintott observed that cruelty, in the political context, was an important category of thought for the Romans but did not have a similar significance in the Greek world.[57] Thus, the unaffective and factual tone of the Eastern accounts may be a result of the tension between the purpose of the narrative, which is to extol the martyr, and the means of expression, which belong to a cultural milieu that is at best ambiguous in its attitude toward the issue of martyrdom. The Latin martyrdoms benefited from a discourse that was already at their disposal, on martyrdom as well as on cruelty, with the necessary modifications occasioned by the shift from a pagan to a Christian context.

These differences in pagan and Christian cultural milieus suggest that the detailed and explicit mode of reference to cruelty emerging from Rufinus's translation is a Latin peculiarity—that is, linked to the Latin classical tradition (as distinguished from the Greek one). In judging the extent of Rufinus's influence during the medieval period, it is difficult to determine whether his work is one of many classical sources of influence, and thus a crystallization of earlier differentiation between Western and Eastern atti-

53. Thus, the messengers who come to take Sophronia are called *stuprorum ministri*, without parallel in the Greek original.

54. Eusebius and Rufinus, *Historia ecclesiastica* 8.14, ed. Theodor Mommsen (Leipzig, 1908), 2:778–87.

55. See earlier, 34–35.

56. Bowersock, *Martyrdom and Rome*, 59–74.

57. Lintott, "Cruelty in the Political Life."

tudes, or whether his Latin version created this difference.[58] Either way, the *Historia ecclesiastica* is the single most important source for early medieval martyrologies and, consequently, also for much of subsequent medieval hagiography. Thus, even if the Latin translation reflects Rufinus's personal eccentricities and not an already existing difference between Greek and Latin Christians, it was influential enough to create such a difference in the centuries that followed.

In sum, cruelty seems to have been an important cultural issue in late antiquity, particularly in the pagan cultural milieu. Cruelty was an object of theoretical and philosophical discussions. It was also amply represented in literature and historiography. Cruelty was a significant issue in two principal contexts: In the legal and political context, it was perceived as excessive punishment or as the violence of tyranny. It was also seen as an un-Roman quality characterizing some of the barbarian "others" who came into contact with the Empire.

The Christian attitude toward cruelty can be seen both as a continuation of the pagan modes of reference to the issue and as a break away from them. The two main contexts of reference to cruelty remain tyranny and the cruelty of the "other," yet cruelty is no longer a subject of theoretic speculation: Christian thinkers refer to this subject only in passing. Some of the reasons for this change have been discussed in the previous chapter. The diminishing importance accorded to the physical aspects of existence by Christian thinkers and the rising importance of spiritual aspects are reflected also in the categories of cruelty represented: Sexual cruelty is represented in Christian sources less than in pagan sources. Conversely, violence against the Christian religion is increasingly characterized as cruelty and becomes an important attribute of the cruelty of the "other." The overall lack of interest in the issue and the new emphases in its representation in those instances in which the subject *is* dealt with are the legacy bequeathed by the Christian writers of late antiquity. These trends become more and more pronounced with the transition to the early medieval period.

58. Similar differences can be observed when earlier Greek and Latin *passiones*, such as those of Musurillo's collection, are compared. Yet the differences are not nearly as clear as they are in Rufinus's version and may not have been noticed without the benefit of hindsight.

CHAPTER THREE
THE EARLY MIDDLE AGES —
AN AGE OF SILENCE?

E arly medieval sources present a stark incongruity between medium and message. Western Christendom in the post-Constantinian age was afflicted by a high level of internal violence and multiple sources of severe external violence by Muslims, Magyars, and later Vikings. Yet contemporary authors report these events in a detached, brief, and factual manner.

Cruelty is absent from the large majority of early medieval sources, and not only as a topic for philosophical speculation. Even when violence is represented, it is seldom characterized explicitly as cruelty. Thus, a work such as the *Histories* of Gregory of Tours, which represents violence in an unusually graphic and detailed manner, mostly ignores the issue of cruelty.

This phenomenon is puzzling, not only on account of the mismatch between the subject matter and its presentation but also because it is a break with the developments observed in the preceding period—namely, the increasing importance of the issue of cruelty in late antiquity. Early medieval martyrdom accounts do not seem to be the heirs of Prudentius's *Peristephanon*, and the historical sources written at this period are even less similar to predecessors such as the works of Ammianus Marcelinus or Victor of Vita.

This seemingly detached attitude toward violence is not merely a stylistic issue. The endemic violence of the period renders this problem central to any scholarly attempt to understand the view early medieval people had of their world. The apparent aloofness of the sources to the violence they describe has been taken by some modern historians as an indication that people grew accustomed to the high levels of violence and, consequently, such events did not seem exceptional to contemporaries. Alternatively, the break with the sources of late antiquity could be seen as the result of the general decline in learning, especially that of the pagan classical heritage.

Yet a closer inspection of early medieval sources reveals that this mode of reference to violence and cruelty was not a deterministic result of historical circumstances. Moral judgment of violent actions is at times conveyed implicitly, by structural means. Moreover, a thin thread of an explicit mode of reference to cruelty persists throughout the early Middle Ages and shows that the classical tradition concerning cruelty was not extinct. Thus, the early medieval silence seems to be a result of a cultural choice: It was neither a result of the violence not being recognized as cruelty by the writers (who were its victims), nor was it due to a lack of cultural means to represent cruelty explicitly.

In this chapter, I outline the general tendencies in the early medieval treatment of cruelty and the ways in which it is modified by the peculiar aspects of each context. Early medieval violence had three main focal points in the period between the sixth and twelfth centuries: intra-Christian conflicts, the Muslim conquests, and the raids of the Vikings. I begin by examining intra-Frankish violence in the Merovingian period, mainly as reflected in accounts of rulers and prelates who were its victims. I then examine Christian-Muslim violence through the prism of texts whose purpose is to celebrate the martyrdom of Christians at the hands of Muslims in ninth- and tenth-century Spain. For the purpose of reconstructing the principles organizing the representation of violence in these texts, they are compared with contemporary reprocessed accounts of martyrs of the pre-Constantinian persecutions, such as the historical martyrologies of Usuard and the works of Hrotswitha of Gandersheim. Most of this chapter, however, deals with the Viking violence as experienced in the early medieval West.

INTRA-FRANKISH VIOLENCE

King Sigismund, the Burgundian king, converted from Arianism to Catholicism, and his violent murder by Clovis's son Chlodomer in 523, together with his religious merits, earned him recognition as a martyr by his contemporaries. The Merovingian *passio* devoted to King Sigismund describes his execution in the following terms: "And as they came there upon a well constructed by the ancients, so that they shall satisfy their madness with treachery, he was sentenced to capital punishment, his head was plunged downwards, he was thrown in the well together with his wife and children."[1]

The murder of the king is described in a factual manner, even though the author considers him a martyr. The drowning of his wife and chil-

---

1. *Passio sancti Sigismundi regis. MGH SSRM* 2:338. On the martyrdom of Sigismund, see also André Vauchez, *La sainteté en occident aux derniers siècles du Moyen Age* (Rome, 1988), 188.

dren together with him is mentioned without any comment, almost as a casual *post scriptum*.[2] In the *Passio Sancti Iuliani martyris*, the weight shifts from the martyr's endurance and death to the posthumous miracles, which occupy about half of the account.[3] Cruelty is not an issue in these texts: It is not mentioned explicitly, and even the descriptions of violence are brief.

The writings of Gregory of Tours display similar emphases. In the *Liber de passione et virtutibus sancti Iuliani martyris*, only the first of fifty chapters is devoted to a brief relation of the *passio*. The remaining chapters deal with the posthumous miracles of the saint. In his version of King Sigismund's death, the narration is sketchy, and the chapter ends with the posthumous miracles.[4] Gregory was preoccupied with violence to a larger extent in his major work, the *Historiae*. The scope of this work enables a partial reconstruction of the mechanisms that shape the degree of the writer's explicitness in expressing his attitude toward violence.

Dealing with an internal strife within the Merovingian dynasty, Gregory describes King Lothar's execution of his son, Chramn, and his family:

> [Chramn] lost time trying to rescue his wife and daughters: as a result he was overrun by his father's army, made prisoner and bound. When this was announced to King Lothar, he ordered Chramn to be burnt alive with his wife and daughters. . . . Chramn was held down at full length on a bench and strangled with a piece of cloth. Then the hut was burnt down over their heads. So perished Chramn with his wife and daughters.[5]

The account of Chramn's death is quite similar to that of King Sigismund's death, with the exception that Chramn did not have the luck to be considered a martyr. Using the somewhat outmoded but useful distinction between narrative techniques termed *telling* and *showing*, Gregory's narrative can be characterized as nearest to "pure" *showing* as possible.[6] He

2. The *Passio Ragneberti martyris Bebronensis* and the *Passio Praeiecti episcopi et martyris Averni* display the same detached manner in reporting the violent deaths of their subjects (*MGH SSRM* 5:207–11, 212–248, respectively).

3. *Passio Sancti Iuliani martyris. MGH SSRM* 1.2:428–31.

4. Gregory of Tours, *Liber in gloria martyrum. MGH SSRM* 1.2:87.

5. Gregory of Tours, *Historiae* IV.20 (*Gregorii episcopi turonensis historiarum libri decem*, ed. Rudolf Buchner [Berlin, 1956], 1:222–24; English version: Gregory of Tours, *The History of the Franks*, trans. Lewis Thorpe [Harmondsworth, 1974], 216).

6. Much of the objection to this terminology centers on the notion that showing can occur only in drama, and every narrative is a type of telling. See Gerard Genette, *Narrative Discourse* (Ithaca, 1980[1972]), 186, 189–90; Shlomith Rimmon-Kenan, *Narrative Fiction* (London, 1983), 96–100; and Seymour Chatman, *Story and Discourse* (Ithaca, 1978), 197–252.

describes events with graphic realism and usually without authorial comment.[7]

But despite its apparent detachment, the *Historiae* does pass moral judgment in several ways. It even offers some indications regarding which violent actions would be considered cruelty. Generally, it can be said that Gregory contributes his own moral judgment when there is a risk that mere factual narration would give the impression that violence goes unpunished. Thus Gregory most commonly criticizes violence by *showing* the operation of divine justice. When the plunderers of a monastery are transfixed by their own lances as their boat breaks, he merely remarks that this did not "happen by chance."[8] In other cases, divine justice is less apparent, and Gregory is more explicit. He tells of Theudebert, son of King Chilperic, who ravaged the district of Cahors, pillaging and burning on his way. Theudebert did not hesitate to plunder monasteries and rape the nuns as well. On these events, Gregory comments that "there was even more weeping in the churches at this period than there had been at the time of Diocletian's persecution." This comparison is an implicit but forceful accusation of cruelty, and Gregory develops it by contrasting the people of his days with their forefathers: In the earlier generation, people reverted from paganism to Christianity, but the people of Gregory's time turned into persecutors instead.[9]

It is worth noting that severe physical violence is implicitly defined as cruelty by linking it to paganism, which in this case is probably more of a label than an indication that the people mentioned were indeed involved in pagan practices. The tendency to associate cruelty with a pagan context is reflected in early medieval martyrdom accounts that are set in the pagan past. These texts, such as Gregory of Tours' *Passio sanctorum martyrum septem dormientem apud Ephesum*, the *Passio Acaunensium martyrum*, or *Passio Floriani*, contain more explicit references to cruelty than do contemporaneous texts that take place in a Christian setting.

These cases suggest that Gregory criticizes, explicitly or implicitly, severe physical violence, especially when it is addressed to representatives of the Church or its property. Examining Gregory's few explicit references to cruelty in the *Historiae* enables us to refine these conclusions: Cruelty is primarily

7. Erich Auerbach writes: "all this has such a visual vividness and testifies to such an endeavor to imitate the occurrence directly . . . Gregory relates the whole incident without personal commentary, purely dramatically" [*Mimesis*, trans. Willard R. Trask (Princeton, N.J., 1953[1946]), 86]. Walter Goffart claims that in such episodes Gregory consciously adopts the ironic mode: "Chains [of events] are broken by the omission of links; the author focuses attention on isolated, discontinuous scenes; and every effort is bent, as irony demands, on conveying a vivid and unforgettably negative impression without betraying overt disapproval" (Walter Goffart, *The Narrators of Barbarian History*, [Princeton, N.J., 1988], 182).

8. Gregory of Tours, *Historiae* IV.48, 1:286; Thorpe, *History of the Franks*, 244–45.

9. Gregory of Tours, *Historiae* IV.47–48, 1:266; Thorpe, *History of the Franks*, 244.

associated with violence against the defenseless (women, children, slaves) and against the Church. The latter category consists of three main subcategories: clerics and nuns, Church property, and the Church's status as a place of asylum (that is, violence against people who sought refuge on Church property).[10]

The tendency to associate cruelty with these types of action and with a pagan historical setting is evident in the *passio* of St. Leudegar, one of the few early medieval martyrs whose popularity survived into the central Middle Ages. Leudegar, bishop of Autun, was entangled in an internal Frankish power struggle and became the victim of Ebroin, the *maior domus* of one of the contending kings. Ebroin severely mutilated Leudegar by cutting his lips and amputating his tongue, so as to render him unfit to remain in his see. When by divine intervention Leudegar was healed and this stratagem failed, Ebroin executed him in 678. The story achieved wide popularity in the centuries subsequent to the anonymous contemporary version. Three other versions of it were written until the end of the tenth century.

The early *passio* has more references to cruelty and related issues than most early medieval martyrdom accounts. There are references to the *furor* (frenzy, madness) and *crudelitas* of Ebroin, and in the paragraph dealing with the mutilation of the martyr, Ebroin is called *saevum tyrannum*. The subject matter is similar to that treated by Gregory of Tours and other early medieval *passiones*: violence against clerics in the context of intra-Frankish violence. Yet the factual details resemble, or are made to resemble, the famous martyrdom of Romanus of Antioch. Similar to Romanus's torture, Leudegar's tongue is cut off, and his speech is miraculously preserved while he continues to praise God: In the words of the author of the first *passio*: "a devoted mind could not be silent" (silere Deo laudes non potuit mens devota).[11] It is probably the fusion

10. Thus, for instance, the word *crudelis* and its derivatives appear twenty-two times in the *Historiae*. Of these, eight are related to violence against the Church and five to violence against persons who cannot defend themselves (three others are related to violence committed by non-Christians [pagans and barbarians], and six cannot be associated with any specific category).

11. Various versions of the martyrdom of Romanus record similar reactions: "Christum loquenti lingua numquam defuit" [Prudentius, *Peristephanon liber* X, l. 927, in *Prudentius*, ed. and trans. Henry J. Thomson (Cambridge, Mass., 1961[1953]), 2:290]. In a Latin *passio*, immediately after his tongue was cut, Romanus declares, "Deus tuae virtuti gratias ago" (Hippolyte Delehaye, "S. Romain martyr d'Antioche," *Analecta Bollandiana* 50 [1932]: 267). Other martyrs who subsequently suffered the same punishment are Eugenius, Menas, Isidore, Potitus, Christine, Polychronius, and Terentianus [Hippolyte Delehaye, *Les passions des martyres et les genres littéraires* (Brussels, 1966[1921]), 203]. This type of mutilation was popular in the Eastern accounts as well. The later Coptic version of the martyrdom of Coluthus adds the cutting of the tongue to the ordeals of the saint, whereas there is not trace of it in the first version. See E. A. E. Reymond and J. W. B. Barns, *Four Martyrdoms from the Pierpont Morgan Coptic Codices* (Oxford, 1973). On the *passio* of Leudegar, see Paul Fouracre, "Merovingian History and Merovingian Hagiography," *Past and Present* 127 (1990): 3–38.

of the contemporary violence with the quasi-pagan setting that made the issue of cruelty more explicit in this martyrdom. The same factors probably made Leudegar's story popular in the centuries that followed. The link to the early, pre-Constantinian martyrdoms provided a meaningful context for the execution of the prelate, which was not an extraordinary event in itself.[12]

Yet even in Leudegar's case one must bear in mind that the treatment of cruelty is restricted and does not deviate from the general lack of preoccupation with the issue. For all their explicitness, the references to cruelty do not deal with cruelty in the elaborate manner of texts from late antiquity. In addition, later versions of the story do not expand on the issue of cruelty beyond the early *passio*, again unlike successive versions of martyrdom accounts in late antiquity. Finally, Leudegar's case, although important in revealing some of the mechanisms involved in the treatment of cruelty, is exceptional.

The high level of internal violence among the Frankish population in the early Middle Ages did not elicit a matching preoccupation with cruelty. Explicit references to cruelty in incidents involving violence were few. When they did occur, however, they can be identified with two principal contexts. First, when a violent event is explicitly labeled as cruel, violence infringes on "natural" immunities, such as those accorded to women, children, Churchmen, or people who seek sanctuary in Church property. That does not mean that all such instances are explicitly labeled as cruel; in many cases this kind of violence is not characterized as cruelty. The second principal focus for explicit references to cruelty is the recycling of traditional contexts of cruelty from late antiquity by early medieval authors. Such references can be found, for example, when early medieval authors relate to the persecution of Christians in pre-Constantinian times or persecution of Catholics by Arians (such as the Vandals). This latter practice seems more a matter of association than of copying: References to cruelty were not necessarily copied from earlier sources, but the writer's knowledge that the topic was associated with cruelty in antiquity induced him to do the same. This associative procedure seems to be at work in the case of Leudegar: The apparent similarities between his death and the martyrdom of Romanus (and a long list of martyrs after Romanus) prompted a more explicit reference to cruelty, similar to the genre to which it was perceived as belonging—the *passiones* of late antiquity. The *passio*'s late popularity, in turn, seems a result of its being a successful emulation of this well-known and popular prototypical model.

12. The commemoration of Leudegar is one of the only three entries in Rabanus Maurus's martyrology that contain words derived from *crudelis*.

At the beginning of the eighth century, Christianity was faced anew with a major threat from the rise of Islam. Within a century from Muhammad's death and within two decades from their initial crossing of the Gibraltar straits, the Muslims conquered Spain and reached Poitiers in France. How did this threat and the subjection of Christians by non-Christians affect the issue of cruelty in the early medieval West? Islamic rule was not a return to the pagan persecutions of late antiquity for Christians who lived under it. In theory and usually in practice as well, Christianity was a tolerated religion, and not one that was persecuted.

Nevertheless, violence did break out at times. The execution of more than 50 members of the Christian community of Cordova between the years 850–59 is one of the more discussed and contested instances of medieval martyrdom in recent research.[13] Many of the Christians executed in this outburst actively sought martyrdom at the hands of the Muslim authorities, mostly by publicly attacking the doctrines of Islam or by insulting the Prophet, an offense that requires the death penalty according to Islamic law. The leading members of the martyr movement were aware of the impression that these martyrdoms seemed self-inflicted, and much of the contemporary literature dealing with these martyrs is apologetic—that is, trying to present the martyrdoms as the result of genuine religious persecution.

The attempt to present these executions as "classic" martyrdoms bears directly on the issue of cruelty because cruelty is one of the more common attributes of the persecutor. Therefore, one would expect that the apologetic effort to create an atmosphere of persecution would lead to a demonization of the Muslim authorities and to their representation as cruel.

The treatment of cruelty in relation to this movement is directly related to the nature of the sources documenting it. The Cordovan martyrdoms were recorded primarily by the leader of that movement, Eulogius, who was among the last to be martyred. Eulogius faced the question of voluntary martyrdom in the first part of his *Memoriale sanctorum*. Thus, the issue of cruelty is important, particularly in the context of book I, in which he tries to justify the presentation of these executions as martyrdoms (and of the

13. The most recent study is Ann Christys, *Christians in al-Andalus 711–c. 1000* (Richmond, Surrey, 2002). Other studies are Benjamin Z. Kedar, *Crusade and Mission* (Princeton, N.J., 1984), 14–18; Kenneth B. Wolf, *Christian Martyrs in Muslim Spain* (Cambridge, 1988); Clayton J. Drees, "Sainthood and Suicide: The Motives of the Martyrs of Córdoba, A.D. 850–859," *Journal of Medieval and Renaissance Studies* 20:1 (1990): 59–89; Jessica A. Coope, "Religious and Cultural Conversion to Islam in Ninth-Century Umayyad Córdoba," *Journal of World History* 4 (1993): 47–68; and Coope, *The Martyrs of Córdoba: Community and Family Conflict in an Age of Mass Conversion* (Lincoln, Neb., 1995).

Muslims as persecutors). Most of the lexical references to the cruelty of the Muslims are from this apologetic first book.[14]

The lexical references are mostly limited to expressions such as *mucro saeviens* (cruel [raging] sword), or *judex ferocissimus* (a most ferocious judge) and are not developed beyond the appearance of a word from the semantic field of cruelty. Thus, the account of the martyrs Christophorus and Leovigildus refers to the *saevus furor* (savage fury) of the judge who sends them to prison but does not deal further with the Muslims' cruelty.[15]

Most accounts of execution and martyrdom in Eulogius's narrative are brief and factual, even somewhat detached. The death of Paul, a deacon of Cordova, is described by Eulogius in this manner: "The servant of God consumed his martyrdom in peace." The utmost inconvenience he was previously subjected to was incarceration with common criminals.[16] The death of Emila and Hieremias is summed up in one sentence: "Those which were tormented in prison were later slain by the liberating sword."[17]

Thus in the *Memoriale sanctorum*, cruelty is not part of the martyrdom accounts themselves. The lexical references to cruelty in the accounts are rare, as are references to torture, pain, or suffering. The issue of cruelty is important primarily as part of the apologetic effort to promote the martyr status of the executed Christians. Many of Eulogius's Christian contempo-

14. Fourteen in book 1 and seven each in books 2 and 3. The picture is much the same when the distribution is viewed according to the individual accounts: Only four accounts out of fourteen refer explicitly to the cruelty of the Muslims in book 2, and four out of eleven in book 3. The accounts are in book 2, chapters 1, 4, 11, and 13; book 3, chapters 7, 11, 16, and 17. Book 2, chapter 15 and book 3, chapter 5 refer to the cruelty of the Christians who do not support the martyrs. Book 3, chapter 1 contains two references to cruelty; however, this chapter is not an account of a martyrdom but rather narrates the historical background linked to the reign of Muhammad I, which began in 852.

15. Eulogius, *Memoriale sanctorum* (hereafter *MS*) 3.11, *PL* 115:792.

16. *MS* 2.6, *PL* 115:773–74.

17. *MS* 3.12, *PL* 115:793. Most of the accounts of the martyrs of Cordova survived only in the sixteenth-century edition of Ambrosio de Morales (which was reproduced by Migne). The accounts of those martyrs whose relics were brought by Usuard to Paris survived in their original form in a ninth-century manuscript. An examination of these, besides revealing the generous liberties taken by Morales in editing the text, does not require a modification of the findings based on Morales's version: They, too, contain no explicit references to cruelty, and the changes between the two versions are not significant insofar as cruelty is concerned. The parallel texts are edited in R. Jimenez Pedrajas, "San Eulogio de Córdoba, autor de la Pasión francesa de los mártires mozárabes cordobeses Jorge, Aurelio y Natalia," *Anthologica Annua* 17 (1970): 465–583.

raries—who probably found Muslim rule less unbearable—were not at all enthusiastic about the martyrdom movement and were not ready to accept the executed Christians as martyrs. Their objections, as presented (and refuted) in Eulogius's apology of the martyrs, refer to the incompatibility of these martyrdoms with the traditional Christian ones: The persecution, it was claimed, was not real because Christians were allowed by the Muslims to practice their religion. Therefore, the Muslims could not be represented as similar to the pagan persecutors of old. Moreover, the Cordovan martyrdoms were unlike the early pre-Constantinian martyrdoms for two reasons: The Muslims were not pagans, and the Cordovan martyrs were summarily executed without suffering the variety of torments inflicted on the early martyrs.[18] These factors prevented the demonization of the persecutor. And in fact Eulogius's account celebrates the intention of the martyrs, their *zelus Dei et amor regni perpetui* (zeal of God and love of the eternal kingdom) and their readiness to die rather than their physical endurance under torture.

The close acquaintance of the Cordovan Christian community with the martyrs on the one hand, and with their persecutors on the other hand, was an obstacle to the presentation of these accounts as traditional martyrdoms. It is not accidental that even though these martyrs appear in Mozarabic lists of martyrs, their cult achieved its greatest success (limited in itself) only beyond the Pyrenees, when Usuard included them in his martyrology. The geographic distance and the struggle between the Franks and the Muslims enabled a more traditional view of the latter as persecutors and, consequently, of the executed Christians as true martyrs.

Usuard is the link between the Cordovan martyr movement and the most concentrated martyrological production of the early medieval period, the compilations known as "historical martyrologies." These compilations deal with martyrs from the earliest persecutions to the times of the authors of the collections. They provide an additional perspective on the Cordovan martyrdoms by examining the issue of cruelty both with respect to these specific martyrdoms and within a wider frame of early medieval attitudes toward cruelty in the context of martyrdom in general.

The historical martyrologies are collections of references to martyrs arranged according to the calendar; that is, each saint is mentioned in the day of year commemorating him. Each day contains multiple such commemorations; martyrs are celebrated in the day of their martyrdom, which

18. See Wolf, *Christian Martyrs*, 77–104.

was considered their true birthday. The individual entries are brief, although their length can vary from a mere commemoration of the martyr's name to a basic outline of the full story of his martyrdom. Bede's martyrology, written in the middle of the eighth century, served as the basis for subsequent collections. Later compilers in the ninth and tenth centuries besides Usuard included Florus of Lyons, Rabanus Maurus, Ado, and Notker the Stammerer (*Balbulus*).[19]

The early medieval martyrologies generally ignored the issue of cruelty, and this disregard is particularly evident in the way in which Usuard incorporates the Cordovan martyrs into his martyrology. Usuard was on a relic-collecting journey to Spain in 858 when the martyrs' movement was still active. In fact, Usuard was the main promoter of the cult of the martyrs outside Cordova.[20] Therefore, there can be no question that Usuard viewed the executed Cordovan Christians as true martyrs, unlike some of their Spanish contemporaries. Nonetheless, his commemoration of these martyrs is quite brief and reflects the same lack of preoccupation with cruelty as the texts written by their Cordovan fellows. Thus, Usuard's entry on Maria and Flora, two Muslim girls who converted to Christianity, is representative of his procedure: "In the city of Cordova, [the day of birth] of the holy virgins Flora and Maria who, after a long period of incarceration, were slain by the sword for Christ."[21] The martyrdom of Perfectus, the first of the Cordovan martyrs, is described even more briefly in less than a full sentence,[22] and even the martyrs whose relics were brought to France by Usuard himself do not fare much better.[23]

How do the contemporary accounts of the Cordovan martyrs compare with those of the pre-Constantinian persecutions? The lack of concern with cruelty is representative of Usuard's martyrology in general and of other martyrologies as well. Rabanus Maurus's entire martyrology has only three words derived from *crudelis*. Of these, two are clearly copied from the

19. The discussion of the early medieval martyrologies is heavily indebted to the study of Henry Quentin, *Les martyrologes historiques du moyen âge* (Paris, 1908). An important updated survey is Jacques Dubois, *Les martyrologes du Moyen Age latin* (Turnhout, 1978).

20. See Bonnie Effros, "Usuard's Journey to Spain and its Influence on the Dissemination of the Cult of the Cordovan Martyrs," *Comitatus* 21 (1990): 21–37; and Drees, "Sainthood and Suicide," 80.

21. *PL* 124:729–30.

22. *Cordubae, sancti Perfecti presbyteri et martyris* (*PL* 123:945–46).

23. Eodem die, natalis sanctorum Georgii diaconi, Aurelii, Felicis, Nathaliae et Liliosae, quorum primus mirae abstinentiae monachus, ab Hierosolymis Cordubam adveniens, cum reliquis ex eadem urbe claro germine ortis diu optatum sibique a Domino praemonstratum meruit assequi martyrium (*PL* 124:405–6).

sources used for the compilation.[24] So in the final count we are left with one reference—in the entry on Pontianus of Spoleto—that may be an original addition of the compiler.

Although in most cases, repetitions, omissions, and additions are all significant in the transmission of texts, the case of the martyrologies is an exception to this rule because subsequent compilers do not always copy the earlier texts they are using. The references to a saint in the earlier version may be used only as a pointer, with the text taken from a source different from the one used in the "original compilation."

This procedure can be observed in the entry on Peter of Nicomedia in the martyrologies of Bede, Ado, and Usuard. Rufinus's Latin version of the *Historia ecclesiastica* served as the source for all three authors. Bede's account of Peter of Nicomedia is much briefer than that of Rufinus. Ado's version is much longer than Bede's and contains a detailed account of tortures. Yet, this is not Ado's own expansion: Ado used Bede only for the association of the name with the date and went back to cite directly and accurately from Bede's source—that is, Rufinus's version. Usuard once more abbreviates the entry.[25]

In handling their sources, the martyrologies do not, in general, systematically add or delete references to cruelty, which indicates that the authors are quite indifferent to the issue. When the compilers skip or abridge certain passages, cruelty also falls prey to this abridgment. The editorial decisions concerning these additions or deletions seem to be length driven rather than content driven. Thus, if the original source refers to cruelty, the longer the citation the greater the chance that it will also contain references to cruelty. The numeric data support these conclusions: The number of lexical references to cruelty is proportionate to the relative length of the texts. Thus, Bede's martyrology has nineteen words derived from *crudelis*, Ado's

---

24. The relevant passage in the martyrdom of Marcellus of Chalon-sur-Saône is an almost verbatim repetition of the *passio* (*AASS*, September 4, 2 [1869]: 200; *PL* 110: 1166). The entry on Leudegar echoes the continuator of Fredegar:

CONTINUATOR OF FREDEGAR	RABANUS MAURUS
Sanctum Leudegarium episcopum *crudelissimis tormentis* caesum *gladio peremi* iussit (ed. B. Krusch, *MGH SSRM* 2:169).	*Crudelissimis tormentis* afflictus oculorumque effusione cruciatus: ad extremum *gladio peremptus* est (*PL* 110:1172).

25. Eusebius and Rufinus, *Historia ecclesiastica* 8.6.1–4, ed. Theodor Mommsen (Leipzig, 1908), 2:749; *PL* 94:858 (Bede); *PL* 123:238 (Ado); *PL* 123:835–36 (Usuard). See also the entries on Blandina, Phileas, and Philomore, all taken from *Historia ecclesiastica*. Other sources are also treated in a similar manner; see for instance the entry of October 22 in the Martyrology of Florus of Lyons, which abbreviates from Victor of Vita's chronicle (Quentin, *Les martyrologes historiques*, 352).

has forty-three words, and Usuard's has twelve. Those figures, which are extremely low considering the length of the texts, coupled with the lack of editorial preferences concerning cruelty, reflect a lack of interest in this issue. This attitude is not influenced by the particular historical context, whether it is the contemporary struggle with Islam or the older contest of Christianity versus paganism.

Three quarters of a century later in 925, the execution of another Christian in Cordova occasioned more passionate responses from hagiographers. The account of this martyrdom was written by a contemporary, Raguel the Presbyter. According to him, Pelagius was ten years old when he was sent to the court of the Cordovan king 'Abd al-Raḥmān as a hostage. After three years, the Muslim ruler noticed his beauty and became infatuated with him. Pelagius was offered to convert in return for riches and honors for him and his relatives, but he refused. During this exchange, the king tried to touch him and was repulsed by Pelagius with insults: "Take off [your hands], dog, said saint Pelagius; do you suppose me to be like your effeminate [servants]?"[26] In Raguel's account, the threat of religious coercion is combined with that of sexual coercion, but the first seems to be of greater importance. Following this exchange, Pelagius is executed by being gradually dismembered. Raguel describes the executioners working simultaneously: one amputating his arm from the root, another cutting off his leg, while yet another wounds him in the head.

This punishment is evidently more painful than those of the ninth-century Cordovan martyrs; it recalls the Muslim punishments for apostates and heretics.[27] Raguel emphasizes this aspect in his *passio*, implicitly presenting suffering as a requirement for martyrdom. He represents Pelagius as "invoking the Lord Jesus Christ, for whom he was not reluctant to suffer, and saying: Lord, take me away from the hands of my enemies."[28] Raguel does not refer, however, explicitly to the cruelty of the Muslims.[29]

---

26. Interea cum eum joculariter Rex tangere vellet: Tolle, canis, inquit sanctus Pelagius; numquid me similem tuis effeminatis existimas? (*AASS*, June 26, 5 [1709]: 208).

27. See *Qur'an* 5:33; and Joel L. Kraemer, "Apostates, Rebels, and Brigands," *Israel Oriental Studies* 10 (1980): 34–73.

28. *AASS*, June 26, 7 (1867): 184. Raguel also comments "et qui jam electus manebat in coelis, adhuc duriter patiebatur in terris."

29. Because in the accounts of the Cordovan martyrs most references to cruelty belong to the apologetic effort to prove that they are martyrs, the violent and painful nature of Pelagius's execution may have rendered such references unnecessary. Pelagius is commemorated as well in Mozarabic liturgy. See *AASS*, June 26, 5 (1709): 215ff. See also *Missa S. Pelagii martyris*, PL 85:1041–50.

The story of Pelagius was taken up a few decades later by Hrotswitha of Gandersheim (ca. 935–ca. 1001/1003), one of the outstanding literary figures of the post-Carolingian period. Hrotswitha's treatment of this story is interesting not only because of her importance as a cultural figure but also because it is much more polished and literary than Raguel's *passio*. As such, one can compare it to "second-generation" *passiones* of late antiquity, which emphasized cruelty (whereas the earlier and less polished *passiones* or *acta* did not).[30]

In Hrotswitha's version, it is clear that the lack of reference to cruelty is intentional and part of a consistent ideology. Hrotswitha ignores pain altogether, and this attitude is evident in her other martyrdom accounts as well. She emphasizes the affronts to the sexual purity of the saints and their heroic attempts to preserve it. Thus, it is evident that Hrotswitha perceives martyrdom as the saint's departure from his physical nature. The importance of virginity fits with this conception as do the marginalization of pain and cruelty. The comparison with second-generation accounts of antiquity, such as those written by Prudentius, only reflects the significant shifts in the perception of martyrdom. Cruelty, similar to other physical aspects of existence, becomes marginal in these tenth-century accounts.

THE VIKINGS

The sources dealing with the Muslims are similar to those dealing with intra-Frankish violence in their general lack of interest in the issue of cruelty. The Christian-Muslim confrontation in Cordova and its later repercussions did not elicit detailed explicit references to cruelty, either. The cruelty of the Muslims was not a major issue in the accounts referring to these incidents for various cultural and factual reasons—namely, because in certain respects it was difficult to cast the historical situation into the traditional images of martyrs and persecutors.

The Vikings, who plagued Western Europe in the ninth and tenth centuries, present a new type of "other," whose characteristics are a partial return to the traditional mold of barbarian invaders.[31] The destruction

---

30. Hrotswitha's account is probably not a simple adaptation of Raguel's text; she probably relied on an eyewitness account as well. See *Hrotsvithae Opera*, ed. Helene Homeyer (Munich, 1970), 123–26; Elizabeth A. Petroff, "Eloquence and Heroic Virginity in Hrotsvit's Verse Legends," in *Hrotsvit of Gandersheim: Rara Avis in Saxonia*, ed. Katharina M. Wilson (Ann Arbor, Mich., 1987), 231; and Katharina M. Wilson, *Hrotsvit of Gandersheim: The Ethics of Authorial Stance* (Leiden, 1988), 40.

31. I shall not distinguish here between the various Northern peoples and shall refer to them generally as Vikings.

they caused and the fear they inspired are reflected in the contemporary chronicles. The anxiety caused by the Vikings could be better understood if the difference between them and the Muslims were translated into modern terms. The conflict with the Muslims could be seen as equivalent to modern warfare in the sense that it was conducted between two territorial entities with a defined, although shifting, geographical frontier between them. The modern approximation of the Vikings' raids is terrorism: In most cases there was no definable frontier, they were short outbursts of concentrated violence, and they involved surprise in terms of timing and choice of target. This atmosphere of terror was consciously created by the Vikings: Robert Bartlett shows how they committed actions aimed at shocking outside observers and opponents, and the terror evoked by these acts served as an effective tool of "psychological warfare."[32] The paganism of the Vikings added another dimension to their "otherness" and evoked the contest between pagans and Christians in the late Empire.

In light of the early medieval sources reviewed thus far, it is not surprising at this stage to find the following entries in the *Annales Bertiniani:*

(836) At that same time, the Northmen again devastated Dorestad and Frisia.
(844) The Northmen sailed up the Garonne as far as Toulouse, wreaking destruction everywhere, without meeting any opposition.
(848) The Northmen laid waste the township of Melle and set it on fire.[33]

Other early accounts of the incursions, such as the Anglo-Saxon chronicle, are similarly dry and brief.[34]

The writers of such entries do not specify exactly what happened when the Vikings ravaged a city, unlike the detailed descriptions of the actions of the Vandals in Victor of Vita's account. Moreover, whereas the texts relating to the Vandals explicitly characterized some of their actions as cruelty, such as violence against clerics, the references to the Vikings do not clearly indicate that the actions described were perceived as cruelty. Therefore, these texts pose methodological problems similar to those raised by Gregory of

32. Robert Bartlett, *The Making of Europe* (Princeton, N.J., 1993), 85–90.

33. *Annales de Saint-Bertin*, ed. Felix Grat, Jeanne Vielliard, and Suzanne Clémencet (Paris, 1964), 19, 49, 55; English translation: *The Annals of St. Bertin*, trans. Janet L. Nelson (Manchester, 1991), 35, 60, 66.

34. For instance, *s.a.* 835: "In this year heathen men ravaged Sheppey" (*Anglo-Saxon Chronicle*, ed. and trans. Dorothy Whitelock [London, 1961], 41).

Tours' *Historiae*: How can we know that the Vikings were seen as "other" and their actions as cruelty? The Vikings were evidently perceived as violent, but were they in fact considered to be a separate category, or merely as somewhat more violent than one's everyday acquaintances or superiors? And if they were perceived as cruel "others," do we have enough information to characterize the cruelty attributed to them?

The answers to these questions are complex and elusive. The brevity and aloofness of these chronicles led some scholars to claim that the actions of the Vikings were not extraordinary when compared to the high level of internal violence in these early medieval societies. Accordingly, the reports of their atrocities that do exist are exaggerated, as they were written by Churchmen who were the main target of the raids. Moreover, these accounts are usually not contemporary but later, "fanciful" elaborations of the events. Conversely, other scholars claim that the incursions of the Vikings were indeed perceived as extraordinary by contemporaries.[35]

To interpret the reports of the Vikings' incursions, it is necessary to use a combined approach that focuses on the scarce information supplied by the chronicles themselves and supplements it with external information from other types of reports of these incursions. As in Gregory of Tours' *Historiae*, one must look in the chronicles for the rare instances in which the author supplies a more detailed narrative of the actions of the Vikings and for formulations that enable us to deduce his attitude toward the events.

One indication that the Vikings are classified as "other" by the chronicle writers is their recurrent characterization as "pagans" in some of the chronicles (*pagani* in Asser's chronicle; heathen [hæðene] in the Anglo-Saxon chronicle). In contrast, the Muslims in the Cordovan martyrs accounts were only rarely

---

35. The main exponent of the view that underplays the violence of the Vikings is Peter H. Sawyer, *Age of the Vikings* (London, 1962), 117–44; this position is repeated in Sawyer, *Kings and Vikings: Scandinavia and Europe A.D. 700–1100* (London, 1982), 95. See also Thomas Lindkvist, "The Politics of Violence and the Transition from Viking Age to Medieval Scandinavia," in *Crudelitas: The Politics of Cruelty in the Ancient and Medieval World*, ed. Toivo Viljamaa, Asko Timonen, and Christian Krötzl (Krems, 1992), 141; Luigi de Anna, "Elogio della crudeltà. Aspetti della violenza nel mondo antico e medievale," in *Crudelitas: The Politics of Cruelty*, 102. An argument against such views can be found in John M. Wallace-Hadrill, *The Vikings in Francia* (Reading, 1975). In the context of medieval drama, Jody Enders has recently argued against the view that a high level of actual violence causes audiences to "get used" to violence and not react to it (*The Medieval Theater of Cruelty: Rhetoric, Memory, Violence* [Ithaca, 1999], 22–23, 231–32). An intermediate position was put forward by Guy Halsall, "Playing by Whose Rules? A Further Look at Viking Atrocity in the Ninth Century," *Medieval History* 2:2 (1992): 2–12.

presented as pagans.[36] This careful and correct distinction on the part of the medieval authors is significant: Pagans were perceived as the worst type of unbelievers and, by association with the pagans of late antiquity, as the most dangerous. This typology is reflected in cases in which the appellation is knowingly applied incorrectly, with a pejorative purpose, to unbelievers who are not pagans. Thus, Hrotswitha uses this term for the Muslims in *Pelagius*, and in the late eleventh century it was used in the same manner in crusading propaganda.

But these terms (pagans, heathens) are not common to all chronicles; in some of them, the Vikings are merely termed *Nordmanni*. Therefore, one must turn to the places in which the actions of the Vikings are described with less brevity than usual. The *Annales Bertiniani* provide some instances of this sort: "(842) At that time, a fleet of Normans made a surprise attack at dawn on the *emporium* called Quentovic, plundered it and laid it waste, capturing or massacring the inhabitants of both sexes. They left nothing in it except for those buildings which they were paid to spare."[37]

The chronicler relates the killing of the inhabitants and is even more precise in specifying that they were of both sexes. The reference to the killing of women (or children), as we have seen, is one of the traditional characteristics of cruelty (particularly attributed to the "other"). In the following year, 843, the chronicle specifies that in Nantes the Vikings "slew the bishop and many clergy and lay people of both sexes, and sacked the *civitas*."[38] The reference to violence against holy people or places is a common attribute of the "other." The entry for 837 refers to the *furia* of the Vikings. This term has connotations of madness and irrational urges and passions in contrast to the rational attributes and behavior usually expected of human beings. Thus, although not synonymous with cruelty, this term nevertheless sets the Vikings in the context of the "other."[39]

36. See, for instance, the distribution of the terms used for Muslims by Alvar of Cordova (Eulogius's friend and the other important exponent of the martyr movement ideology) and Eulogius (the list includes also words derived from these adjectives):

	pagani	*infideles*	*gentiles*
Alvar	—	6	38
Eulogius	5	5	24

As this table shows, Alvar does not use *pagani* at all, and Eulogius uses it only rarely.

37. *Annales de Saint-Bertin*, 42; *Annals of St. Bertin*, 53.

38. *Annales de Saint-Bertin*, 44; *Annals of St. Bertin*, 55–56.

39. Similar characteristics were ascribed to a second "other" of the early Middle Ages, the Muslims. Thus, for instance, in the popular chronicle of Sigebert of Gembloux, one finds references such as, "Saraceni . . . Garunnam transeunt, omnia devastant, aecclesiasque Dei cremant" or "Mady amiras multos utriusque sexus pro Christo martyrizat." (*Chronica*, MGH SS 6:330, 334). Similar entries can be found in the chronicle of Ademar of Chabannes—for instance, "Mauri quoque de Hispania Corsicam ingressi, in sabbato sancto Paschae civitatem quandam diripuerunt, et preter episcopum et paucos senes et infirmos nihil in ea reliquerunt" (*Chronicon*, 2.21, ed. Jules Chavanon [Paris, 1897], 99).

The more detailed entries indicate that the violence of the Vikings may have been perceived as similar to that of earlier barbarian invaders, such as the Vandals in late antiquity. Nevertheless, here there are no explicit references to cruelty. In the somewhat later *Annales Vedastini*, there are more explicit references to the cruelty of the Vikings. However, they are still a small minority among all other references to the Vikings, and they are still brief. Thus, in one place the chronicler uses the adverbial form atrociously (*atrociter*) to describe the devastation caused by the Vikings. The nominal form *atrocitas* is one of the parallel (although not always synonymous) terms to *crudelitas*. Another entry is even more explicit, relating that "the Normans began to be cruel [*sævire cœperunt*], athirst for burnings and killings; and they kill the Christian people, take captives, tear down churches, with no one resisting them."[40] The reference to violence against religion recalls the actions attributed to the Vandals in late antiquity. The depiction of the Vikings as a force that cannot be resisted evokes the Old Testament characterization of the "other" (Assyrians and Babylonians) as a punishment sent by God. Such a view of the Vikings was also expressed explicitly by chroniclers.[41]

Were the Vikings perceived as "other" and presented as such? The early sources imply, indeed, that this is the case but do not provide an unequivocal answer. When their actions are described in more detail, or when they are linked explicitly to cruelty, they seem very similar to the barbarian peoples of antiquity who were unambiguously "other" for the Christians describing them and in whose eyes cruelty was part of this alterity. Nevertheless, in the case of the Vikings, only a minority of the passages describing them can be linked to this tradition.[42]

40. *Les Annales de Saint-Bertin et de Saint-Vaast* (*s.a.* 882, 885), ed. Chrétien C. A. Dehaisnes (Paris, 1871), 313–14, 322. *Saevire* is the only verb form whose precise meaning is "being cruel"; no parallel form exists from *crudelis*.

41. See for instance the *Annales Bertiniani s.a.* 845 (after a report of a Viking incursion): "Sed licet peccatis nostris diuinae bonitatis aequitas nimium offensa taliter christianorum terras et regna attriuerit"; *s.a.* 881 (after the Franks are defeated in a battle): "Diuino manifestante iudicio quia quod a Nortmannis fuerat actum non humana sed diuina uirtute patratum extiterit" (*Annales de Saint-Bertin*, 50, 244). On the origin of the concept of defeat as punishment of sin, see Elizabeth Siberry, *Criticism of Crusading 1095–1274* (Oxford, 1985), 70–72. On the specific application of this conception to the Vikings (and references to more sources expressing this position), see Simon Coupland, "The Rod of God's Wrath or the People of God's Wrath? The Carolingian Theology of the Viking Invasions," *Journal of Ecclesiastical History* 42:4 (1991): 535–54.

42. On interpreting implicit references to violence and suffering in complaints from twelfth-century Catalonia, see Thomas N. Bisson, *Tormented Voices* (Cambridge, Mass., 1998), 143–55.

More information can be obtained when one studies the chain of transmission of texts dealing with the Vikings. The later versions can inform us about how the earlier texts were understood and interpreted by later compilers, and, because the differences in the representation of the Vikings between the links of the chain are tendentious, they reveal also the changes in the manner of reference to cruelty.

Such a process can be best observed in the English chronicles, which cite earlier sources at length. One of the first Viking incursions in Britain led to the destruction of the church of St. Cuthbert in Lindisfarne in 793. The descriptions of this event suggest that it was indeed perceived as extraordinary and not as an outburst of local violence. Alcuin (ca. 735–804), for instance, referred to the attack on Lindisfarne in more than one place as a catastrophe laden with metaphysical significance. He considered this event together with other portents (such as bloody rain) as a warning on the impending judgment on account of the sins of the English.[43] Yet the entry devoted to the event in the Anglo-Saxon chronicle is very brief, telling only that "the ravages of heathen men miserably destroyed the church of God on Lindisfarne, with plunder and slaughter," thus conveying little of the significance of the event.[44]

The Anglo-Saxon chronicle served as a source for the *Historia regum* attributed to Simeon of Durham (fl. ca. 1130), although much of it is believed to be the work of Byrhtferth of Ramsey around the year 1000.[45] The account of the same event in the *Historia regum* is significantly different. The Vikings are described primarily by means of animal imagery as "stinging hornets" and "fearful wolves." Then the *Historia regum* proceeds to narrate their deeds, specifying first the plunder and devastation of the church and then the violence done to the clerics, some of whom were killed, some taken as captives, and some driven away "naked and loaded with insults."[46]

There is no explicit reference to cruelty in this passage, yet there are elements that are traditionally associated with the "other"—for instance, the image of the hornets, depicting the Vikings as a group of indistinguishable

43. See his letters to King Ethelred of Northumbria and to the bishop of Lindisfarne (both from 793), in *Alcuini Epistolae, MGH Epist. Karol. Aevi* 2:16, 20, pp. 42–44, 56–58; English translation: *English Historical Documents*, 2nd ed., ed. Dorothy Whitelock (London, 1979), 1:842–46. See also the poem composed by Alcuin on the event, *De clade Lindisfarnensis monasterii, MGH Poetae Latini Aevi Carolini*, 229–35.

44. *Anglo-Saxon Chronicle*, 36.

45. John Marsden, *Fury of the Normans* (New York, 1993), 42.

46. Simeon of Durham, *Historia regum*, ed. Thomas Arnold (*RS* 75) (London, 1885), 2:55; *English Historical Documents*, 1:273.

but noxious insects, like the locusts that serve as a biblical image of the "other."[47] This image, which dehumanizes the Vikings by presenting them as a faceless collective, also recalls the utterly dehumanized portrait of the Huns, painted several centuries earlier by Ammianus Marcelinus.[48] The violence against Church property and clerics (in this order) is also a common denominator of "otherness," as seen in Victor of Vita's portrayal of the Vandals. Thus, although cruelty does not figure explicitly in this passage, one can see a clear intensification of the signs pointing to the actions of the Vikings as cruelty and, more specifically, of the types of cruelty attributed to the "other."

For the events of the latter part of the ninth century, the *Historia regum* is the third link in the chain of transmission, going from the Anglo-Saxon chronicle through Asser's chronicle (*De rebus gestis Alfredi*), written at the turn of the tenth century. The passage between the first two sources to the *Historia regum* reveals the same increase in the number of explicit references to cruelty. Thus, the *Historia regum* is in many cases the only source that offers moral criticism of the Vikings.[49] The *Historia regum* also provides more detail concerning the specific actions of the Vikings, which are absent from the sources it uses. These actions are all stock elements of the cruelty of the "other": violence against men *and* women, the burning of monasteries, looting, and sexual violence.[50]

Later English chronicles present a further extension in the explicitness of references to the cruelty of the Vikings. Henry of Huntington wrote his *Historia Anglorum* around the middle of the twelfth century and devoted the fifth book to the Vikings. In the prologue to this book, Henry states his opinion that the Vikings were the worst of the afflictions that befell Britannia because they were "by far more brutal [*longe immanior*], by far more cruel [*longe crudelior*] than the others." He explains that previous invaders, such as the Romans, Saxons, or Normans (those that conquered England in

47. See, for instance, Jeremiah 46:23, 51:14; Joel 1:4, 2:25; see also Revelation 9:3, 9:7.

48. Ammianus Marcellinus, *Rerum gestarum libri* 31.2.1–12, ed. and trans. John C. Rolfe (Cambridge, Mass., 1950–52[1936–39]), 3:381–87. Marcellinus's text is much longer and more explicit; he writes that the people of the Huns *omnem modum feritatis excedit* (31.2.1; 3:381).

49. Thus, *s.a.* 878 the Vikings are compared to ferocious wolves only in the *Historia regum* (Asser, *Life of King Alfred* [*De rebus gestis Alfredi*] 54 [*s.a.* 878], ed. W. H. Stevenson [Oxford, 1904], 43; Simeon of Durham, *Historia regum* [*s.a.* 877], 1:83). Likewise, the actions of the Vikings in the year 864 are introduced in the *Historia regum* with the interjection *sed o nefas*. For a parallel presentation of these texts referring to the events of 865–66, see Appendix 4. On this passage, see Raymond I. Page, "'A Most Vile People': Early English Historians on the Vikings" (Dorothea Coke Memorial Lecture in Northern Studies, 19 March 1986) (London, 1987), 10–11. Page points to the varied representations of the Vikings but does not suggest any development.

50. See the references in note 49. Sexual violence is implied in the phrase "non parcentes viris vel feminis vel viduis nec virginibus" (*Historia regum s.a.* 864).

1066), conquered to rule and consequently developed and built the country. The Picts or the Scots attacked only in some places, were repulsed, and ceased to invade. But, unlike any of these, the Danes (Vikings) attacked everywhere and did not want to possess the land but only to destroy and despoil it. Henry explains the Viking invasions as punishment for the decline of religion in England. He characterizes the Vikings as "swarms of bees, most cruel people, who do not spare neither age nor sex."[51]

The same process of multiplying references to cruelty in the central Middle Ages continues in the subsequent transmission of Henry's chronicle. Matthew Paris used Henry's text as one of his main sources when he compiled his *Chronica majora* in the thirteenth century. Matthew summarizes Henry's explanation of the causes of the invasions and his characterization of the Vikings' cruelty.[52] He also adds his own references to cruelty, as can be seen in the following examples:

HENRY OF HUNTINGTON

In the year 1003 the anger of the Danes was inflamed, as if someone should want to extinguish [fire] with grease. Flying therefore like a multitude of locusts, they came to Exeter, and destroyed the whole town from the ground, and took with them all the spoils, with only ashes left.[53]

The fourth year [1004], Swein, the most powerful king of the Dacians [Danes], to whom God destined the realm of England, came with many ships to Norwich, and plundered it and burned it.[55]

MATTHEW PARIS

[1004] This year the Danes burnt with unheard of cruelty [*crudelitate inaudita*], and covering the whole of England like locusts, taking everything as spoils, delivering men to death, and there was no one who stood against the enemies.[54]

The year of the Lord 1007. Swein, the king of the Danes, a strong and cruel man [*vir potens et crudelis*],[56] came with a great fleet to England, and they were followed everywhere by looting, burning, and killing; the whole of England shook [gnashed], like reeds struck by the blowing Zephyr.[57]

51. Immisit ergo Dominus omnipotens, velut examina apium, gentes crudelissimas, quae nec aetati nec sexui parcerent, scilicet Dacos cum Gothis, Norwagenses cum Suathedis, Wandalos cum Fresis (Henry of Huntington, *Historia Anglorum*, ed. Thomas Arnold [*RS* 74] [London, 1879], 137, 139).

52. Matthew Paris, *Chronica Majora*, ed. Henry R. Luard (*RS* 57) (London, 1872), 1:378; Paris is a little more explicit here, as he specifies women and children instead of Henry's more general terms ("quae ne quidem sexui muliebri aut parvulorum parcerent aetati").

In Paris's borrowings, one can see the addition of minor details relating to cruelty, either by the insertion of factual details in the manner observed above (such as the addition of *occisio* to the actions ascribed to the Danes in the second passage) or by the introduction of explicit authorial comments on cruelty. Such, for instance, are the additions of *crudelitate inaudita* to Henry's summary of the events of 1003 and the additional characterization of Swein as *crudelis*. It should be noted that the additions to cruelty cannot be explained away as being merely the result of the expansion of earlier texts; Paris's entry for 1004 is shorter in the original Latin than is Henry of Huntington's. Similar changes can be pointed out for Paris's references to the Vikings borrowed from other sources.[58]

The thickening of the references to the cruelty of the Vikings in the later chronicles is indicative of the rising importance of the subject in historical discourse. This process has already been observed in the treatment of cruelty by medieval thinkers, for instance. The references to the Vikings are particularly significant in this respect, as they run counter to the real historical process: The Vikings are presented as more and more cruel just as they are becoming more integrated in Western European society and culture.[59]

The chronological survey of references to the Vikings has shown that the factual and cryptic references to their actions in the early chronicles have

53. Henry of Huntington, *Historia Anglorum*, 174.

54. *Chronica Majora*, 1:481.

55. *Historia Anglorum*, 175.

56. This combination of adjectives is used also in relation to two other Danish chieftains, Inguar and Hubba, characterized as *viros potentes et crudeles* (*Chronica Majora*, 1:395).

57. *Chronica Majora*, 1:481.

58. Paris's entry is twenty-seven words long versus thirty-five of the original. For other instances, see the *Historia regum s.a.* 794, in which the verb *praedarunt* is used, and *Chronica Majora s.a.* 800, in which he uses the expression *crudeliter spoliavit* (*Historia regum*, 1:56; *Chronica Majora*, 1:367).

59. A critical view of the pre-Christian violence is evident also in some of the Norse and Icelandic sagas. The representation of pagan Viking practices as more and more cruel in the central Middle Ages can be observed in relation to the blood-eagle method of sacrificial execution attributed to the Vikings. Those accounts, which are detailed enough so that their literal meaning would not be debated, date from the twelfth century, and the execution procedure, as Roberta Frank remarks, becomes "more lurid, pagan, and time-consuming with each passing century" ("Viking Atrocity and Skaldic Verse: The Rite of the Blood-Eagle," *English Historical Review* 99 [1984]: 333. This article occasioned a lively debate: Bjarni Einarsson, "*De Normannorum atrocitate*, or on the Execution of Royalty by the Aquiline Method," *Saga-Book* 22:1 [1988]: 79–82; Roberta Frank, "The Blood-Eagle Again," *Saga-Book* 22:5 [1988]: 287–89; and Einarsson and Frank, "The Blood-Eagle Once More: Two Notes," *Saga-Book* 23:1 [1990]: 80–83).

indeed been interpreted as cruelty by later users of these texts. It has also shown that the references to cruelty multiply with time, and that there are also changing emphases and additions in the building blocks used for characterizing the cruelty of the "other" in historical writing. Of these, indiscriminate massacres of women and children remain constant from late antiquity to the accounts of the Vikings. Other characteristics, such as sexual cruelty, virtually disappear with the passage to the Middle Ages, while new ones, such as violence against religion, achieve prominence. A more general change in the portrayal of the "other" is the conception that its violence is a punishment for the sins of the Christians. The view of the "other" as a tool in the hands of God involves a totally depersonalized characterization. Thus, in contrast to anthropologically oriented classical accounts of the "other"—in the rare cases that the issue of cruelty came up—the reference to cruelty pointed to the actions committed rather than to the character of the Vikings.

Following the characterization of the Vikings over five centuries, however, still leaves out another problem: It is possible to assume that the killing of women and children was seen as cruelty by the later chroniclers but not by earlier ones. The fact that such actions were evidently considered negative and violent by the early writers does not imply that they were necessarily categorized as cruelty.

This issue can be addressed only by looking for other voices among early medieval sources—that is, those that are contemporary to the chronicles. And although the chroniclers' handling of Viking violence is the representative one, there *are* sources that deal with the issue differently. The paganism of the Vikings facilitated the representation of their victims as martyrs. And it is in hagiographic sources, to which a morally judgmental context is intrinsic, that we find another mode of representing cruelty.

The chronicles themselves describe some of the Vikings' victims as martyrs in a manner that conforms to the pattern observed earlier: short and factual in earlier chronicles and becoming longer and more affective with time. The difference between the accounts of the martyrdom of St. Edmund in the *Historia regum* and that in the *Chronica majora* of Matthew Paris is significant. Even more significant is the difference between the early chronicles and the *passio* of St. Edmund written by Abbo of Fleury (d. ca. 1004). Written in the tenth century, it is nearly contemporary with these early chronicles.

Immediately in the introductory paragraphs to the *passio*, Abbo refers in detail to the cruelty of the Vikings in a manner not encountered thus far in early medieval sources:

In fine it is proverbial, according to the prediction of the prophet, that from the north comes all that is evil, as those have had too good cause to know, who through the spite of fortune and the fall of the die have experienced the savagery [cruelty] of the races of the north. These, it is certain, are so cruel by the ferocity of their nature, as to be incapable of feeling for the ills of mankind; as is shown by the fact that some of their tribes use human flesh for food, and from the circumstance are known by the Greek name *antropofagi*. Nations of this kind abound in great numbers in Scythia.[60]

Such a representation of the Vikings goes back to classical representations of the "other." The reference to the Greek expression points explicitly in this direction and more specifically to the *Histories* of Herodotus. This imagery is the inspiration to the return of the classical images of the cruelty of the "other," evident in the references to cannibalism and to the Scythians and in the attempt to present an anthropological profile of the Vikings, however biased.

Besides such general remarks, Abbo supplies in the introductory paragraphs specific instances of Norman cruelty and refers to the ravages of two notorious chieftains, Inguar and Hubba. Abbo describes in detail one of these attacks, in which Inguar massacred women and children and raped ("ordered the modesty of women and virgins to be given to shame"). Abbo elaborates on Inguar's gratuitous cruelty, exercised only for his pleasure: Children were killed "before their mothers' gaze, so that the wailing will be greater," and the innocent were killed for the "zeal of cruelty."[61]

This passage contains several elements that were absent in the chronicle accounts. Abbo explicitly characterizes the actions attributed to the Vikings in the chronicles as cruelty and includes rape in this category. In addition, the overall tone is affective, and the Vikings are presented as enjoying their cruelty. Abbo already referred to this quality of the Vikings in his quasi-

60. Some passages of the Latin are problematic. The following is the original: "Denique constat, juxta prophetae vaticinium, quod ab aquilone venit omne malum, sicut plus aequo didicere perperam passi adversos jactus cadentis tesserae, qui [quo] aquilonialium gentium experti sunt saevitiam. Quas [quos] certum est adeo crudeles esse naturali ferocitate, ut nesciant malis hominum mitescere; quandoquidem quidam ex eis populi vescuntur humanis carnibus, quo ex facto Graeca appellatione antropofagi vocantur. Talesque nationes abundant plurimae infra Scythiam" (Abbo of Fleury, *Passio Sancti Eadmundi*, in *Memorials of St. Edmund's Abbey*, ed. Thomas Arnold [RS 96] [London, 1890], 1:9; English translation: *Corolla Sancti Eadmundi*, ed. and trans. Francis Hervey [London, 1907], 19 [translation modified]).

61. "Quo posset placere tyranno qui solo crudelitatis studio jusserat perire innoxios." There is an additional lexical reference to cruelty in this short passage, in which Abbo refers to Hubba as "*crudelitatis socium*" (*Passio Sancti Eadmundi*, in *Memorials of St. Edmund's Abbey*, 1:9–10).

anthropological introductory paragraph and mentions it once more in his description of Edmund's torture and execution.[62] Adding to the density of references to cruelty is Inguar's appellation as "tyrant." While the link between tyranny and cruelty is not new, it is less common in the early chronicle accounts of the Vikings.

This mode of reference can be found in a variety of hagiographic sources dealing with the Vikings. In a series of miracles attributed to St. Germain, the writer reports massacres, burning of churches and villages, plunder, and, as in Abbo's *passio*, refers explicitly to the cruelty of the Normans in a manner emphasizing the pleasure they derived from these acts. He writes that they "reveled with every cruelty" and "exercised their desires" against their victims.[63] When the Vikings kill 111 captives in front of the king and other Christians in order to mock them, they are characterized by a long epithet that mentions cruelty as one of their principal traits: "the impious and most cruel Normans, blasphemers of God."[64] The similarity between these hagiographic sources and the *passiones* is not surprising. The attacks against the saint's relics or against churches or monasteries dedicated to him were considered as attacks on the saint himself, and thus by implication the attackers became persecutors.

The return of this mode of reference is linked to the reappearance of pagan persecutors. Much of the ambiguity of Merovingian *passiones* can be attributed to the fact that the persecutor could not be presented as a complete "other." The context of intra-Christian and intra-Frankish political violence was by nature equivocal. The case of the martyrs of Cordova is similar from this perspective. The Muslims were better candidates for being

62. "*Pascantur hominum cruiciatibus*"; the Vikings make Edmund a target for their arrows "*quasi ludendo*" (ibid., 9, 15). The association of cruelty and martyrdom is also evident in the use of the verb *martyrizare* in the early medieval chronicles to indicate inflicting death with suffering.

63. Et cum omni crudelitate in populo quondam Dei debachari suamque in eum ob enormitatem peccatorum exercere libidinem (*Ex miraculis Sancti Germani in Normannorum adventu factis, cap. 4*, ed. G. Waitz, *MGH SS* 15.1:11). Toward the end of *De infantia Sancti Eadmundi*, written around the middle of the twelfth century by Galfridus de Fontibus, we find the following reference to the Vikings: "Isti [Hingwar, Ubba, and Wern] in aquilonali sinu Dacorum propter Gothos commanentes, ex antiqua consuetudine piraticam rabiem exercentes, latrociniis et depraedationibus ex toto se mancipaverant, et plurimas provincias crudeli exterminio dederant" (Galfridus de Fontibus, *De infantia Sancti Eadmundi*, in *Memorials of St. Edmund's Abbey*, 1:102).

64. Impiissimi ac crudelissimi Normanni, blasphematores Dei (*Ex miraculis Sancti Germani, cap. 12*, 12). The tendency to refer more explicitly to cruelty in hagiographic sources is evident also in the works of Simeon of Durham; see, for instance, *Symeonis monachi historiae Dunelmensis ecclesiae auctarium*, in *Simeonis monachi opera omnia*, ed. Thomas Arnold (London, 1882) (*RS* 75), 202–3, esp. 229–30.

represented as "other," yet even they could not be represented as pagan persecutors because Christianity was tolerated under Muslim rule, and the martyrdoms were basically self-inflicted rather than a result of persecution. The association of cruelty specifically to Viking violence bears out Wallace-Hadrill's claim that the conception, or myth, of "Norman atrocity" owes much of its formation to the fact that the Vikings were pagans.[65]

This mode of reference to cruelty, however, characterizes only the first part out of four distinct sections that make up the *passio* of St. Edmund.[66] The section dealing with the martyrdom itself contains only two brief explicit references to the cruelty of the Danes, even though the *passio*'s account of Edmund's execution is detailed.[67] It tells that Edmund was bound and tortured like Christ.[68] He was bound to a tree and made "as if in play" (*quasi ludendo*) a target for the arrows of the Vikings, similar to St. Sebastian. He was made to suffer the contested "blood-eagle" punishment and finally decapitated.[69] Thus, the references to cruelty are scant in the passage in which one would expect them to be the most numerous and most explicit.

The *passio* seems to be speaking about cruelty in two different voices: The introductory section resembles representations of cruelty from late antiquity in the types of cruelty attributed to the persecutors and in the explicit nature of the references to it. The narration of the martyr's execution belongs to the tradition of the early medieval chronicles, which represent cruelty implicitly by *showing*. In this sense, Abbo's text is like a two-faced Janus: The main section looks back to earlier medieval sources, such as the Merovingian *passiones*, the martyrologies, and to the works of Gregory of Tours. The introductory section is a prefiguration of the renewed interest in cruelty in the central and late Middle Ages.

65. And thus intrinsically different from perpetrators of intra-Frankish violence; see Wallace-Hadrill, *Vikings in Francia*, 9–10. See also Sarah Foot, "Violence against Christians? The Vikings and the Church in Ninth-Century England," *Medieval History* 1:3 (1991): 3–16.

66. Although not formally divided, the *passio* is made up of four parts of almost equal length: an introduction dealing with the Vikings (par. 1–5); the account of Edmund's martyrdom (par. 6–10); the account of the discovery of Edmund's body (par. 11–15); and some of the miracles produced by it (par. 16–19).

67. "*Adversarii in* furorem *versi*" and "saevis *tortum ungulis*." The latter expression is used to describe the "blood-eagle" procedure performed on Edmund (Abbo of Fleury, *Passio Sancti Eadmundi*, 15–16). Later, Abbo uses the expression *asperitate tormentorum* when he compares Edmund's passion with that of Christ.

68. This is an important point for Abbo; after telling of Edmund's death he comes to this issue again, comparing in detail the execution of Edmund with that of Christ.

69. On the scholarly dispute about the "blood-eagle," see note 59, above.

Although the hagiographic sources that deal with the Normans stand apart from other early medieval sources in preserving the ancient mode of explicit representation of cruelty, they are part of the overall process of the increasing preoccupation with cruelty in the twelfth and thirteenth centuries. This tendency is evident, for instance, when the *passio* of Edmund is compared with that of Elphegus, a bishop killed by the Vikings in 1012, written by Osbern (d. ca. 1100). As in the *passio* of St. Edmund, that of Elphegus contains a long historical introduction concerning the Norman incursions that precedes the account of the martyrdom, in the course of which Osbern remarks that "piety decreased, while cruelty increased from day to day."[70] He refers to the cruelty of the Vikings explicitly and in detail, emphasizing its gratuitous nature.[71] The number of explicit lexical references to cruelty is greater here than in the *passio* of St. Edmund, and they are dispersed throughout the account.[72]

Most of the medieval sources examined in this chapter do not refer explicitly to cruelty, or do so in a very cursory manner. When the texts from this period are compared with earlier and later ones, the early medieval period appears as a gap between late antiquity and the central Middle Ages—periods in which cruelty was treated much more extensively. This absence does not mean that cruelty was missing completely from historical sources. Cruelty in early medieval texts was represented implicitly (by *showing*), rather than explicitly (by *telling*). When early medieval sources, particularly those relating to the Vikings, are examined in a comparative context, it appears that some of the violence represented implicitly is similar in its forms and imagery to violence that is explicitly characterized as cruelty in earlier and later periods. Moreover, some of the early medieval

70. Minuebatur pietas, crudelitas indies augebatur (*Passio Sancti Aelfigi*, *AASS* 3rd ed., April 19, 1866[1668], 2:633). *Pietas* is a term that has no exact equivalent in English.

71. Ibid., 635–36; Osbern stresses the Vikings' cruelty to children.

72. Another eleventh-century source that refers explicitly and in detail to the cruelty of the Vikings is the *Gesta Normannorum* of Dudo of St. Quentin. Although cast in the form of a chronicle, it is a hagiographic work, recounting the conversion of the Normans from pagan raiders to a Christian nation. Looking back to the prototypical conversion of St. Paul, this genre emphasizes the cruelty of the persecutor before the conversion in order to convey the magnitude of the transformation (the thirteenth- and fourteenth-century references in Norse literature to the cruelty of the pagan Scandinavians may be similarly motivated). Dudo's account of the Norman incursions is similar to Abbo's in naming Scythia as the Vikings' place of origin and in the types of cruelty assigned to them (Dudo of St. Quentin, *Gesta Normannorum*, ed. Felice Lifshitz, 1996. http://orb.rhodes.edu/ORB_done/Dudo/chapter02.html [accessed 6/10/02]).

texts were interpreted as referring to cruelty by authors who used them in the central Middle Ages.[73]

But even though silence was indeed the default choice regarding cruelty in the early Middle Ages, there are exceptions. Most notably, some of the hagiographic material that deals with the Vikings treats cruelty explicitly and represents it in a very detailed and graphic manner. These exceptions are important for understanding the place of cruelty in early medieval culture. They indicate that the implicit and brief mode of reference to cruelty cannot be attributed to a disappearance of the earlier modes used in antiquity. It was a conscious cultural choice, which may be seen as similar to the conventions of Greek drama: Similar to the unity of time, the exclusion of "low" speech, and the aversion to onstage violence, explicit references to cruelty were left out of most early medieval sources. The brief descriptions of the Vikings' actions are signs, pointers to cruelty. This technique of representation, a very minimalist type of *showing*, recalls the medieval practice of symbolic (rather then mimetic) representation in the plastic arts. Taking up a related issue, rape was represented in many instances by depicting the rapist grasping the wrist of the victim (and not in the actual action of rape). This synecdochic mode of reference does not imply, of course, that the missing action was not important but rather reflects a choice of style.[74] The reluctance to represent rape explicitly may also account for its very minor role in the early chronicle accounts of the Vikings.

The conclusion that the violence of the Vikings was indeed perceived as cruelty does not imply that most medieval accounts of violence can be interpreted in this manner. And the following passage from *Njal's Saga* makes this point forcibly: "Brodir was taken alive. Ulf Hreda slit open his belly and unwound his intestines from his stomach by leading him round and round an oak-tree; and Brodir did not die before they had all been pulled out of him."[75]

The execution of Brodir, one of the principal villains of *Njal's Saga*, is neither explicitly nor implicitly presented as cruel. If this passage can be understood at all, it seems to show the operation of divine justice. One cannot impose an interpretation of cruelty on such a text. Nor can one use it to reach the opposite, and equally erroneous, conclusion that the Middle Ages were a "cruel period."

73. The more numerous references to cruelty in the later chronicles—whether in the form of more detailed representation or addition of explicit references to cruelty—cannot be attributed to a general tendency to expand the narrative. In some cases, the addition of an explicit reference substituted a more detailed account of the events; see p. 66 above for Matthew Paris's account of the Viking incursions of 1007.

74. Diane B. Wolfthal, "'A Hue and Cry': Medieval Rape Imagery and its Transformations," *Art Bulletin* 75:1 (1993): 39–64.

75. *Njal's Saga*, trans. Magnus Magnusson and Hermann Pålsson (Harmondsworth, 1960), 348.

Thus, the claim that the Vikings were perceived as cruel was not based on the intuitive assumption that extreme violence *should* be perceived as cruelty. Three independent threads of evidence led to this conclusion: (1) Cross-references within the early medieval chronicles and annals describing and defining the actions of the Vikings, (2) a comparison between the early medieval texts and representations of the "other" in historical writings of other periods, and (3) representations of the incursions of the Vikings in early medieval hagiography.

Within the fairly uniform mode of reference to cruelty in the early Middle Ages, there are two factors that have some influence on the way in which cruelty is treated: genre and historical context. The more explicit references to cruelty in this period can be found in hagiographic, mainly martyrological, texts. The characteristics of the perpetrators of cruelty also have some influence: Cruelty is represented more explicitly when its perpetrators can be clearly represented as "others." Because the Vikings were pagans, they were more readily characterized as cruel than were the Muslims or the violent Franks.

The genre differences regarding the treatment of cruelty are not merely lexical and quantitative—that is, the hagiographic sources are not merely chronicle entries that were expanded and into which words for cruelty were inserted. The words themselves (*crudelitas, saevitia*) are labels that are part of a wider context. The lexical field of cruelty is part of a specific cultural tradition that goes back to antiquity. For this reason, the explicit mode of reference to cruelty is linked to the paganism of the perpetrators, to the proto-martyrdoms of early Christianity, to tyranny in the political context, and to classical images of the "other," such as the barbarous and cannibalistic Scythians. The presence of this cultural matrix in hagiographic material contemporary to the incursions of the Vikings indicates that its absence from the chronicles is a conscious choice.

Finally, some of the general trends mentioned in the first chapter as shaping the treatment of cruelty also influence early medieval sources by their absence. The relative obscurity of the issue at this period is related to contemporary attitudes toward the body and to classical culture. Negative attitudes toward the body and toward the physical aspects of existence, which were dominant in the early medieval period, run counter to detailed representations of cruelty. In addition, there was at this period an ambivalent, even negative, attitude toward Latin classical culture, which was the only precedent for a cultural approach to cruelty. One needs only to remember St. Jerome's nightmare of being tried in the heavenly tribunal and beaten for being, in spite of his protestations, a *Ciceronianus* instead of *Christianus*.[76]

76. *Sancti Eusebii Hieronymi epistulae* 22.30, ed. Isidor Hilberg (*CSEL* 54) (Vienna, 1996[1910]), 189–91.

CHAPTER FOUR
THE CENTRAL MIDDLE AGES —
A RENAISSANCE OF CRUELTY

The twelfth century marks the beginning of rapid Western European development, evident in the buildup of military power, increased economic activity, technological and scientific advancement, and the "restoration" of classical learning. The consolidation of the medieval West into a strong political and military entity also meant that there were fewer external enemies posing a real threat.

The increased sense of confidence and security is accompanied, oddly at first sight, by an increasing cultural preoccupation with cruelty. The issue became increasingly important in the twelfth and thirteenth centuries, as reflected in the emergence of cruelty as a legitimate subject for philosophical speculation. The rising status of the issue can be noted as well in various areas of medieval culture. Thus, Alan of Lille (ca. 1120–1202/3) refers to cruelty in his *Ars praedicandi* (Art of Preaching), a model collection of sermons. In the texts on *misericordia* and *justitia*, Alan paraphrases Seneca's position in *De clementia*, defining cruelty as a perversion in the exercise of justice and as the opposite of mercy. He also claims that *crudelitas* and *clementia* characterize, respectively, the tyrant and the king.[1] Cruelty as overly rigorous justice is also mentioned briefly in the *Livre des vices et des vertus* (Book of Vices and Virtues) written by the Dominican Frère Laurent around 1280. In courtly poetry, cruelty appears as one of the attributes of the Lady in the treatment of her suitors. In the thirteenth century, cruelty also emerges as a marginal legal category: *Saevitia* is mentioned by canonists as one of the few grounds for divorce.[2]

The greater visibility of cruelty as a cultural issue is accompanied by another development. The agents of cruelty are mainly internal to Euro-

1. *PL* 210:148, 149; English version: Alan of Lille, *The Art of Preaching*, trans. Gillian R. Evans (Kalamazoo, Mich., 1981), 80, 83.

2. See James A. Brundage, *Law, Sex, and Christian Society in Medieval Europe* (Chicago, 1987), 510–11; Richard H. Helmholz, *Marriage Litigation in Medieval England* (Cambridge, 1974), 100–1. On intra-marital violence, see, for instance, Gregory IX, *Decretales* 4.19.1 and 4.19.5 (Rome, 1582); Felino Sandeo, *Consilia* 14 (Venice, 1582), fol. 13ra.

pean society. They are no longer external invaders such as the Vandals or the Vikings. In this chapter, I concentrate on four topics that best reflect the increasing preoccupation with the issue of the "internalization" of cruelty and the amalgam of cultural, social, religious, and political factors involved in this process: (1) the martyrdom of William of Norwich, (2) the murder of Thomas Becket, (3) the Albigensian crusade, and (4) the Mongol conquests.

In the middle of the twelfth century, the Jews emerged as a group that was collectively characterized as cruel. The most detailed and influential case that reflects this development is the account of the martyrdom of William of Norwich, who was said to have been the victim of ritual murder practiced by the Jews. Later in this century, the martyrdom of Thomas Becket showed how the issue of cruelty was manipulated by Church authorities in their political struggle with secular authorities. This process continued in the thirteenth century with the joint effort by secular and ecclesiastical authorities to depict another internal group, the Albigensian heretics, as similar to the cruel "others" of the past. The cultural preoccupation with cruelty culminated in the thirteenth century with the last outburst of real external enemies, the Mongols, who reached the outskirts of Western Europe around 1240. The accounts relating to the Mongol conquests presented the new contours of cruelty as represented from the thirteenth century to the early modern period. The main manifestations of this view of cruelty are indiscriminate massacres, sexual violence, and cannibalism. Although the first seems to be a constant and characterized also the cruelty of the Vikings, the latter two categories are new. In addition, violence against religion, which was a major aspect of the Vikings' cruelty, seems to have had only a minor role after the early medieval period.

One topic is ostensibly absent from this list: the Crusades. The issue of cruelty did have a role in the recruitment and in the actual conduct of the Crusades. The cruelty of the Muslims figured as an incentive in some of the Crusade propaganda.[3] Yet, in Western eyes, the Muslims presented on the whole a lesser degree of "otherness" than the Vikings or the Mongols.[4] Their status as lesser "others" was due in part to their not being pagans and also to the reciprocity of violence in their relations with the medieval West. With the Vikings and the Mongols, the roles of victims and victimizers were fixed—the "others" were the sole victimizers. In contrast, in the rela-

3. See, for instance, the acts of violence and sacrilege attributed to the Muslims in Guibert of Nogent, *Gesta Dei per francos* 1:5, *RHC HOcc.* 4:131ff.; and Robert the Monk, *Historia Hierosolimitana* 1.1, *RHC HOcc.* 3:727–28.

4. See Paul Freedman, "The Medieval 'Other': The Middle Ages as 'Other,'" in *Marvels, Monsters, and Miracles: Studies in the Medieval and Early Modern Imagination* (Kalamazoo, Mich., 1999), 1-24.

tions between the Muslims and the West, the roles were constantly changing during the twelfth and thirteenth centuries. Due to the ambiguity of the Muslims' "otherness," the references to their cruelty are less useful for reconstructing the perceptions of cruelty in the medieval West.[5]

The internalization of cruelty was, in part, a direct result of the decline in external threats to Western Christendom. Among internal groups, the Jews were the foremost candidates to become associated with cruelty.[6] Living as a minority within Christian society, they were very different from peoples such as the Vikings. Nevertheless, they were still outsiders and, more important, were still remembered as persecutors. This characterization is evident already at the end of the eleventh century at the beginning of the first Crusade. The Hebrew chronicle describing the massacres of the Rhine communities tells that the crusaders considered the killing of Christ's crucifiers in Europe a logical beginning for the crusade against the enemies of the faith in the East.[7] Guibert of Nogent echoes the same logic in his description of the crusaders reasoning between themselves: "Here we are . . . going off to attack God's enemies in the East, having to travel tremendous

---

5. See the Introduction, 9.

6. There have been numerous studies of the blood libel accusations; for the more general and recent ones, see: Gavin I. Langmuir, *Towards a Definition of Antisemitism*, part 4 (Berkeley, Calif., 1990); Gavin I. Langmuir, "The Tortures of the Body of Christ," in *Christendom and Its Discontents*, ed. Scott L. Waugh and Peter D. Diehl (Cambridge, 1996), 287–309; Robert I. Moore, "Anti-Semitism and the Birth of Europe," in *Christianity and Judaism*, ed. Diana Wood (*Studies in Church History* 29) (Oxford, 1992), 33–57; Christopher Ocker, "Ritual Murder and the Subjectivity of Christ: A Choice in Medieval Christianity," *Harvard Theological Review* 91:2 (1998): 153–92. See also Robert Chazan, "Twelfth Century Perceptions of the Jews: A Case Study of Bernard of Clairvaux and Peter the Venerable," in *From Witness to Witchcraft: Jews and Judaism in Medieval Christian Thought*, ed. Jeremy Cohen (Wiesbaden, 1996), 187–201. Jeremy Cohen identifies the twelfth century as a period of change in regard to the Jews as killers of Christ: The Augustinian position attributing the Jews' actions to their blindness was gradually replaced by a view ascribing intentionality to their actions. Cohen effectively links this change to various contemporary developments but does not relate to the more general shift in this period toward *ethics of intention*. In an ethical system in which action as such does not have a moral significance, the age-old guilt of the Jews would be meaningless without ascribing intentionality to their actions (Jeremy Cohen, "The Jews as the Killers of Christ in the Latin Tradition, from Augustine to the Friars," *Traditio* 39 [1983]: 1–27). See also Robert Chazan, "The Deteriorating Image of the Jews—Twelfth and Thirteenth Centuries," in *Christendom and Its Discontents*, 220–33.

7. Sefer gezerot shnat de'tatnu lerabi Shlomo bar Shimshon [גזירות שנת ד'תתנ'ו לרבי שלמה ב'ר שמשון], in *Sefer gezerot ashkenaz vetsarfat* [ספר גזירות אשכנז וצרפת], ed. A. M. Haberman (Jerusalem, 1945), 24.

distances, when there are Jews right here before our very eyes. No race is more hostile to God than they are."[8]

The cruelty of the Jews was not an issue raised by the official Church: Some of the bishops in the Rhine cities actively tried to help the Jews, and some of the chroniclers of the Crusades expressed varying degrees of criticism of these massacres.[9] The cruelty of the Jews, however, figures prominently in an even more important undercurrent of central and late medieval culture—the accounts of Christian children allegedly martyred by the Jews. Again, the papacy did not encourage the development of this trend: None of these saints was canonized during the Middle Ages. But they do hold a central place in the conception of martyrdom during this period.

There have been various attempts to account for rise of the image of the cruel Jew as reflected in these martyrdoms. This development is most closely linked with the contemporary yearning for apostolic Christianity, however, and the increasingly affective attitude toward the passion of Christ that was part of it.[10] Yet the *imitatio Christi* was not confined to the martyr's side alone. The conception that it was possible to reenact the passion of Christ led to the search for contemporary persecutors, and what choice was more natural than the direct heirs of the old ones, the Jews? I argue that it is the conjunction of these two currents—the fact that the Jews were the most readily available "other" and the increasing spiritual importance of the *imitatio Christi*—that enabled the creation of the child martyrs of the central Middle Ages. These children were represented as the victims of Jewish ritual sacrifice, in itself a reenactment of the original crucifixion.[11] The focus on children rather than adults is probably related to the sentimental spirituality associated with the passion of Christ.

Because these saints were not canonized in the Middle Ages, most of them do not have a *vita* or *passio* to commemorate them. William of Norwich is one

8. Guibert of Nogent, *De vita sua* 2.5, *PL* 156:903; English translation: *A Monk's Confession*, trans. Paul J. Archambault (University Park, Pa., 1996), 111.

9. The most explicit criticism of these massacres is Albert of Aachen, *Historia Hierosolymitana* 1:26-28, *RHC HOcc.* 4:292–93. But see also William of Tyre, *Chronicon*, 1:29, ed. Robert B. C. Huygens (Turnhout, 1986), 1:156; English translation: William of Tyre, *A History of Deeds Done beyond the Sea*, trans. Emily A. Babcock and August C. Krey (New York, 1943), 1:112–13.

10. See Chapter 5.

11. Robert I. Moore links the growth of medieval anti-Semitism to twelfth-century reform and the increasing awareness of the early patristic accounts of the role of the Jews in Christian society, but he emphasizes the social roots of this anti-Semitism and the marginalization of the Jews ("Anti-Semitism," 33–57; on the reform and the link to early Christianity, 37). On the related but later genre of accusations against the Jews for desecrating the Host, see Miri Rubin, "Desecration of the Host: The Birth of an Accusation," in *Christianity and Judaism*, 169–185; and Miri Rubin, *Gentile Tales: The Narrative Assault on Late Medieval Jews* (New Haven, Conn., 1999).

of the few unofficial saints who has a *vita*.[12] The *Vita et passione Sancti Willelmi Martyris Norwicensis* was written in the third quarter of the twelfth century by Thomas of Monmouth and is one of the very first blood libel accusations.[13] The *vita* tells that William, a twelve-year-old boy living in the vicinity of Norwich, was taken to the city by a mysterious stranger who convinced his mother that he was going to work in the archdeacon's kitchen. On the next day, the stranger visited William's aunt together with the boy. The aunt suspected the stranger and sent her daughter to follow them. She saw them entering the house of a Jew. Then, according to Thomas's narrative, William spent the next day with the Jews. The following day, at the table, they seized him, tortured him, and finally murdered him. The body was thrown in Thorpe wood and was discovered by the forester, who immediately suspected the Jews of the deed.

The account of William's torture and martyrdom is unsettling in the amount of detail it supplies, especially concerning the torture instrument used by the Jews (*teseillun* [teazle]). This instrument was forcibly introduced into William's mouth and was fastened to both jaws and then to the back of the neck. Another rope was fastened with knots applying pressure to the forehead and temples, and then it was tied around the back of the head and the neck. This intricate torture instrument presumably applied increasing pressure to the most sensitive parts of the head. The mention of the torture instrument is important in establishing systematic cruelty as a basic trait of the Jews. It emphasizes that this was not an outburst of violence and hatred against Christians but an established procedure that the Jews were well equipped to implement. Thomas does not neglect, however, the other aspect of cruelty—that is, that of excess which is motivated by pleasure—and it is in this context that Thomas refers explicitly and elaborately to the cruelty of the Jews:

> But not even yet could the *cruelty* [*crudelitas*] of the torturers be satisfied without adding even more severe pains. . . . And *cruel* [*crudeles*] were they and so

12. See André Vauchez, *La sainteté en occident aux derniers siècles du Moyen Age* (Rome, 1988), 173.

13. There has been a debate in recent years of whether the case of William of Norwich is indeed the first appearance of such an accusation and the extent to which the author of his *passio* is the inventor of the blood libel motif. See Gavin I. Langmuir, "Thomas of Monmouth: Detector of Ritual Murder," in *Towards a Definition of Antisemitism*, 209–36; Israel J. Yuval, "Vengeance and Damnation, Blood and Defamation: From Jewish Martyrdom to Blood Libel Accusations," in *Zion* 58:1 (1993): 33–90 [in Hebrew]; John M. McCulloh, "Jewish Ritual Murder: William of Norwich, Thomas of Monmouth, and the Early Dissemination of the Myth," *Speculum* 72:3 (1997): 698–740. The outline of William's story is prototypical of these accusations, but some cases differ in some of the details: The incidents do not always happen during the Passover, and in some cases the victims are adults (as in Bray-sur-Seine in 1192).

eager to inflict pain that it was difficult to say whether they were more *cruel* [*crudeliores*] or more prompt in their tortures. For their skill in torturing kept up the strength of their *cruelty* [*crudelitati*] and ministered arms thereto. . . . But while in doing these things they were adding pang to pang and wound to wound, and yet were not able to quench the madness of their *cruelty* [*crudelitatis*], and satisfy their inborn hatred of the Christian name.[14]

The density of references to cruelty is in itself a novel feature not encountered to this extent in martyrdom accounts of the early Middle Ages. References to the cruelty of the Jews recur on the occasion of the finding of the body. Henry of Sprowston, the forester, notices the wooden torture instrument in the boy's mouth, and it is the *unusual* character of the torments (*inusitatis penis*) suffered by the boy that leads him to conclude it is the work of a Jew. He then notifies a priest that he has found the body of a boy who was "most cruelly treated."[15]

The cruelty of the Jews is an issue in the case of other child martyrs as well. Hugh of Lincoln, who died in 1255, achieved even greater fame than William and is commemorated in a number of chronicles and popular songs.[16] His death is presented, much more so than that of William, as a reenactment of the crucifixion of Christ. In the most famous account of his martyrdom, from Matthew Paris's *Chronica majora*, the Jews put up a perverted "mystery play," with a Jew assuming the role of Pilate.[17] Most of the sources refer explicitly to the cruelty of the Jews in this episode. The most outspoken and affective are the *Burton Annals*, which are also the earliest. They refer to the "cruelty [of the Jews], which should be detested and abhorred."[18] Nevertheless, in none of these sources is the cruelty of the Jews as important an issue as it is in the *vita* of William of Norwich. This emphasis indicates that the genre differences in the treatment of cruelty observed in the sources dealing with the Normans are still relevant in the middle of the twelfth century—that is, cruelty belongs more to the realm of the *passio* than to that of the chronicle.

14. *Vita et passio Sancti Willelmi Martyris Norwicensis* 1.5, in *The Life and Miracles of St. William of Norwich*, ed. and trans. Augustus Jessopp and Montague R. James (Cambridge, 1896), 20–22 (translation modified).

15. "Crudelissimis attrectatus modis" (ibid., 1.6, 34–35).

16. For an analysis of this case, see Langmuir, *Towards a Definition of Antisemitism*, 237–62.

17. This version, via the mediation of John Capgrave, was the one incorporated later into the *Acta Sanctorum*.

18. *Annales monastici*, ed. Henry R. Luard (*RS* 36) (London, 1864), 1:340–44. On this source, see Langmuir, *Towards a Definition of Antisemitism*, 239. See also the *Waverly annals* in *Annales monastici*, ed. Henry R. Luard (*RS* 36) (London, 1865), 2:346–48. Matthew Paris does not refer explicitly to the cruelty of the Jews but mentions the testimony of a Jew to the effect that they crucified Hugh "without pity" ("immisericorditer crucifixerunt," *Chronica majora*, ed. Henry R. Luard [*RS* 57] [London, 1880], 5:518).

The marginalization of the Jews was a social and political process, part of what Robert I. Moore referred to as the formation of a "persecuting society."[19] The cruelty attributed to the Jews had a major role in this development. But the references to the cruelty of the Jews were only the beginning of the progress of cruelty toward the center of the cultural scene: The child martyr phenomenon was not well regarded by Church authorities and hence did not become a mainstream religious movement.

The martyrdom of Thomas Becket, only several decades later than that of William of Norwich, presents a significant leap forward in the role assigned to the issue of cruelty. In Becket's case, the highest levels of the Church hierarchy manipulated the treatment of cruelty and rendered it an integral part of one of the most popular medieval cults.

The murder of Thomas Becket by the emissaries of Henry II was part of a high-profile conflict between Church and State, one that was not devoid of personal aspects. The Church was quick to exploit the opportunity and presented the dead prelate as a martyr. Unlike William of Norwich, an uncommon consensus concerning Becket evolved almost immediately between popular opinion and Church authorities. The rapidity of his canonization was matched by the almost instantaneous development of the cult at his grave in Canterbury.

The intense martyrological activity in the case of Becket is reflected in the production of a number of contemporary or nearly contemporary accounts of his passion. Three of the major contemporary accounts of Becket's death continue the trends noted in relation to the *passio* of William of Norwich.[20] These are John of Salisbury's *Vita S. Thomae*[21]; the extant fragments from Benedict of Peterborough's *passio*; and the *Vita S. Thomae*

19. Robert I. Moore, *The Formation of a Persecuting Society* (Oxford, 1987). I have not dealt here with the stories charging Jews with tormenting the Host. Gavin Langmuir convincingly argues that the emergence of these stories reflect—in addition to the social and political processes that made the Jews "other"—Christian anxieties concerning the doctrine of transubstantiation. It is significant, nevertheless, that these stories were also modeled, similar to the blood libel accusations, on the model of the Jews persecuting Christ and were not attributed to a different type of "other," such as the Muslims. See Langmuir, "The Tortures of the Body of Christ," 287–309.

20. A fourth account, *Vita et passio S. Thomae*, ascribed to William of Canterbury and written very close to Becket's murder, is an exception as it is casual and unaffective. It contains no explicit references to cruelty. This *passio*, however, is not representative. On the apparent emotional detachment of contemporary accounts in general, see Chapter 2, 37ff.

21. John of Salisbury's *Vita* is an exception in certain respects. Although composed within seven years of Becket's death, it already uses material from other *vitae*, composed at a somewhat earlier stage (Anne Duggan, *Thomas Becket: A Textual History of His Letters* [Oxford, 1980], 176, citing Emanuel Walberg, *La tradition hagiographique de S. Thomas Becket avant la fin du XIIe siècle* [Paris, 1929], 173–85).

attributed to Edward Grim, an assistant of Thomas Becket who was wounded while trying to defend the archbishop.

Becket was assassinated and died on the spot, so there is naturally no reference to his suffering, and the accounts deal mostly with the murderers. In all three accounts, the reference to the murderers' cruelty is triggered not by the murder itself but by the episodes that immediately follow in which Becket's brains are dashed all over the floor of the church (by one of the murderers or by a malicious cleric in another version), and the archbishop's palace is plundered.[22] All three versions draw on the martyrdoms of the ancient martyrs and try to cast the *passio* as a direct heir to them. Thus, the murderers are explicitly demonized: Benedict calls the soldier who delivered the final blow to Becket's head "son of Satan" (*filius Sathanae*); John of Salisbury refers to the murderers as "attendants of Satan" (*satellites Satanae*).[23] Benedict repeats the ancient identification of the persecutor as tyrant.[24]

All three versions base their representation of the cruelty of the murderers mainly on explicit parallelisms with the passion of Christ. Thus, the dashing of his brains is compared to the lance thrust in Christ's side after he was already dead, and the plundering of the palace is compared to the division of Christ's clothes among his executioners. Benedict of Peterborough's account contains a scene of mockery of the dead Becket, recalling the mockery of Christ.[25]

The reference to the ancient martyrs and particularly to the passion of Christ has a double purpose: First, it employs the basic elements of the discourse of cruelty used in the prototypical *passiones* of antiquity. The mere reference to these elements evokes the context of cruelty, even if it is not detailed. Second and more important, however, is the manner in which this reference transforms the ambiguous political context of the martyrdom. The factual circumstances would not naturally allow the authors of these *passiones*

22. For instance, "injecto in sanctissimum caput ejus gladio, jam defuncto cerebrum ejiceret, et per pavimentum crudelissime spargeret," in Benedict of Peterborough's version (in *Materials for the History of Thomas Becket*, ed. James C. Robertson [*RS* 67] [London, 1876], 2:13); or "cerebrum . . . cum cruore et ossibus crudelissime spargerent," in John of Salisbury's version (*Materials for the History of Thomas Becket*, 2:320). The transition to the relation of the plunder occasions a renewed reference to the cruelty of the murderers: "non minus cupidi quam crudeles" (Edward Grim, in *Materials for the History of Thomas Becket*, 2:439; John of Salisbury, in *Materials for the History of Thomas Becket*, 2:320).

23. Benedict, in *Materials for the History of Thomas Becket*, 2:13; John of Salisbury, in *Materials for the History of Thomas Becket*, 2:318, 322.

24. *Materials for the History of Thomas Becket*, 2:14.

25. Alii autem insultabant dicentes, 'Voluit esse rex, voluit esse plusquam rex; modo sit rex, modo sit rex; . . . et inter cetera dicentes: 'Dixit enim, 'Filius Dei sum' (ibid., 2:14).

to present the king as an "other" and would therefore prevent his identification with the prototype of the cruel persecutor. Using a clever rhetorical move, however, the parallel drawn with the ancient martyrdoms does present the murderers (and implicitly their master) as the ultimate "other." This characterization is accomplished by pointing toward the outward similarity in action and condemning it as much graver because it was performed not by pagans or Jews, who were ignorant, but by Christians who should have known better. Thus, these Christians become more cruel than the already acknowledged "others." John of Salisbury refers to the murderers as "savage executioners, forgetful of any humanity . . . more savage than the crucifiers of Christ."[26] In this manner, the allusion to the ancient martyrdoms serves as a rhetorical device, the purpose of which is to present Becket's opponents as unambiguously conforming to the prototype of the cruel persecutor.

Two other *vitae* by William FitzStephen and by Herbert of Bosham further develop these trends and introduce another aspect to the representation of the murderers' cruelty. The greater density of references to cruelty is coupled with an affective description of the murder. FitzStephen's account, nearly contemporary, follows the account of the desecration of Becket's body with the following comment: "Oh sad spectacle, oh unheard of cruelty [*crudelitas inaudita*] of those who should have been Christians! But they are worse, who under the name of Christian[s] do the deeds of pagans."[27] The affective exclamations in this context are new, and they change the character of the whole account. And although none of the other components of this paragraph is new, bringing together elements that were dispersed in other accounts enhances the effect. William resorts also to stock images, which were used since late antiquity as pointers to cruelty— the killing of children in their mothers' wombs and the desecration of temples. But he uses them metaphorically: The Church is the mother and Thomas its son who is killed inside the church building (the mother's womb).[28] William, like the other authors but with more pathos, claims that the murderers are worse than the crucifiers of Christ (who sincerely believed him to be a man who was attacking their traditions).[29] Completing the transforma-

26. Carnifices immanissimi, totius humanitatis immemores, . . . immaniores Christi crucifixoribus (ibid., 2:320).

27. William FitzStephen, *Vita S. Thomae*, in *Materials for the History of Thomas Becket*, 3:142. FitzStephen refers to the cruelty of the murderers more than other authors: "tam crudeles dextras; tam cruentos gladios," "saevo mucrone" (3:143).

28. Occiderunt filii patrem in utero matris suae (ibid., 3:143).

29. In his *Ethics*, Abelard claims that the persecutors of Christ did not sin because they really believed him to be a criminal [Peter Abelard, *Ethics*, ed. and trans. David E. Luscombe (Oxford, 1979[1971]), 66–67].

tion of Becket's enemies into "others," he compares them unfavorably to the old "others"—Jews and pagans—who had reverence at least for their own sacred places.[30] The allusion to older martyrdoms is more detailed here and contains additional comments on cruelty. William goes back to John the Baptist and comments on the fact that not only did Becket not merit his death, but he, unlike John, was not even given a chance to present his version in trial.[31]

Herbert of Bosham, writing sixteen years after the murder, completes this movement of increased affectivity and greater density of references to cruelty. He presents his reflections on the murder in a chapter entitled *On the Enormity of the Sacrilege*, in which he links the murder to ancient persecutors. Herbert claims that all of them are justified by the present sacrilege, as they committed their deeds against the faith of their adversaries. This claim emphasizes the "otherness" of Becket's opponents, who committed a crime against their own religion.[32] The same point is emphasized by the use of the ancient terms *athleta* and *gladiatores* for the saint and his murderers throughout the account.[33] Similar to the account of William FitzStephen, Herbert's is very affective and contains long passages expressing his horror at the murder.[34]

The political context of Becket's murder could potentially cast a doubt on his being a martyr, at least in the sense of the term derived from the early Christian martyrs. This possibility rendered it necessary to *prove* that he was a martyr, and the need for proof was augmented by the tightening of the ecclesiastical constraints on the establishment of new saints.

The somewhat problematic attempt to establish Becket's murder as a martyrdom reveals the contours of a developed and fairly sophisticated dis-

30. William's original contribution to the list of historical parallels is the mention of St. Elphegus, who was martyred by the Normans, as a predecessor bishop-martyr (ibid., 3:141).

31. The persecutors of Becket are compared to "fratres Herodiadis crudelissimae" (ibid., 3:146).

32. Hoc quippe sacrilegii opus si quis attendat et inspiciat, omnem Diocletiani, Neronis, Maximini, aliorumve hostium Christi excedit debachantiam, omnem Antiochi profanationem, omnem Juliani perfidiam et Herodis saevitiam, omnius his justificatis ex sacrilego facto hoc. Isti quippe in fidei suae adversarios, aut quos hostes jam habebant vel suspicabantur futuros, saeviebant (Herbert of Bosham, *Vita S. Thomae*, in *Materials for the History of Thomas Becket*, 3:509–10).

33. See for instance ibid., 3:508ff. The image of the son killed in his mother's womb is used by Herbert as well (3:510).

34. For instance, "O vos omnes quit transitis per viam, attendite et videte si ab initio nascentis ecclesiae, vel etiam a prima saeculi origine, fuerit dolor sicut dolor iste. Sto hic et haesito, ultra progredi non possum, singultus et suspiria erumpunt magis quam verba. Stupet animus, plorat oculos, tremit manus, haeret stylus" (ibid., 3:507).

course of cruelty, which has three main characteristics. One is the adoption of an affective mode of reference to the issue of cruelty. Another is the explicit and extensive analogy to Christ and the early martyrs and to the cruelty of their persecutors. A third related aspect is the reference to the cruelty of the "other," which serves primarily as a means of characterization and as a measuring rod for cruelty. All three characteristics point to the decline of the implicit mode of reference to cruelty and to the ascendance of an explicit mode of treating this issue.

The cruelty attributed to the Jews in the cases of the child martyrs reflects the internalization of the "other" with regard to internal minorities being characterized in a manner that was usually reserved for external invaders. Becket's case reflects a further development of this process in the sense that the construct of the "other" was applied in an intra-Christian context, and was used, to a limited extent, for political purposes. The shift to internal agents of cruelty and the use of cruelty as a label in a political context were combined at the beginning of the thirteenth century in the crusade against the Albigensians.[35]

The Jews were geographically internal to European society, but they were ethnically and religiously different, and thus still external to some extent. Cruelty was further internalized in the case of the Albigensians. They differed from the mainstream Catholics mainly in their beliefs, and ethnic difference was no longer in itself an identifier of "otherness." In this they were unlike the barbarians of late antiquity and the Normans of the early Middle Ages. More simply put, Jews, Muslims, and barbarians were externally different: They might be distinguished from the Catholics by their physiognomy, by their clothes, by their language, or by any combination of these parameters. Conversely, heretics differed from Catholics only in their interiority.

The threat of these "others" was also internalized. Obviously enough, the heretics did not and could not pose a real physical threat but only a spiritual one—that is, leading believers astray. The vast effort invested in the suppression of this heresy was politically motivated in part: These heretics endangered the dominance of the Church, and the leaders of the crusade against the Albigensians had additional local political motives as well.

Thus in the Catholic sources dealing with the Albigensians, the issue of cruelty is manipulated as a label that has political significance. These sources represent the heretics as extremely cruel and essentially similar to

35. This is the appellation given to the adherents of a heresy that flourished in the twelfth and thirteenth century, mainly in southern France and Italy, and maintained anticlerical and moderately dualist beliefs.

the "others" of earlier times. This mode of reference to the heretics served a double purpose. The extremely violent means used to suppress these heresies were presented as a form of retaliation, even self-defense, against the cruelty of the heretics.[36] In addition, the insistence on the cruelty of these heretics and on their "otherness" was part of a demonization process that was necessary to distinguish them from the society to which they belonged.[37]

The rhetorical construct that uses cruelty for marginalizing and suppressing deviant groups is still imperfect in the case of the Albigensians. Thus it draws attention to itself and makes its operation visible. These imperfections in the manipulation of the issue of cruelty are present in the most detailed and partisan account of the Albigensian crusade written by Peter of Vaux-de-Cernay, himself a participant in this crusade.[38]

Peter tells of a knight, Giraud de Pépieux, characterized as a "most cruel enemy of the faith,"[39] who mutilated two Catholic knights who were his prisoners. Subjecting them to a fate more cruel than death, in Peter's view, he gouged out their eyes, cut their noses, ears, and upper lips, and sent them back naked to Simon of Monfort. One of them died on the way (as these events took place in the winter), and the other managed to reach Carcassone. This story, however, is recounted in order to represent Simon's disproportionate revenge as justified. Capturing the castle of Bram, Peter tells, the crusaders took the defenders, more than a hundred people, "gouged out their eyes, and cut their noses, sparing one of them a single eye, so that as a mockery of our enemies, he will lead all the others to [the town of] Cabaret."[40]

36. See Luigi de Anna, "Elogio della crudeltà. Aspetti della violenza nel mondo antico e medievale," in *Crudelitas: The Politics of Cruelty in the Ancient and Medieval World*, ed. Toivo Viljamaa, Asko Timonen, and Christian Krötzl (Krems, 1992), 81. Much in the same way, the cruelty of the Muslims was used as one of the justifications for the Crusades to the East.

37. The Social Identity Theory, from the field of social psychology, applies to this situation. It stipulates that in certain cases, similarity rather than difference between the ingroup and another group is detrimental to the relations between the two groups. See Henri Tajfel, "Social Identity and Intergroup Behaviour," *Social Science Information* 13 (1974): 65–93; Michael Hogg and Dominic Abrams, *Social Identifications* (London, 1988); and Sonia Roccas and Shalom H. Schwartz, "Effects of Intergroup Similarity on Intergroup Relations," *European Journal of Social Psychology* 23 (1993): 581–95.

38. On Peter of Vaux-de-Cernay's *Hystoria Albigensis* as the representative source for the crusaders' point of view, see Yves Dossat, "La croisade vue par les chroniqueurs," *Cahiers de Fanjeaux* 4 (1969): 221–59.

39. Nequissimus proditor et fidei crudelissimus inimicus, negans Deum fidemque abjurans (Petrus Vallium Sarnaii monachus, *Hystoria Albigensis* 142, ed. Pascal Guébin and Ernest Lyon [Paris, 1930], 1:129).

40. Ibid., 1:148.

This lack of proportion between Catholic and heretic violence is related to the very vivid representation of cruelty in Peter's account: He supplies names of people and places and detailed accounts of the actions performed by the heretics. Thus, for instance, he recounts the exploits of a couple, Bernard of Cazenac and his wife, belonging to the heretic gentry. Having characterized Bernard as a most cruel man (*homo crudelissimus*) and his wife as a second Jezebel (*altera Jezabel*), Peter proceeds to describe their actions:

> These two, then, as they were most wicked, plundered, or rather destroyed churches; attacked pilgrims, oppressed widows and orphans; mutilated the innocent, so as in a single Benedictine monastery called Sarlat, our [people] found 150 men and women, with arms or legs amputated, eyes gouged out or other members cut, mutilated by the aforesaid tyrant and his wife. This same woman, devoid of any pity, cut out the breasts of poor women or tore away their thumbs, thus rending them incapable of work.[41]

The detailed narration creates an impression of volume and at the same time enhances the credibility of the account.

In other cases, the attribution of cruelty to the Albigensians is not only disproportionate to the violence committed by the Catholics but blatantly absurd. The destruction of Béziers and massacre of its inhabitants have become one of the most well known instances of Catholic violence in this crusade, occasioning a variety of comments and references on the issue. The justification of this massacre, attributed by Caesarius of Heisterbach to the papal legate to the crusade, Arnald-Amalric, is particularly notorious. Asked what to do with the inhabitants, his reply was "kill them [all], God will know his own."[42] Most references to the event, however, even those written by Catholic writers, adopt a critical attitude toward the indiscriminate slaughter committed there. Thus, the anonymous writer of the *Histoire de la guerre des Albigeois* writes that the papal legate "has sworn that in the aforesaid Béziers he will not leave stone over stone, that all will be put to the fire and the sword, men as well as women and little children; not one he will be ready to spare; and the thing was done."[43] The writer, who is perhaps unwilling to condemn explicitly, points to the traditional elements used for describing cruelty in such a context: the massacre of women and children.

41. Ibid., 2:225–26.

42. Caesarius of Heisterbach, *Dialogus Miraculorum*, ed. Joseph Strange (Cologne, 1851), 1:303. Aron I. Gurevich briefly discusses this episode in the chapter "'High' and 'low': The medieval grotesque," in his *Medieval Popular Culture* (Cambridge, 1998[1981]), 197–98.

43. *Histoire de la guerre des albigeois*, ed. Michel-Jean-Joseph Brial, *RHGF* 19 (Paris, 1880), 120.

Peter of Vaux-de-Cernay attempts to justify the massacre by pointing to the cruelty of the city's inhabitants, narrating several incidents under titles such as *crudelitas quedam* (a certain [act of] cruelty) or *crudelitas alia* (another [act of] cruelty). But the stories themselves have no relation to their titles: They tell how the citizens beat priests, desecrated the chalice and the Host, and, their most violent action, killed their lord Raymond Trencavel in the church of Mary Magdalene. The incompatibility of the cruelty charges stands out in comparison to the general slaughter committed by the Catholics, which is described only briefly, telling that the Crusaders "killed all, from the smallest to the greatest [of age]."[44] Peter then proceeds to praise divine justice for this outcome. In addition to the brevity of the reference, the massacre is played down by the use of neutral terms (*minimus* [smallest], *maximus* [greatest]) instead of the explicit reference to children and old men.

Peter supplements the construct of the Albigensian cruelty by adding the context of tyranny; he refers to heretic leaders as tyrants. As in the case of cruelty, the term itself is sometimes out of place—tyranny being used as a synonym for cruelty. Thus, a long section (chapters 197–209) is devoted to the cruelty of the count of Foix.[45] Most of the examples are of violence against religion. Under the heading *crudelitas mirabilis*, Peter narrates how the "tyrant" and his soldiers mock and beat a crucifix in church. Raymond, the lord of Termes, is termed *tirannus*, and his aides ("extraordinary and most cruel enemies of the Christian religion") are charged with actions that have nothing to do with tyranny in the political sense, such as mutilation and violent execution of Catholic prisoners.[46]

The reference to tyranny enhances the delegitimization effort aimed at the Albigensians and their leaders.[47] It points to a process by which the explicit references to cruelty—that is, words related to the concept—function as a label that has social significance. That the appearance of the word does not have a merely descriptive function is reflected by the inappropriateness of the labels for cruelty or tyranny to the overall context of the narration.

44. Quid plura? Statim intrantes, a minimo usque ad maximum omne fere necant, tradentes incendio civitatem (*Hystoria Albigensis* 90, 1:91).

45. The section is entitled *Hic narrat de crudelitate et malicia comitis Fuxi*. The link between cruelty and tyranny is demonstrated by the variants to this title; one of the manuscripts has instead "*De malitia et tyrannide comitis Fuxensis contra ecclesiam et ejus ministros.*"

46. *Hystoria Albigensis* 173, 1:175–76.

47. A similar attempt of delegitimization is evident in the case of King John of England (1167[r. 1199]–1216), who aided the Albigensians. Guillaume le Breton describes him as a lecherous glutton who despoiled churches and brought paganism back to England (*Philippidos* 8:887–913, in *Oeuvres de Rigord et de Guillaume le Breton*, ed. Henri F. Delaborde [Paris, 1885], 2:244).

The growing sensitivity to cruelty, rooted in the political aspects of the concept, is reflected also in the emergence of explicit apologetics of cruelty. Peter of Vaux-de-Cernay, for instance, follows his description of Simon of Monfort's violent conquest of the castle of Bram with the comment that "the count ordered this to be done, not because he took pleasure in mutilation such that was carried out. . . . Never did the noble count enjoy any cruelty or the suffering of others; he was the most gentle of men."[48] Peter's comments indicate that he assumed that his audience, or part of it, might possess this new sensibility to cruelty and interpret the action as such rather than as justified violence.

These central medieval developments in the treatment of cruelty culminate in the middle of the thirteenth century in the sources dealing with the attacks of the Mongols in central Europe. The political role of the issue of cruelty is relatively insignificant in the case of the Mongols. But in no previous medieval context is cruelty represented so vividly and to such an extent as in these texts.

The internalization of the agents of cruelty—evident in the case of the Jews, Albigensians, and the political enemies of the Church—was largely the result of the diminishing external threats to Western Christendom, as reflected in the assimilation of the Normans into the mainstream of Western medieval civilization and in the Spanish *Reconquista*. Western Europe did not encounter major external threats until the Turkish offensives of the fifteenth century. In the first decades of the thirteenth century, the Mongols started their rapid expansion from central Asia in all directions. Toward 1240, they reached Europe and wreaked havoc for a short period in Hungary, Poland, and Dalmatia. This invasion was a brief but shocking setback from the relative tranquility and safety of the central Middle Ages.

The Mongol conquests were, in certain respects, the medieval predecessor of the *Blitzkrieg*: They were swift and extremely violent by medieval standards. The Mongol interlude in Europe occurred at a period of significant changes in the treatment of cruelty, providing an opportunity to observe how these changes are reflected and further developed in the representation of their actions in contemporary chronicles. The accounts of previous "others," such as the Normans, provide a background for noting the extent of these changes.

The historical accounts of the Mongols also provide an external observation post on the Western mode of reference to cruelty. The Mongol invasions affected vast areas, although more in the Far and Near East than in

48. *Hystoria Albigensis* 142, 1:148.

Western Europe. All sources, Western and Eastern alike, attest to the unprecedented violence that accompanied the Mongol conquests. Thus, they serve as focus for a cross-cultural comparison of modes for representing cruelty and of cultural attitudes toward it. The wide spectrum of sources, which includes, in addition to Western sources, Muslim and Eastern Christian ones as well, can also help in clarifying the role of religion (Christianity or Islam) versus that of the cultural *koine* (Western or Eastern) in shaping the various ways of addressing the issue of cruelty.

THE MONGOLS IN WESTERN SOURCES

The Mongols were perceived in the West as the contemporary reincarnation of the invading "others." To cite one instance, Salimbene of Adam refers to the Mongols as the present link in the chain of invaders starting with the Vandals and continuing through the Huns, the Goths, and the Lombards.[49] I return later to the actions and characteristics attributed to the Mongols; but those cannot be fully interpreted without considering an element that consistently comes out of the sources relating to the Mongols: fear.

The terror inspired by the Mongols permeates almost every account of them, whether written by a European, a Muslim, or an Eastern Christian. The magnitude of this fear can be grasped from a personal account of a Hungarian cleric, Master Roger (d. 1266), later archbishop of the Dalmatian city of Salona, who was for a brief period a prisoner of the Mongols:

> Immediately afterwards the rumors became widespread that the Tartars [Mongols] occupied at dawn the aforesaid Pont-Thomas, the village of the Germans, and those whom they did not want to keep, the horrendous cruelty of harshness killed direfully with the sword. When [this] was heard, the hairs of my flesh bristled, and my body started to tremble and quake, my tongue [started] to stammer miserably, observing that the dire moment of death, which by now could not be avoided, was imminent. I contemplated the killers with the eyes of my heart, and my body emitted the most cold sweat of death.[50]

49. Salimbene did not deal with the Mongols per se and can be thus assumed to offer a consensual view when he mentions them in passing. *Cronica fratris Salimbene de Adam*, *MGH SS* 32:209–10; English translation: Salimbene de Adam, *Chronicle*, trans. Joseph L. Baird and Giuseppe Baglivi (Binghamton, N.Y., 1986), 199–200.

50. In Latin, the reference to the Mongols' cruelty is "et quos tenere noluerunt horrenda crudelitas acerbitatis gladio dire iugulavit" (*Epistola Magistri Rogerii in miserabile carmen super destructione regni Hungariae per Tartaros, MGH SS* 29:562). The account is in the form of a letter addressed to Johannes, the bishop of Pest. The excerpt quoted comes before the account of the author's capture by the Mongols but was of course written subsequently. *Tartari* is the term used for the Mongols in the Latin sources.

Although this might be expected in the areas directly affected by the Mongols, the extent of the terror is evident from reports in chronicles whose geographic focus lies outside those areas, such as England. Thus, for instance, the *Annales Cambriae* report for the year 1260 that "all Christendom was seized by the fear of the Mongols."[51] Matthew Paris also uses similar terms: "They inspired the whole of Christendom with inordinate fear."[52]

This reaction, especially in English chronicles, seems at odds with the relatively limited scope of the Mongol conquests in Europe. They were restricted geographically to Hungary, Poland, and Dalmatia, and the threat was short lived (1240–1241). What was the source of this "inordinate fear?" The concurrence of the non-Western sources, which are discussed later, rules out that this is an overreaction to the sudden irruption of violence after the relative security of the twelfth century in the West. The fear was, in fact, the calculated effect of the extreme and systematic violence used by the Mongols in the course of their conquests.

The principle adopted by the Mongols was simple, and they applied it methodically: They spared cities that capitulated in advance of the Mongol approach and offered no resistance; they destroyed and massacred mercilessly in cities that offered the slightest resistance, even if this resistance was followed by capitulation. This procedure was very effective in inducing other prospective targets of the Mongols to surrender. This terror tactic, or psychological warfare, was not new in itself: Ṭāriq, the Muslim conqueror of Spain in the eighth century, ordered during the first siege of a Spanish city (Carteya) that some of the prisoners be killed and their bodies be cut to pieces and cooked in cauldrons. He also ordered that the story be spread, and the chronicler reported that the purpose of this procedure—inspiring terror—was achieved.[53] Severe mutilation was used by both sides during the Albigensian crusade for the same purpose.[54] Yet the case of the Mongols is different: Violence was not the initiative of a local commander, nor was it the case of undisciplined soldiers looting, raping, or slaughtering. It was a systematic

51. *Annales Cambriae*, ed. John W. A. Ithel (*RS* 20) (London, 1860), 99.

52. *Chronica Majora*, 4:109; see also ibid., 3:488–89; and *Flores Historiarum s.a.* 1238, ed. Henry R. Luard (*RS* 95) (London, 1890), 2:229.

53. Ibn al-Qawṭiyya, *Ta'rīkh iftitāḥ al-andalus*, ed. Julian Ribera (Madrid, 1926), 9. There are also other reports of dissimulated cannibalism by the Muslims during the conquest of Spain; see Ibn 'Abd al-Ḥakām, [*Futūḥ ifrīqiya wal-andalus*] *La conquête de l'Afrique du Nord et de l'Espagne*, ed. and trans. Albert Gateau (Algiers, 1947), 92–93. Significantly, in accounts of the Muslim conquest written in the central Middle Ages, the simulated cannibalism of the Muslim conquest becomes real; see *Poema de Fernán González*, ed. John Lihani (East Lansing, Mich., 1991), 15. See also the biblical story of Rabshakeh, who insists on addressing the defenders of Jerusalem in Hebrew, conducting a similar kind of psychological warfare (2 Kings 18:17–37).

54. See above, 86–87.

procedure, used on a large scale, and its application, cessation, or non-application was based on the strict discipline of the Mongol troops.[55]

The unprecedented magnitude of the Mongols' violence is central to the main questions of this study—that is, when and why is cruelty an important cultural issue—because it eliminates some of its relativist aspects. The extent of their violence would render the Mongols cruel in any cultural context that is preoccupied to some extent with cruelty. Therefore, in such a context it would produce explicit references to the issue. Conversely, the lack of such references would be significant because it cannot be explained away as "normal violence," as some scholars attempted to do in the case of the Vikings. Thus the absence of references to cruelty would indicate that cruelty is not a major issue in the culture that produced such texts.[56]

In contrast to the accounts of the Vikings, the Western sources dealing with the Mongols explicitly characterize their violence as cruelty. The detail with which their actions are described may raise the question *which* of their actions are characterized as cruelty? Paradoxically, the brevity of the reports on the Vikings made their interpretation easier when they did contain explicit references to cruelty. The proximity of the label to the action enabled the association of the two. In the detailed accounts of the Mongols' violence, some of which are several pages long, it cannot be expected that each of the actions described will be modified by one of the lexical pointers to cruelty. Master Roger, for instance, completes one report by mentioning the rape of nuns in a monastery destroyed by the Mongols and sums it up with an affective comment on his inability to record every instance of the cruelty of the Mongols.[57] In such cases, it is evident that the writer categorizes all the violent actions committed by the Mongols as cruel, even if the label itself is attached only to one of them.

What types of cruelty are attributed to the Mongols? The primary attribute of the Vikings' cruelty was indiscriminate massacres. This type of activity has a prominent place in the accounts of the Mongols as well. Nevertheless, it appears in a new form and with new emphases. Most of the

---

55. The promise of security to besieged cities was kept only if *no resistance at all* was offered. In any other case, the Mongols slaughtered the population (even if they did promise to spare the inhabitants). Thus, the fear induced by these massacres functioned as a stimulus to give up any thought of resistance.

56. Under the assumption that the texts are representative.

57. Quid amplius? Si describerentur singulariter pugne singule et crudelitates nimie, que fiebant, legentium corda perterrerent et terribili sonitu tinnire facerent aures (*Epistola Magistri Rogerii, MGH SS* 29:564). See also *Ex Thomae Historiae Pontificum Salonitanorum et Spalatinorum, MGH SS* 29:589.

accounts underline the *systematic* nature of the Mongol massacres and the care they invested to ensure that no survivors would be left. Master Roger relates that after the conquest of Estergom in Hungary only 15 survivors were left from the whole city.[58] Thomas of Spalato (ca. 1200–1268), another eyewitness, writes that 100,000 men were killed in one day until the water of the Danube turned red.[59] Although some of these figures may be attributed to conventions of report, the wealth of details about the procedures taken indicate that the authors indeed wished their words to be taken literally. Master Roger describes how the Mongols took care not only to kill everybody in the conquered cities but also to kill the survivors who managed to escape. For this purpose, the Mongols used to assign a task force to remain inside the conquered city or in its neighborhood and wait until hunger compelled the survivors to come out and look for food.[60]

The Mongols did not always execute the conquered population on the spot, but would gather them together, lead them into a deserted place, and execute them there. Thomas of Spalato describes the procedure of such mass executions, which he calls immense savagery (or cruelty) in terms that evoke modern genocides: The Mongols took all women, children, and old men (Thomas emphasizes that they took those who did *not* fight); made them sit in a line and take off their clothes so that they would not be stained by blood; and then killed them all.[61] The systematic nature of the Mongol massacres is brought into relief by these procedures and by the effort invested to maximize efficiency (such as the care taken to assure that the clothes of the victims will not be stained). The writers emphasize this point even further by indicating that the precise procedure was a matter of choice—taking into account the desired effect—and not an action committed in the heat of battle: Thomas of Spalato describes how in their initial incursions into Hungary, the Mongols did not apply their "whole cruelty" and indulged more in taking spoils rather than in killing.[62] Yet when they

58. *Epistola Magistri Rogerii, MGH SS* 29:565.

59. On Thomas's account, see James R. Sweeney, "Thomas of Spalato and the Mongols: A Thirteenth-Century Dalmatian View of Mongol Customs," *Florilegium* 4 (1982): 156–83.

60. *Epistola Magistri Rogerii, MGH SS* 29:562–63.

61. Quid vero commemorem de immani sevicia, quam in civitatibus et villis diebus singulis exercebant, cum imbellem turbam mulierum, senum et infancium congirantes faciebant uno ordine considere, et ne vestes macularentur sanguine, neve carnifices lassarentur, indumenta prius omnibus detrahebant. Et tunc missi carnifices, singulorum brachia elevantes, figebant leviter telum in corde et extinguebant omnes. (*Ex Thomae Historiae, MGH SS* 29:588. See also *Epistola Magistri Rogerii, MGH SS* 29:563–64.)

62. Non totam sue atrocitatis seviciam a principio ostenderunt, sed discurrentes per villas predasque facientes, non magnam stragem ex ominibus faciebant (*Ex Thomae Historiae, MGH SS* 29:586).

wished to make the massacre as great as possible, they ignored the spoils altogether, and with "unheard of cruelty" (*Tartarorum inaudita crudelitas*) concentrated only on killing.[63]

Beyond the method of execution, the systematic mode of operation extended to the choice of the victims. The inhabitants of a conquered city underwent a careful process of selection that determined who would be assigned to various types of servitude and who would be executed. The Mongols left alive those who could be of some use to them: artisans whose craftsmanship could be put to use and women who could be exploited sexually or as slaves.[64]

The emphasis on massacres in eyewitness accounts is perhaps to be expected, but similar descriptions appear in other types of sources as well. Besides chronicle accounts written by eyewitnesses, there are two other types of sources: general chronicles that refer to the Mongols among other subjects and anthropologically oriented accounts devoted specifically to the Mongols written mainly by missionaries. These types of Western sources concur with the eyewitness accounts on most issues, even if they differ in some of the factual details and in the manner of presentation. The systematic massacres committed by the Mongols figure prominently in the accounts not written by eyewitnesses to the Mongol massacres. The *Annales Cambriae* tell that "all the kingdoms of the East were destroyed and all Saracens were killed," and Matthew Paris writes that the Mongols "destroy the lands of the Christian with horrible extermination."[65] In the accounts of missionaries such as John of Plano Carpini, one finds similar statements about the habit of the Mongols to kill rather than take captives and to divide the task of executing the captives among the soldiers.[66]

63. Ibid., 588.

64. The issue of the artisans is a recurring motif in Eastern accounts of the Mongols; in Western sources, it is mentioned by Simon of St. Quentin and by William of Rubruck, who refers to German gold miners and a French goldsmith (Simon of Saint Quentin's work did not survive independently, but was reconstructed as *Histoire des Tartares* [*Historia Tartarorum*] 30.83, ed. Jean Richard [Paris, 1965], 48; William of Rubruck, *Itinerarium* 23, 29, trans. Peter A. Jackson, in *The Mission of William of Rubruck* [London, 1990], 144–46, 183). The selection of women is discussed in detail later in the chapter.

65. *Annales Cambriae*, 99; *Chronica Majora*, 4:109. For more detailed references in Matthew Paris, see *Chronica Majora*, 4:76; 110ff. (*passim*), 387–89. Another chronicle states that "partes Aquilonares Orientis miro vastarunt exterminio" (*Flores historiarum*, 2:229).

66. Occidendos autem diuidunt per centenarios [Johannes de Plano Carpini, *Liber Tartarorum cap.* 6, in *The Texts and Versions of John de Plano Carpini and William de Rubruquis*, ed. C. R. Beazley (London, 1903), 65; English translation: Christopher Dawson, ed., *The Mongol Mission* (New York, 1966[1955]), 35–38].

The accounts of the Mongols focus on different types of cruelty than did the chronicles of the Vikings. The primary manifestations of the cruelty attributed to the Mongols are sexual cruelty and cannibalism. Writers referring to the Mongols consistently emphasize sexual cruelty, whereas chroniclers of the early medieval period concentrated on violence against clerics and church property committed by the Vikings. The transition between the two modes of reference stands out clearly when it becomes obvious that even when the accounts of the Mongols describe the "old" type of cruelty, they are in fact referring to the new one. Thus, when Master Roger relates how the Mongols desecrate churches, he tells that they rape both men and women inside the building.[67] Likewise, he tells of the capture of a monastery in which they killed most of the monks and retained some of the women and beautiful girls "for their abuse" [*ad abusum eorum*].

The most recurrent manifestation of this type of cruelty is rape with aggravating circumstances—for example, that committed in front of family members, followed by murder, or both. As with the accounts of the Mongol massacres, these accounts accord equal weight to the systematic manner of committing these actions and to the actions themselves as representations of the Mongols' cruelty.

Thus, the Mongols decide the fate of each woman after a process of meticulous selection. Master Roger describes how conquered soldiers and "useless" women captives who are destined to be executed are set apart from the peasants, property, and some of the women who are "reserved for their [the Mongols'] sport."[68] As in the case of the nuns left alive for the same purpose in the captured monastery, it is difficult to separate here the massacre from the sexual abuse of the women. In both cases, the narration of facts is followed by an affective exclamation as to the cruelty of the action: "Oh the pain, oh the cruelty and the immense frenzy of the savage people!"[69] Here, too, the reference to cruelty applies both to the massacre and the rape, actions that are presented in the text as complementary.

It may seem an overstatement of the obvious that the victims of this kind of cruelty were the more beautiful women among the conquered popula-

67. In aliis vero ecclesiis tot scelera de mulieribus patrabant, quod tutius est subticere, ne homines ad nequissima instruantur. . . . Post hec sanctorum sepulchra totaliter everterunt et pedibus sceleratis reliquias calcaverunt . . . Introducebant in ecclesias mixtim viros et mulieres et post turpem illorum abusionem eosdem ibidem necabant (*Epistola Magistri Rogerii, MGH SS* 29:562).

68. Milites igitur et dominas, que multe erant extra in campo, in una parte et rusticos in alia posuerunt, ac pecunia, armis, vestibus et aliis bonis receptis ab eis, et quibusdam dominabus puellis reservatis ad vitam et ad lusum eorum deductis, cum securibus et gladiis omnes crudeliter interfecerunt (*Epistola Magistri Rogerii, MGH SS* 29:564).

69. O dolor, o crudelitas, et rabies immanis populi immensa! (ibid., 564).

tion. The accounts emphasize this, however, to present the systematic and calculated nature of the actions committed. This sometimes involves the assignment of what seems to be overrationalized motivations to the Mongols by contemporary writers. The Templar Ponce de Aubon, who writes to the king of France concerning the ravages of the Tartars in Eastern Europe, explains that captive women are killed after they are raped so that they cannot divulge military information concerning the Mongols.[70]

Matthew Paris, one of the principal Western authors dealing with the Mongols, refers in detail to this aspect of their cruelty. Thus, he mentions that the Tartars demanded from the prince of Antioch 3,000 virgins.[71] In another place, he is much more specific when he quotes from the letter of Ivo of Narbonne to the archbishop of Bordeaux. Ivo describes a selection between the women destined to serve as food and the more beautiful ones who are raped by the multitude of Mongols.[72] The rape scene itself is extremely violent. In modern terms, it is a gang rape, and the great number of times that each woman is raped is conveyed by telling that the women are raped until they are suffocated (it is not clear whether they die or not). In an apt *finale* for this violent scene, the nipples of the raped virgins are cut and are served as a delicacy to the Mongol magistrates.[73]

This passage from Paris comes after an explicit remark on the cruelty of the Mongols, which was actualized by two previous examples: the indiscriminate slaughter effected by them and their cannibalism, which was manifested in eating the bodies of the slain. It serves as the culminating instance of their cruelty as it combines, in fact, three types of cruelty: murder of women, sexual cruelty, and cannibalism. Thus it introduces cannibalism, in addition to sexual cruelty, as the second new aspect of the Mongols' cruelty.

Cannibalism as an aspect of cruelty is not a new theme; it is part of classical mythology, fully developed particularly in the plays of Seneca and in Ovid's *Metamorphoses*. Pagans charged early Christians of cannibalism.[74] The cases of ritual murder attributed to the Jews, discussed earlier, were

70. Et sachiez qu'il n'espargnent nului, mes il tuent touz, povres et riches et petis et granz, fors que belles fames pour faire lor volonte d'elles; et quant il on fait lor volonte d'elles, il les ocient pour ce qu'eles ne puissent riens dire de l'estat de leur ost (*Ex historiae regum Franciae continuatione Parisiensi, MGH SS* 26:604).

71. In addition to lowering the walls of his towns and castles and to the revenues from his lands (*Chronica Majora,* 4:389).

72. The text is ambiguous as to whether they, too, are eaten afterward.

73. The phrases used are *in multitudine coituum suffocabant* and *usque ad exanimationem opprimebant* (*Chronica Majora,* 4:273).

74. See, for instance, Eusebius's account of the Martyrs of Lyons, in which Christians are accused of "Oedipean marriages and dinners in the manner of Thyestes" (*Historia Ecclesiastica* 5, 1.14).

also a variation on ritual cannibalism, and so by extension are some of the stories describing the desecration of the Host by Jews. As a characteristic of the "other," cannibalism has its roots in the representation of the Scythians by Herodotus.[75] Abbo of Fleury accuses the Vikings of cruelty and cannibalism in his *passio* of St. Edmund, but it does not appear as one of their characteristics in historical writings. In the case of the Mongols, this issue becomes central, and it continues to be a prominent characteristic of the cruelty of the "other" well into the early modern period. The perception of Jews and Mongols as cannibals indicates that it is not a coincidence that the Mongols were linked in the West to the Jews and were seen as the lost ten tribes.[76]

In his analysis of the Latin texts dealing with Mongol cannibalism, Gregory G. Guzman proposes a tripartite typology of cannibalism, all parts of which were attributed to the Mongols:

1. Survival cannibalism: eating human flesh in cases of dire necessity.
2. Preference cannibalism: eating human flesh "as a regular source of food."[77]
3. Ritual cannibalism: eating the bodies of the dead for ritual purposes.

The scheme is useful enough for discussing Mongol cannibalism, even though the episode just quoted (the eating of the nipples) does not fall neatly into any of these categories; it is nearest, perhaps, to the second. The first two categories are directly related to the cruelty of the Mongols, but there is not always a clear demarcating line between these categories. The issue of cruelty, however, is related precisely to the distinction between them: Preference cannibalism is a dietary choice, with the moral implications of a choice. Cannibalism committed out of necessity would not generally be considered as cruelty, or at least it would be a milder form of cruelty.[78] Albert of Aachen,

75. François Hartog, *The Mirror of Herodotus: The Representation of the Other in the Writing of History*, trans. Janet Lloyd (Berkeley, Calif., 1998[1980]), 187.

76. *Chronica Majora*, 4:77ff. On this link, see Andrew C. Gow, *The Red Jews* (Leiden, 1995), 53–56; see also p. 320, n. 36, where Gow cites from the 1571 edition of the *Chronica*, which enlarges on the *crudelitas ferina* of the Jews. See also Francis Martens, "Le miroir du meurtre ou la synagogue dévoilée," in *Le racisme—mythes et sciences*, ed. Maurice Olender and Pierre Birnbaum (Brussels, 1981).

77. Gregory G. Guzman defines this type as "customary cannibalism," but this definition does not emphasize adequately the contrast with the first category—namely, that this is a dietary *choice* ("Reports of Mongol Cannibalism in the Thirteenth-Century Latin Sources: Oriental Fact or Western Fiction?" in *Discovering New Worlds*, ed. Scott D. Westrem [New York, 1991], 31–68, esp. 33).

78. Extreme hunger or famine did not legitimize the violation of dietary taboos, but it did mitigate their gravity; on this subject, see Pierre Bonnassie, "Consommation d'aliments immondes et cannibalisme de survie dans l'Occident du Haut Moyen Age," *Annales E.S.C.* 44:5 (1989): 1035–56, esp. 1042–51.

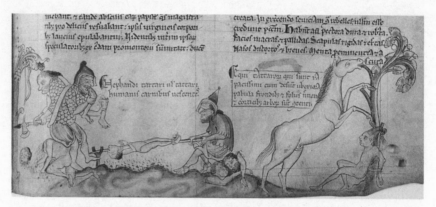

FIGURE 1. Mongol cannibals cooking while a naked woman prisoner is tied to a tree. (The Master and Fellows of Corpus Christi College, Cambridge. Ms. 16, fol. 166r.)

for instance, relates that the crusaders in Syria were also reduced by hunger to eating the bodies of dead Muslims and follows the explicit condemnation of the act with an implicit justification.[79]

Matthew Paris refers extensively to Mongol cannibalism. In addition to the letter of Ivo of Narbonne, which he quotes to that effect, he mentions this as fact on his own authority in two places, once briefly and once in graphic detail:

> And thus they use their captives like beasts of burden. The men are inhuman and bestial, they can be said to be monsters rather than men, they thirst for blood and drink it, they tear to pieces and devour flesh of dogs and of men . . . they drink for their delight blood which they draw from their sheep.[80]

79. Mirabile dictu et auribus horrendum: tanta ipsa famis angustia circa has urbes invaluit (quod nefas est dicere, nedum facere) ut Christiani non solum Turcos occisos vel Sarracenos, verum canes arreptos et igni coctos comedere non abhorrerent, prae inopia quam audistis. Sed quid mirum? Non est acutior gladius quam a longo contracta fames (*RHC HOcc.* 4:450). Albert did not hesitate to condemn the crusaders in other cases (such as the pogroms against the Jews), so it seems that he was not too utterly shocked by the events. Moreover, the phrasing of the sentence implies that Albert found the eating of dogs more repulsive than the eating of dead Saracens. In the *Chanson d'Antioche*, however, a similar episode shows the crusaders as enjoying eating human (Muslim) flesh and remarking that the meat tastes better than pork; the attitude of the writer to the episode is unclear (Jill Tattersall, "Anthropofagi and Eaters of Raw Flesh in French Literature of the Crusade Period: Myth, Tradition, and Reality," *Medium Aevum* 57:2 [1988]: 240–53, esp. 248–49).

80. Et sic captivis suis quasi jumentis abutebantur. Viri enim sunt inhumani et bestiales, potius monstra dicendi quam homines, sanguinem sitientes et bibentes, carnes caninas et humanas laniantes et devorantes . . . sanguinem eliquatum a pecoribus suis pro deliciis bibentes (*Chronica Majora*, 4:76–77). See also *Chronica Majora*, 3:488: "carnibus crudis et etiam humanis vescuntur."

Simon of St. Quentin's *Historia Tartarorum*, which has survived only as quoted by Vincent of Beauvais in the *Speculum historiale*, also refers to preference cannibalism under the heading "On their cruelty and their deceitfulness" [*De crudelitate ipsorum et fallacia*] and adds that the Mongols also drink the blood of their dead enemies (Matthew Paris does not refer specifically to *human* blood):

> [*30.77 - On their cruelty and their deceitfulness*] . . . they devour human flesh like lions, whether roasted on fire or boiled, and this [they do] sometimes out of necessity, sometimes for pleasure, and sometimes to strike with terror the people who should hear of this [practice]. They exult in the slaying of people, and their soul delights extraordinarily in the multitude of killings. [*30.78 - On their food*] . . . they suck the blood [of their enemy] avidly like infernal leeches.[81]

These sources clearly attribute preference cannibalism to the Mongols in addition to cannibalism practiced for survival or as psychological warfare (a type that does not fit into any of Guzman's categories). Simon of St. Quentin emphasizes the pleasure taken by the Mongols in acts of killing and cannibalism.

Not all sources attribute preference cannibalism to the Mongols. Generally, accounts of people who came into direct contact with the Mongols, particularly the accounts of missionaries and travelers, are more reserved on this issue.[82] But one can see how a confluence of facts that most writers agree on can lead to the attribution of cannibalism to the Mongols. Matthew Paris himself quotes an account of the Mongols by a Russian archbishop named Peter that mentions only survival cannibalism as a Mongol practice.[83] John of Plano Carpini relates that once when famine threatened the army of Genghis Khan he ordered that every tenth man should be eaten by his comrades (evidently referring to his own men and not to enemies).[84] Nevertheless, the mention of survival cannibalism makes preference cannibalism more credible. It is a preliminary step in the creation of the image of the Mongols as cannibals.

The dietary habits of the Mongols, as reported even by writers who do *not* characterize them as cannibals, also contributed, significantly, to the for-

---

81. *Historia Tartarorum* 30.77–78, 38–41.

82. See Tattersall, "Anthropofagi and Eaters of Raw Flesh," 244ff.

83. Carnes comedunt jumentinas, caninas, et alias abominabiles, etiam in necessitate humanas, non tamen crudas, sed coctas. Sanguinem, aquam, et lac bibunt (*Chronica Majora*, 4:388).

84. Johannes de Plano Carpini, *Liber Tartarorum* 4, 52; Dawson, *Mongol Mission*, 21.

mation of their image as cannibals. Most writers who refer to their eating habits attribute to the Mongols at least one of the following: eating raw meat, eating all kinds of animals (including unclean ones, such as dogs), and drinking blood. These are violations of medieval dietary taboos, as reflected in the penitentials.[85] All these habits are mentioned in the account of the Russian archbishop who links them to cannibalism but are also pointed out by other writers who do not make this connection.[86] One can see how the image of the Mongols as cannibals emerged out of the amalgam of repulsive dietary habits, a reputation of practicing survival cannibalism, and reports of their cruelty in Hungary and Dalmatia. The image of the Mongols as practicing preference cannibalism further reinforced, in its turn, their reputation for cruelty. The attribution of cannibalism to the Mongols is not due only to fact or to a circumstantial apposition of facts, however. The topos of cannibalism appears also in reference to different "others" beside the Mongols (such as the Saracens) in French literature of the twelfth and thirteenth centuries.[87] In itself, the appearance of this motif in the central Middle Ages is part of the revival of Latin classical culture at this period.

The thirteenth-century accounts of the Mongols represent changes in the building blocks used for representing cruelty. Two new categories of cruelty emerge from these sources: sexual violence and cannibalism. These new types of cruelty echo classical models rather than early medieval ones. The image of the inordinate cruelty of the Mongols is constructed with these new categories in conjunction with indiscriminate massacres, which have been a constant identifier of the cruelty of the "other" since antiquity.

The novelty of the thirteenth-century representations of cruelty, however, is deeper than a mere change of building blocks. A whole new mode of reference to cruelty emerges from the accounts of the Mongols. The external characteristics of this new discourse are the detailed descriptions, the den-

---

85. See Bonnassie, "Consommation d'aliments immondes," 1036–40. The infringement of taboos in general is one of the more common ways of characterizing the "other" as such (see Syed M. Islam, "Marco Polo: Order/Disorder in the Discourse of the Other," *Literature and History* 2:1 [1993]: 1–22, esp. 10–12). Cannibalism is not the only taboo violated by the Mongols but is the one most directly related to their cruelty. In most accounts, the Mongols are also represented as violating Western taboos on incest.

86. The account of the Russian archbishop Peter, quoted by Matthew Paris, refers to all three elements: raw meat, "unclean" animals, and blood drinking (*Chronica Majora*, 4:388); Simon of St. Quentin refers to blood drinking (quoted earlier); Joinville refers to their eating raw meat, although only when the blood is extracted ("quant le sanc en est bien hors, si la manjuent toute crue") (*Histoire de Saint Louis*, ed. Pierre-Claude-François Daunou and Joseph Naudet, *RHGF* 20 [Paris, 1840], 264).

87. Tattersall, "Anthropofagi and Eaters of Raw Flesh."

sity of references to cruelty they contain, and their affective tone. Beneath the surface, this development regarding cruelty is linked to two other processes: the emphasis on intentionality and the classical revival of the central Middle Ages.

The impression of a dense "narrative of cruelty" in the thirteenth-century chronicles is the result of a new method of representing cruelty, not merely of a greater number of references. Cruelty is no longer represented as a sequence of isolated actions or episodes but rather as "compounds of cruelty"—that is, acts that simultaneously combine several types of cruelty: The desecration of churches and of holy objects is combined with acts of sexual cruelty committed in churches or monasteries, and sexual cruelty is coupled with cannibalism. These compounds are an instance of the whole being greater than its components. The combination of the acts produces an impression of greater cruelty than if they were related sequentially because it implies that the Mongols practice all these kinds of cruelty simultaneously, and, moreover, it evokes once more the calculated and systematic nature of Mongol cruelty.

The focus on cruelty and its systematic aspect and the emergence of rape and cannibalism as primary themes in representations of cruelty are related to a process of interiorization that takes place in twelfth-century philosophy and theology and that emphasizes intentionality. Thus, discussions of ethics lean more and more toward judging morality almost exclusively on the basis of the intentions of the actor. Virtues and vices, as the writings of Bernard of Clairvaux indicate, are judged by their effect on the subject's soul and not on their external object.[88] The institution of private confession and the establishment of the Inquisition are also part of the same process.

The concentration on intentionality is particularly evident in the explicit reference to the pleasure that the Mongols derived from their acts of cruelty. Thomas of Spalato describes the Mongols watching the slaying of children with cruel eyes and laughing together at the spectacle.[89] Master Roger relates how the Tartars were overjoyed to see men ransom their lives by their beautiful wives, daughters, or sisters, who were then raped before their family

88. See Chapter 1, 19–20. Traces of this type of emphasis on intentional violence can be found also in legal texts. The *Freisinger Rechtsbuch*, for instance, deals with the death of serfs as the result of flogging. The master is not accused of murder if the serf lingers for more than a day after the flogging, probably because in this case the intention to kill is not beyond doubt (Ruprecht of Freising, *Freisinger Rechtsbuch*, c. 46, ed. Hans-Kurt Claussen [Weimar, 1941], 52; I am indebted to Paul Freedman for this reference).

89. Ipse vero sedentes et crudelibus oculis intuentes corridebant ad invicem (*Ex Thomae historia, MGH SS* 29:588–89).

members' eyes.[90] Simon of St. Quentin likewise mentions that the Mongols enormously enjoy committing massacres.[91]

Preoccupation with intent and pleasure can also be seen as the backdrop to the rise of the new categories of sexual cruelty and cannibalism. The two are transformations, or aberrations, of the elemental pleasures of food and sex. Thus Matthew Paris uses the expression "for their delights" (*pro deliciis*) when referring to the two issues, and Simon of St. Quentin emphasizes that cannibalism is practiced at times out of necessity and at times "for pleasure" (*causa delectationis*). Münster, a Renaissance scholar, likewise defines the purpose of Mongol cannibalism as "taking [their] pleasure" (*uindicandi desiderium*).[92]

The emphasis on intentionality is related to the revival of classical anthropology and to the emergence of cruelty as an anthropological category, perhaps the most important one in the Westerners' perception of the Mongols. In late antiquity, there was a certain degree of anthropological interest in such peoples. Works such as Herodotus's *Histories*, Tacitus's *Germania*, and Ammianus Marcelinus's *Rerum gestarum libri* displayed an aspect of intercultural polemics as well as a genuine interest in the life and culture of the peoples they dealt with. Cruelty was one of the characteristics of such people, one that was considered an innate quality of the barbarians by both pagan and Christian authors.

The attitude toward peoples perceived as "other" changed in the early Middle Ages. Such peoples were viewed as agents of divine punishments, and their incursions were seen as no different than attacks of locusts, to which they were explicitly compared at times.[93] And as the attribution of intentions is of little relevance to locusts, the intentions of such peoples were also ignored.

The European expansion of the central Middle Ages brought Westerners into contact with other cultures. In conjunction with the revival of classical

90. Stabant nobiscum Tartari et Comani simul, videbant quamplurimi et gaudebant, letabantur, quod patres per filias, mariti per uxores, fratres per sorores pulchras vitam redimebant, illas ad libitum eorum conservantes; et pro quodam illis fiebat solatio, ut in conspectu patris vel mariti uxor vel filia stuprabatur (*Epistola Magistri Rogerii*, *MGH SS* 29:563).

91. See above, 99.

92. *Chronica Majora*, 4:76-77, 273; Sebastian Münster, *Cosmographia* (Basel, 1550), 1060.

93. The Danes, for instance, are described as "advolantes . . . quasi multitudo locustarum" (Henry of Huntington, *Historia Anglorum*, 174). The attribution of cruelty, or other intentions, to animals in the Middle Ages (in the West) is problematic. Intentional cruelty *is* attributed to various animals, but in this context the type of animal is significant. It seems that such motivations are assigned to "higher-order" animals and not to locusts, whose representation as a mass of unindividualized creatures excludes the possibility of referring to them in the same manner as to lions or bears.

culture in general, this contact renewed the old mode of approaching other peoples, including those who were perceived as barbarians, or "others." The focus on intention made possible a view of the "other" that was more complex than the early medieval approach; now the "other" could be presented as a faceless god-sent punishment but at the same time as intentionally cruel. The distinction between the action and the intention makes it possible, as Thomas Aquinas does in his discussion of cruelty, to distinguish between the categories of justice and cruelty—the administrator of justice can be cruel if his intentions are so, regardless of the fact that the action is just. These developments focused the attention on the Mongols as subjects accountable for their deeds and made the reference to their cruelty more relevant.[94]

The anthropological interest is evident in a number of accounts that take a broader view of the Mongols, looking beyond their military victories and including descriptions of their outward appearance, their women, their laws (or lack of laws), their diet, and their character.[95] These accounts follow the classical models in their interests and in their biases toward other peoples. As shown by Brent D. Shaw, since the times of Homer and Herodotus, nomadism was perceived as the lowest stage of human development. This characterization was reflected in the diet attributed to the Mongols, which consisted of *unprocessed* food: the eating of raw flesh (sometimes human) and the drinking of milk or water (instead of a processed product like wine). This level of human existence was also associated with savagery and cruelty. Such a picture was the prism through which various nomadic peoples were described from the ninth century B.C. to the seventeenth century.[96]

The anthropologically oriented accounts of the Mongols join together classical and purely medieval points of view. As in the classical model, the

94. Roger Bacon attributes the victories of the Mongols to their practice of magic and sorcery. Thus, their achievements are still supernatural, but they are active subjects using these powers and not tools in their hands (*Opus majus*, trans. Robert B. Burke [New York, 1962], 1:416–17). The focus on intentions is evident also in another place in the *Opus majus* where Bacon analyzes the motivations of various sects; the Tartars and Saracens are "sects" whose aims of felicity regard only the present life: The Muslims seek pleasure, and the Tartars lust for dominion (ibid., 2:788).

95. In addition to the well-known accounts, such as the ones by John of Plano Carpini and William of Rubruck, similar anthropological interest is betrayed by the contents of a now lost manuscript containing an account of the Mongols by David of Ashby (Clovis Brunel, "David d'Ashby auteur méconnu des *Faits des Tartares*," *Romania* 79 [1958]: 39–46, esp. 41).

96. Brent D. Shaw, "'Eaters of Flesh, Drinkers of Milk': The Ancient Mediterranean Ideology of the Pastoral Nomad," *Ancient Society* 12 (1982): 5–31. The mention of the Mongols as drinkers of milk in the account of the Russian archbishop Peter (see note 83) is significant in this context.

Mongols are systematically differentiated from the medieval West.[97] But the descriptions are cast into the mold of contemporary discussions of virtues and vices. Thus, in Matthew Paris's accounts of the Mongols, cruelty appears as one of their main characteristics (listed among others, such as their physical appearance, their horses, their women, their laws, their matrimonial habits). In Simon of St. Quentin's *Historia Tartarorum*, various qualities of the Mongols are discussed in several chapters according to the following headings: "On the external characteristics of the Tartars," "On their pride [*superbia*] and impiety [*impietas*]," "On their greed [*cupiditas*] and avarice [*avaricia*]," "On their lack of restraint [*effrentatio*] and lust [*luxuria*]," "On their cruelty [*crudelitas*] and their deceitfulness [*fallacia*]," and "On their food [*De victu eorum*]." One notices here the addition of new vices, such as cruelty and lack of restraint, to the traditional list of vices and deadly sins such as *cupiditas, avaritia, superbia, luxuria,* and *gula* (gluttony, dealt with in the chapter *De victu eorum*).[98] Even in Thomas of Spalato's chronicle, which does not deal primarily with the Mongols, there are two chapters with the headings "On the nature of the Tartars" (*De natura Tartarorum*) and "On the savagery [or cruelty—*sevicia*] of the Tartars."[99] The appearance of cruelty as an anthropological category (in relation to the "other") implies also that it is a human quality. Admittedly, it is on the borderline between the human and the beastly and perhaps even defines this border, but it nevertheless belongs also to the human side. Although cruelty does not figure in the extensive formal medieval literature on virtues and vices (as one of the deadly sins, for instance), such headings in the literature on the Mongols indicate that it was beginning to be considered a vice. Significantly, this development coincides with the appearance of cruelty as a human characteristic in medieval thought, as treated by Thomas Aquinas in the *Summa theologiae*.[100]

97. On some aspects of this differentiation, see Claude C. Kappler, "L'image des Mongols dans le *Speculum historiale* de Vincent de Beauvais," in *Vincent de Beauvais: intentions et réceptions d'une oeuvre encyclopédique au Moyen Age*, ed. Monique Paulmier-Foucart, Serge Lusignan and Alain Nadeau (Paris, 1990), 219–240.

98. Schemes of deadly sins, usually seven, figured prominently in the central Middle Ages in a variety of sources: theological tracts, literature, drama, and the figurative arts. These lists varied slightly in the sins they included and even more in their hierarchical order. Most commonly, they included pride, wrath, envy, avarice, sloth, gluttony, and lechery (*superbia, ira, invidia, avaritia, acedia, gula, luxuria*). For a good survey of this topic, see Morton W. Bloomfield, *The Seven Deadly Sins* (East Lansing, Mich., 1952).

99. James R. Sweeney remarks that the cruelty (lack of compassion in Sweeney's formulation) of the Mongols is for Thomas "a distinguishing; even a defining characteristic of the invaders" ("Thomas of Spalato," 164).

100. See Chapter 1, 9–11.

This development in the West also reflects the changing importance of two trends of influence—biblical and classical. The view of the "other" as an instrument of punishment in the hands of God is biblical: It was reiterated on numerous occasions by the Old Testament prophets.[101] The more personalized and anthropologically oriented view of the "other" is classical. The two streams of influence cannot be separated in the Western accounts relating to the Mongols because neither appears in a "pure form": The way of looking at other peoples is inescapably Christian and morally oriented; it is not identical to the pagan anthropological outlook. Yet the growing weight of the classical trend, in which the qualities of the "other" are more relevant, is clearly noticeable, and it is not a phenomenon confined to the context of historical writing: The growing importance of the classical elements is reflected also in the emphasis on such classical attributes of the "other" as cannibalism.

THE MONGOLS IN EASTERN SOURCES

The analysis of Western sources dealing with the Mongols shows that Western authors were intensely preoccupied with cruelty. The rise of cruelty to the status of an important cultural issue is related both to the extraordinary level of violence used by the Mongols and to cultural developments in the medieval West. But what is the respective role of actual violence versus that of cultural factors in engendering this preoccupation with the subject in the West? The Mongol conquests in Asia and the Middle East were incomparably greater than those they accomplished in their brief incursion into Europe. Setting the Western accounts of the Mongols against Eastern ones enables a cross-cultural comparison of the ways in which violence of external invaders is represented. Because the historical circumstances are similar, differences between Eastern and Western representations would be due primarily to cultural factors.

The Eastern sources dealing with the Mongols are of a somewhat different nature than the Western ones. The Western outlook is more self-centered, and the Mongols are viewed mainly in terms of their influence on Europe. There are a few Western works whose main subject is the Mongols as a people, such as the now lost *Historia Tartarorum* of Simon of St. Quentin and the works of the missionaries. But even these few are mainly anthropological, and they do not attempt to present a comprehensive history of the Mongols and their conquests. In the East, there are several ambitious works whose purpose is to present a survey of at least a segment of Mongol

101. Isa. 13 is an expressive formulation of this view.

history. Among these are writings by Juvaini, Rashīd al-Dīn, and Nuwayrī. Additionally, similar to the Western chroniclers, other writers deal with the Mongols mainly from the viewpoint of their effects on their countries.

Eastern authors differ widely among themselves, more so than did the Western writers, in their actual relation with the Mongols. Some of them, unlike Western authors, were employed in the Mongol administration or belonged to peoples who were allied to the Mongols (e.g., the Armenians). Others, similar to their Western counterparts, were victims (direct or indirect) of the Mongols. The different circumstances put some constraints on these writers' reports on the Mongols. Authors employed by the Mongols were evidently not in a position to criticize their masters explicitly. Nevertheless, there are no substantial factual disagreements between these authors, such as Juvaini (1226–1283), and others who did not work in the service of the Mongols, such as Ibn al-Athīr (1160–1233). This agreement enables the reconstruction of a fairly accurate picture of the violence committed by the Mongols.

One point of agreement between the chroniclers is the devastating effect of the Mongol incursions into the Near East. Ibn al-Athīr is perhaps the most important Arabic-writing Muslim writer describing as a contemporary the initial phase of the Mongol invasions. He abandons the usual understatement that characterizes his writing by stating that the Mongol invasions are "the greatest catastrophe and the most dire calamity . . . which befell all men in general, and the Muslims in particular . . . since God, be praised and exalted, has created Adam and until now."[102] In comparison, the victories of the Franks—including the conquest of Jerusalem in 1099—are described in considerably milder terms. Juvaini, the author of the most well-known Persian account of the Mongols, refrains from condemning or judging the Mongols explicitly.[103] Similar to European chroniclers of earlier times, Juvaini tends to see the actions of the Mongols as a god-sent plague. This position, however, does not lead him to mitigate the reports of the Mongol devastation and atrocities but rather to adopt the role of a detached observer. Thus, he introduces his account of the actions of the Mongols in Persia with the following comparative summary:

> When, therefore [Genghis Khan] took Bokhara and Samarqand, he contented himself with slaughtering and looting once only, and did not go to the

102. *Al-kāmil fī al-taʾrīkh*, ed. Carl J. Tornberg (corrected edition) (Beirut, 1966[1851–1876]), 12:358.

103. John A. Boyle mentions only three instances in which the author betrays open dislike or condemnation of the Mongols (Juvaini, *The History of the World-Conqueror*, trans. John A. Boyle [Manchester, 1958], 1:xxx–xxxi).

extreme of general massacre. As for the adjoining territories . . . the hand of molestation was to some extent withheld from them. And afterwards, the Mongols pacified the survivors and proceeded with the work of reconstruction, so that at the present time, i.e., 658/1259–60, the prosperity and well-being of these districts have in some cases attained their original level . . . It is otherwise with Khorasan and Iraq . . . every town and every village has been several times subjected to pillage and massacre and has suffered this confusion for years, so that even though there be generation and increase until the Resurrection the population will not attain to a tenth part of what it was before.[104]

This report is very unlike the European reports of the Mongols in its matter-of-fact tone. The magnitude of the devastation is brought home effectively by the probably ironic reference to the luck of Bokhara and Samarqand in suffering slaughter and pillage only once.

The terror inspired by the Mongols recurs in Muslim accounts: Ibn al-Athīr refers in several places to this fear, once from personal experience. He also cites some eyewitness accounts that convey effectively the paralyzing fear inspired by the Mongols. He reports that it is said that even when only one of them enters a populous village, he kills the inhabitants one by one, without meeting any resistance. Another eyewitness reports a similar situation, in which a company of eighteen men met a single Mongol, but none of them except the narrator of the incident dared to strike him in spite of the numeric odds. In another example, Ibn al-Athīr tells how an unarmed Mongol took a Muslim, ordered him to lie with his head on the floor, went away to fetch a sword, and then returned to kill him.[105] Nevertheless, fear figures less prominently in the Muslim chronicles than it does in the Western accounts.

Similar to the European accounts of the Mongol invasions, the main characteristic of the conquests in the East as reported by Muslim chronicles is the large-scale massacres. Ibn al-Athīr attempts to convey the magnitude of these massacres by comparing them to the massacre inflicted by the Romans in Jerusalem when they conquered the city in 70 A.D. and burnt the Temple.[106] Ibn al-Athīr claims that a massacre on such a scale occurred in every city occupied by the Mongols.

As to the conquest itself, he comments that "these [Tartars] did not spare anyone, but killed the women, the men, and the children; and split the bel-

---

104. Ibid., 1:96–97.

105. *Al-kāmil fī al-ta'rīkh*, 12:500–501. For other references to the fear inspired by the Mongols, see ibid., 12:369, 378 (the episode recounting Ibn al-Athīr's personal experience), 384, 497.

106. The choice of this particular example is unusual in Islamic sources.

lies of the pregnant [women], and killed the fetuses."[107] Juvaini emphasizes the extent of the slaughter in almost every account of a Mongol conquest. In some cases, Juvaini is content to refer in general terms to a great slaughter or laconically to the killing of the inhabitants of a whole region.[108] In other instances, he only hints at the numerical magnitude of the slaughter, as in the case of Khawārizm, in which the minority who were spared (craftsmen and artisans) numbered 100,000 and, on the number of the slain, Juvaini says, "I have heard of such a quantity of slain that I did not believe the report and so have not recorded it."[109] This information gap has a considerable rhetorical effect, suggesting that the numbers were much higher than in cases for which he does provide figures: In the city of Merv, the number of the slain was, according to Juvaini's report, 1,300,000. Ibn al-Athīr mentions 40,000 victims at Ray.[110] Describing the capture of Baghdad in 1258, Al-Maqrīzī (1364–1442) mentions 2,000,000 victims.[111] Regardless of whether these figures are exaggerated, it is evident that the Mongol conquests were perceived as being characterized by massacres of unheard of magnitude.

The Muslim writers, Juvaini in particular, emphasize the systematic nature of the massacres. The sources reveal that the method was basically the same in most of the cities in which the population was massacred: The inhabitants were led out of the city, and the minority who were destined to be left alive—artisans, young women, and children—were separated from the rest. Then the task of executing the remaining citizens was divided more or less equally between the soldiers. Juvaini supplies figures concerning this task. After the capture of Khawārizm, each fighting man had to execute 24 persons; after the capture of Merv, the figure rose to between 300 and 400.[112]

As in the Western sources, emphasis is placed on the measures taken to ensure the general nature of the massacre. The Mongols used to leave a rear

---

107. وهؤلاء لم يبقوا على احد, بل قتلوا النساء والرجال, وشقوا بطون الحوامل, وقتلوا الاجنة (*Al-kāmil fī al-ta'rīkh*, 12:359.)

108. "Törbei Toqshin took the fortress of Nandana and wrought great slaughter"; "The Mongols then plundered and massacred throughout the greater part of Iraq" (Juvaini, *History of the World-Conqueror*, 1:141, 147).

109. Ibid., 1:128.

110. *Al-kāmil fī al-ta'rīkh*, 12:374.

111. Al-Maqrīzī, *Kitāb al-sulūk li-ma'rifat duwal al-mulūk*, ed. Muḥammad Muṣṭafa Ziyāda (Cairo, 1936), 1.2:409–10. For another account relating to the capture of Baghdad by the Mongols and its implications, see John A. Boyle, "The Death of the Last Abbasid Caliph: A Contemporary Muslim Account," *Journal of Semitic Studies* 6 (1961): 145–61 (published also by Variorum in J. A. Boyle, *The Mongol World Empire* [London, 1977]).

112. The systematic division of executions is mentioned also by John of Plano Carpini; see earlier, 94.

guard whose duty was to lure and kill the survivors. At Nishapur, it was even commanded "that in the exaction of vengeance not even cats and dogs should be left alive."[113] The Mongols also erected trophies to commemorate their victories: piles of dead bodies or mutilated members, intended to strike terror. Ibn al-Athīr mentions that the Mongols made a pile of bodies "like a hill"; Juvaini mentions more systematic structures, such as separate piles for the severed heads of men, women, and children.

The similarities with the Western accounts do not, however, extend much beyond the accounts of the massacres. In contrast to the Western sources, sexual cruelty and cannibalism are minor issues in the Muslim texts dealing with the Mongols. Writers like Ibn al-Athīr and Juvaini mention the rape of women and virgins, but only in passing and without the wealth of details supplied by Western chroniclers. Later adaptations of Ibn al-Athīr make even these brief remarks ambiguous. A more detailed account of mass rape is recounted by Rashīd al-Dīn but not under the category of cruelty. The scarcity of references to rape does not seem to reflect a different procedure adopted by the Mongols in the East. It rather points to an issue that I discuss later—the different modes used in the West and East for reporting such events. References to cannibalism are lacking, and the significance of this absence is also discussed later.

Another difference in emphases between the Muslim and Western sources is the issue of violence against religion, which is more prominent in the Muslim accounts. As in the West, the Mongols publicly humiliated the religion of the conquered. Ibn al-Athīr refers mournfully to the desecration of mosques and Qur'ans after the capture of Bokhara. Juvaini's accounts of the same event are more detailed. He relates that Genghis Khan cast the Qur'ans in the courtyard of the mosque and brought the horses to feed there. He also ordered dancing girls to perform in the mosques and made the *a'imma* (scholars) and other men of religion keep watch over the horses.[114] For some Muslim authors, the attitude of Mongol leaders toward Islam is the measuring rod for judging acts of violence committed by them. Rashīd al-Dīn, for instance, comments that "the army continued as before to pillage and commit irregularities; but Mubārak Shāh, being a Muslim, would not allow any violence against the peasants."[115] Al-Jūzjānī (1193–

113. Juvaini, *History of the World-Conqueror*, 1:177.

114. *Al-kāmil fī al-ta'rīkh*, 12:366; Juvaini, *History of the World-Conqueror*, 1:103ff.

115. Rashīd al-Dīn, *The Successors of Genghis Khan*, trans. John A. Boyle (New York, 1971), 151. The severity and fear (among other negative traits of character) inspired by Güyük Khan are perhaps implicitly linked by Rashīd to his preference of Christianity and prejudice against Islam (187–88).

after 1260) makes the same link when he describes Chaghatay, who was anti-Muslim, as violent and tyrannical.[116]

It is clear from the Muslim accounts reviewed here that the Mongols are perceived as "other." The same process of "systematic differentiation" and the presentation of the Mongols as destroyers of taboos, or natural immunities, is evident in the Muslim chronicles as it is in the Western ones. They are called unbelievers [*kifār*], and their acts of violence include killing of women and children and profaning of holy places and objects.

But beyond the similarities and shifts in emphases there is one major difference between the Western and Muslim sources: The Western sources refer explicitly and in detail to the issue of cruelty, whereas the Muslim sources do not. This aspect of the Muslim accounts is unrelated to the author's position in relation to the Mongols, to the level of detail in which the action is described, and to the degree of affectivity. The two types of sources present, in fact, two different approaches to cruelty.[117]

The narration in the Muslim chronicles is usually straightforward and unaffective, more so than the Western chronicles, even when the events are described in detail. This mode of representation contrasts with the Western accounts of the Mongols. In one instance, Juvaini relates how the Mongols plan to execute the population of Bokhara after a failed rebellion and quotes them as saying "again we will strike a blow, and satisfy our appetite, and turn these people into fuel for the fire of calamity, and carry off their property and their children." This depiction of the Mongols enjoying their actions does not draw any explicit reference to their cruelty.[118] This representation is consistent even in the rare exceptions in which a more affective tone is used to describe the actions of the Mongols.[119]

The contrast between East and West also stands out in another comparison. In the West, the study of the transmission of early medieval texts conveyed the following process: References to cruelty were absent in the ninth- and tenth-century texts but were added in the twelfth and thirteenth

116. Al-Jūzjānī, *Ṭabaqāt-i Nāṣirī*, trans. Henry G. Raverty (London, 1881), 2:1144–48.

117. A review of the concept of the "other" in Arabic (mainly *adab*) literature can be found in Aziz al-Azmeh, "Barbarians in Arab Eyes," *Past and Present* 134 (1992): 3–18. Al-Azmeh mentions cannibalism as one aspect of "otherness" but does not deal with the issue of cruelty, nor does he refer to the representation of the Mongols in Arabic literature.

118. Juvaini, *History of the World-Conqueror*, 1:115.

119. See, for instance, Juvaini's comments on the rape of women that followed the conquest of Merv (*History of the World-Conqueror*, 1:161–62).

FIGURE 2. Mongols executing prisoners by arrows and by burial upside down. (From a Persian manuscript of the Shah Nameh, ca. 1300. Chester Beatty Library, Dublin. Ms. 104, fol. 64.)

centuries when these texts were "recycled" in later chronicles.[120] In the East, such recycling does not reveal an increasing preoccupation with cruelty. If at all, the opposite is true. Thus, Nuwayrī's (1279–1332) adaptation of Ibn al-Athīr's account of the conquest of Bokhara and Samarqand abbreviates and tones down the references to the Mongols' violence.[121] Nuwayrī takes out the more affective phrases and the more vivid descriptions. Moreover, he modifies some of the factual aspects of the report, leaving out some

120. The change in Western sources is compelling but not universal. Some of Matthew Paris's references to the Albigensians in Spain are similar to early medieval accounts of the "other": He describes them as burning churches and slaughtering women and children (*Chronica Majora*, 3:267). Similar entries referring to the Mongols can be found in German chronicles (see *Notae Altahenses, MGH SS* 17:422; *Hermanni Altahensis annales s.a.* 1241, *MGH SS* 17:394; *Annales Colmarienses maiores s.a.* 1285, *MGH SS* 17:212; *Annales Colmarienses minores s.a.* 1240, *MGH SS* 17:189; *Annales breves Wormatienses s.a.* 1238, *MGH SS* 17:75).

121. See Appendix 5.

of the references to rape and torture.[122] The claim that Nuwayrī is para-phrasing and summarizing earlier accounts is not valid: In the West, even a shorter summary could introduce the issue of cruelty, which was not present explicitly in the earlier text.[123]

This lack of explicit references to cruelty in the writings of Muslim authors cannot be attributed to the individual writers' relations with the Mongols. Al-Jūzjānī, who wrote an account of the Mongols in Persian, leaves no doubt about his attitude toward the Mongols. He invariably refers to the death of a Mongol as to his "going to hell," and he criticizes Muslim rulers who became tributaries of the Mongols.[124] The magnitude of his resentment and hate of the Mongols on account of their massacres are reflected in a personal story that he inserts in the chronicle. He tells how he was taken prisoner by the Mongols during the siege of Harat and became an attendant to Genghis Khan (providing him information on Islam). One day, Genghis Khan asked him, "Will not a mighty name remain behind me?" and Al-Jūzjānī answered—only after his security had been guaranteed—"A name continues to endure where there are people, but how will a name endure when the Khan's servants martyr all the people and massacre them, for who will remain to tell the tale?"[125] Yet, in spite of that, his accounts of the Mongols are even less affective than Juvaini's, and they, too, lack explicit references to cruelty. Thus, in contrast to the accounts of Ibn al-Athīr and Juvaini on the capture of Merv, Al-Jūzjānī limits himself to the following: "In the year 617 H., Tūlī [Tuloi] turned his face from the [great camp at the] Pushtah-i-Nuʿmān towards the city of Marw [Merv] and took that city and martyred its inhabitants."[126]

As can be seen from these examples, the relation of the writer to the Mongols has limited influence on the way their violence is represented in his writings. Those who cooperated with the Mongols usually refrain from overt criticism and do not refer to their cruelty, even when they represent it in detail. But writers who refer to the Mongols as enemies also do not refer explicitly to their cruelty. What are the reasons for this lack of explicit refer-ence to cruelty, so different from the Western accounts of the Mongols?

122. In the case of Bokhara, rape is replaced by the more ambiguous term *fasād* (cor-ruption, a reprehensible act). These tendencies characterize Nuwayrī's use of Ibn al-Athīr in other instances as well. See, for instance, the accounts of the capture of Bailaqan and Merv: Ibn al-Athīr, *Al-kāmil fī al-ta'rīkh* 12:383, 392; and Al-Nuwayrī, *Nihāyat al-arab fī funūn al-adab*, ed. Saʿīd ʿAshūr (Cairo, 1985), 27:319, 326.

123. See Chapter 3, 66–67.

124. Al-Jūzjānī, *Ṭabaqāt-i Nāṣirī*, 2:1228.

125. Ibid., 2:1041.

126. Ibid., 2:1026–27. For Ibn al-Athīr's account, see *Al-kāmil fī al-ta'rīkh*, 12:392–93.

One possible explanation for the lack of references to cruelty is lexical—namely, the lack of an exact equivalent in Arabic for the word *cruelty*. This absence, however, does not seem a very plausible cause, as there *is* a semantic field for expressing the general meaning.[127] Moreover, Jews and Christians writing in Arabic adopted, consistently and exclusively, the term *qaswa* as the equivalent for *crudelitas* or *akhzariut* when translating from Latin or Hebrew.[128]

Alternatively, as has been suggested by several scholars in relation to the incursions of the Vikings in the West, it could be claimed that the actions did not seem cruel to the writers: They were considered a fact of life, a hateful but common prerogative of the conqueror. Yet the horror of the events and their extraordinary nature, even for people who might be used to violence and tyranny, emerges from the words of these authors even without specific references to cruelty. The detailed accounts, the systematic differentiation, and the (admittedly few) affective interjections indicate that the actions of the Mongols were indeed perceived as exceptional.

A more fruitful approach to account for the differences between East and West would be a comparative one. In their lack of references to cruelty and their matter-of-fact style of narration, the Muslim chronicles recall the early medieval chronicles. The similarity extends as well to the perception of the invaders as a divine punishment. Juvaini elaborates the idea at length, incorporating the Mongols in a broader historical mechanism of sin and correction in which every people receives a punishment according to its sins.[129] Al-Maqrīzī, likewise, sees the conquest of Baghdad and the execution of the caliph as a punishment inflicted on the Muslims on account of their sinful behavior, and he even quotes a *ḥadīth* prophesying the subjugation of the Muslims should they act sinfully.[130] The Mongols are also reported as representing themselves in this same manner.[131] Such a view leads by necessity to a

---

127. Besides *qaswa*, there are words such as *satwa* and *salaba*.

128. .קסוة , אכזריות.

129. "Therefore for the admonishment and chastisement of every people a punishment hath been meted out fitting to their rebellion and in proportion to their infidelity, and as a warning to those endued with insight a calamity or castigation hath overtaken them in accordance with their sins and misdemeanors" (Juvaini, *History of the World-Conqueror*, 1:16–18).

130. Al-Maqrīzī, *Kitāb al-sulūk li-maʿrifat duwal al-mulūk*, 1.2:409–10. Al-Jūzjānī, who attributes the caliph's final fate to some mistakes made by him, sees in them the work of destiny ("fate was using the whip of wrath behind the horse of the Khilafat," *Ṭabaqāt-i Nāṣirī*, 2:1248).

131. See two letters sent by Hülegü as cited by Al-Maqrīzī, *Kitāb al-sulūk li-maʿrifat duwal al-mulūk*, 1.2:415–16, 427–28 (in which Hülegü claims that the Mongols are the "soldiers of God [Allah]"); see also the letter sent in 1246 by Güyük Khan to Innocent IV (English version of the Persian text in Dawson, *Mongol Mission*, 85–86).

more resigned perception of the Mongol conquests.[132] Thus, for instance, Ibn Khaldūn presents the Mongols in the *Muqaddima* as a natural link in the succession of dynasties, not as something extraordinary.[133]

Besides highlighting the differences between East and West in the thirteenth century, this comparison points to the extent of the change that the West underwent from the ninth and tenth centuries to the thirteenth. In the Western accounts, the idea that the Mongols are a god-sent punishment is marginal, especially as compared with the prevalence of this view with respect to the Vikings.[134] As has been shown earlier, one of the key aspects of the new outlook on these issues in the central Middle Ages is the ability to present the "other" simultaneously as a god-sent punishment and as cruel.

The different modes of addressing the issue of cruelty in Muslim and Western sources originate in different cultural choices and priorities. Thus, the Muslim sources emphasize different negative characteristics of the Mongols. Prominent among these is their deceitfulness, which is mentioned repeatedly in Muslim sources; deceitfulness has a relatively marginal role in the Western accounts. Most of the references deal with the issue of *amān*, the promise of security made to besieged cities in exchange for capitulation. As mentioned earlier, the Mongols kept such promises only if the capitulation occurred before the start of the military operations. Ibn al-Athīr refers to this aspect of the Mongol conquests in numerous places; it is almost a recurring motif in his accounts, in contrast to the much less frequent references to rape.[135] As his accounts are quite brief, the constant reference to the subject is evidently of importance and shows that he considers this one of the more reprehensible aspects of Mongol behavior. Similar instances are mentioned also by Juvaini.[136] Western writers do not ignore

132. A resigned acceptance of the punishment sent by God does not imply actual passivity and lack of resistance, as shown by Simon Coupland, "The Rod of God's Wrath or the People of God's Wrath? The Carolingian Theology of the Viking Invasions," *Journal of Ecclesiastical History* 42:4 (1991): 547–54.

133. "The dynasty continued in that manner, until the power of the caliph was destroyed by Hûlâgû . . . the ruler of the Tatars and Mongols" [Ibn Khaldūn, *The Muqaddima* 3.45, trans. Franz Rosenthal (Princeton, N.J., 1967[1958]), 2:128].

134. See Kappler, "L'image des Mongols." Kappler mentions as significant the fact that Vincent of Beauvais does not present the Mongols in this way, although she remarks, without specifying, that this idea "avait largement cours chez les Latins contemporains de Vincent" (221). On different attitudes to the failure of the Second Crusade, cf. Giles Constable, "The Second Crusade as Seen by Contemporaries," *Traditio* 9 (1953): 213–79, esp. 266–76.

135. See Ibn al-Athīr's references to the capture of Bokhara, Samarqand, and Merv: *Al-kāmil fī al-ta'rīkh*, 12:366–68, 392.

136. See the capture of Merv in Juvaini, *History of the World-Conqueror*, 1:161ff. Juvaini claims that the Mongols spared cities that submitted (1:150, 173), but his own evidence contradicts this unqualified assertion.

this aspect of Mongol behavior, but they do not attach the same importance to this issue.[137]

What is the role of religion in these divergent attitudes toward cruelty? Do they reflect differences between Christianity and Islam, or between Western and non-Western societies? The religious answer seems, prima facie, less plausible. A crucial aspect of the developments in the West in the central Middle Ages is the existence, for centuries, of a discourse of cruelty that stretches back to Latin classical culture. It was present, even if little used, throughout the early Middle Ages. The lack of references to cruelty in most historical sources before the twelfth century was a deliberate choice on the part of the early medieval authors. In the East, there was no such tradition going back to antiquity, mainly because Greek classical culture was not preoccupied with cruelty.

Nevertheless, this question cannot be answered without examining Eastern Christian sources. Eastern Christians shared their religion with Western authors and a certain cultural koine with the Muslims among whom they lived. The ambiguous status of the Eastern Christians was recognized also by the Mongols, who sought to exploit the religious rivalry between them and the Muslims. Bar Hebraeus's (1225/6–1286) life and writings vividly reflect this situation. In 1243, as a young man of eighteen, he experienced the terror of the oncoming Mongols as his family tried to escape to Aleppo; a year later, his father served as the doctor of a Mongol commander.[138] This duality with respect to the Mongols is reflected in his account of the following incident:

> And [the Mongols] encamped on the canal of the village of 'Karmelīsh,' and the inhabitants fled and went into the church therein. And the Tātārs took the church, and two nobles sat by the two doors of the church. And one of them spared and set free those who went out by his door, and the other with the edge of the sword destroyed the men and women and children who went out by his door.[139]

The Muslims—even those who worked for the Mongols—and the Westerners regarded themselves as the victims and the Mongols as oppressors. The Eastern Christians, as a minority formerly oppressed by the Muslims, collaborated at times with the Mongols against the Muslims. Most promi-

137. See Simon de Saint-Quentin, *Historia Tartarorum* 30.77, 39; and Guillaume de Nangis, *Gesta Sancti Ludovici (Vie de Saint Louis)*, RHGF 20 (Paris, 1840), 340–43.
138. Ernest A. Wallis Budge, Introduction to Bar Hebraeus, *Chronography*, trans. Ernest A. Wallis Budge (Amsterdam, 1976[1932]), 1:xvi–xvii, 408.
139. Bar Hebraeus uses the term *Tātārs* for the Mongols (Bar Hebraeus, *Chronography*, 1:402).

nent in this respect were the Armenians, who became subjects of the Mongols but maintained their own rulers and operated as allies of the Mongols. The Christians were accused by the Muslims of collaboration as a matter of default, even when they did not, and suffered severe retributions whenever the Muslims had the chance to inflict them.[140]

As in the Western and Muslim chronicles, the fear inspired by the Mongols figures prominently in the Eastern Christian accounts. It is mentioned by different authors, such as Bar Hebraeus or Kirakos of Gandzak. Even the *History of the Patriarchs of the Egyptian Church*, which devotes only a few lines to the conquests of the Mongols, mentions the anxiety that seized the local population at the news of the Mongol conquests in Syria.[141] Another angle on the terror that the Mongols inspired even in their ally leaders is supplied by the Armenian historian Smpad, who writes about his brother, King Het'um of Armenia. Het'um was ordered by the Mongols to join them on a campaign, but when he reached the meeting point, the Mongols had already departed, "but because of his fear of them, he did not interrupt his journey, and, though facing death, he proceeded with a few men."[142]

The Eastern Christian sources also refer to the large-scale indiscriminate and systematic massacres committed by the Mongols, although the sources vary significantly in their description of the massacres. Bar Hebraeus refers to both the large scale of the massacres and their systematic aspect. On the capture of Baghdad, he writes, "And the Mongols drew their swords, and slew all the people of Baghdad—tens of thousands of men—the Iberians especially effected a great slaughter."[143] Referring to the capture of Samarqand, he relates how during the conquest of Samarqand the Mongols killed the inhabitants after dividing them in groups, "and they left [alive] only sons and daughters who were under twenty years of age."[144] Bar Hebraeus, however, is brief

140. See Badr al-Dīn al-ʿAynī, *Kitāb ʿiqd al-jumān fī taʾrīkh ahl al-zamān*, RHC HOr. 2a:216; Grigor of Akancʿ, *History of the Nation of the Archers*, ed. and trans. Robert P. Blake and Richard N. Frye, *Harvard Journal of Asian Studies* 12 (1949): 357. Al-Jūzjānī accuses the Christians of Baghdad of conspiracy with the Mongols in the capture of the city (*Ṭabaqāt-i Nāṣirī*, 2:1234).

141. انزعج النلس...انزعاجًا كثيرًا (*History of the Patriarchs of the Egyptian Church*, ed. and trans. Antoine Khater and Oswald H. E. Burmester [Cairo, 1974], 4.2:144).

142. Sirarpie Der Nersessian, "The Armenian Chronicle of the Constable Smpad or of the 'Royal Historian,'" *Dumbarton Oaks Papers* 13 (1959): 141–68, esp. 161.

143. Bar Hebraeus, *Chronography*, 1:431.

144. Ibid., 1:382. The systematic search for survivors is reflected in a Jewish source, a letter relating to the Mongol conquests in Syria. The writer tells how *after* the initial raid and after the Mongols have left, he looked for a hiding place, and Shlomo D. Goitein draws attention to the fact that he acted in this manner because he was familiar with the Mongol procedure of coming back to look for survivors ("Glimpses from the Cairo Geniza on Naval Warfare in the Mediterranean and on the Mongol Invasion," in *Studi orientalistici in onore di Giorgio Levi Della Vida* [Rome, 1956], 1:393–408).

in his descriptions, similar to most of the Muslim sources. He maintains the same style not only when referring to the massacre of Muslims (effected also by Christians) but also when he describes how Christians were slaughtered by the Mongols.[145] Also like the Muslim authors, Bar Hebraeus does not write *about* cruelty. His account is factual (less affective than Ibn al-Athīr's, for instance), and his references to cruelty are only implicit. The large-scale massacres *seem* an indication of cruelty, much in the same way that breaking guarantees of security (*amān*) seem to be criticized. But in many instances, Bar Hebraeus does not even use the conventional signs of cruelty, such as the specific mention of the killing of women, old men, and children.

The differences in the treatment of violence between West and East go beyond the accounts of the Mongols. Whereas in the West cruelty becomes an important issue in martyrdom accounts from the twelfth century onward, Eastern martyrdom accounts reveal no explicit preoccupation with the subject. The Coptic *Synaxary*, the official martyrology compiled from older material around the thirteenth century, contains detailed references to numerous martyrs. Many of these entries, similar to the accounts of the Mongols, narrate at length various torments applied to the martyrs, yet they do not refer explicitly to cruelty.[146]

The difference between these accounts and the Western accounts is evident. Even some of the taciturn accounts of the Viking invasions are more explicit than Bar Hebraeus's accounts. An episode relating how the Mongols cut the ears of their victims and sent them to the Khan is mentioned in Western, Islamic, and Eastern Christian sources. The narration itself is factual in all three types of sources. In the Latin version of Simon de Saint Quentin, however, this episode is part of a chapter entitled *On their cruelty and their deceitfulness*. This categorization demonstrates that cruelty is an important category for the writer, and he explicitly tells this story as an example of cruelty. In the Eastern sources, there is no explicit reference to cruelty in the title or in the narration itself. Simon also mentions another detail that is not present in the Eastern sources: that the ears were put in

145. Bar Hebraeus, *Chronography*, 1:433 (on the systematic execution of Christians), 1:436 (on the capture of Samarqand and Harim).

146. The issue of the formation of the Coptic Synaxary is complex; despite the efforts to create a canonical text there are many variants to the version published by René Basset in the *Patrologia Orientalis* (hereafter *PO*): *Synaxaire arabe jacobite*, ed. René Basset, *PO* 1.3, 3.3, 11.5, 16.2, 17.3, 20.5 (Paris, 1922–1929). For a recent summary of the state of the research, see Gérard Colin, "Le Synaxaire Ethiopien: état actuel de la question," *Analecta Bollandiana* 106 (1988): 273–317. The account of the martyrdom of Thomas of Shandalat is a good example of the matter-of-fact narration of the extreme tortures suffered by the martyrs (*PO* 17:602–3).

vinegar, perhaps an allusion to the cannibalism of the Mongols (although it is possible of course that the sole purpose was the conservation of the ears for the duration of the journey).[147]

The similarity to the Muslim chronicles extends also to the absence of references to rape. This absence may be attributed in part to Bar Hebraeus's ambiguous attitude toward the Mongols. Bar Hebraeus writes, for instance, that Genghis Khan "had mercy upon [the citizens of Bokhara] and did not kill them," contradicting all other reports of this event.[148] The Arabic version of Bar Hebraeus's chronicle is not identical to the Syriac, but its treatment of the Mongols is similar.[149]

The Mongols reached beyond Islam's sphere of influence. Reports of their raids in Russia present another type of non-Western reaction to the Mongols. The Russian *Chronicle of Novgorod* covers the years 1016–1471 and is one of the more important Russian sources dealing with the period of the Mongol expansion.[150] The following excerpts are indicative of the way in which it handles the Mongol incursions:

> 1238: That same year foreigners called Tartars came in countless numbers, like locusts, into the land of Ryazan . . . But it was too late to oppose the wrath of God, as was said of old by God to Joshua the son of Nun, when leading them to the promised land, then he said: "I shall before you send upon them perplexity, and thunder, and fear, and trembling." Thus also did God before these men take from us our strength and put into us perplexity and thunder and trembling for our sins.

> [Same year, on the capture of Ryazan] They likewise killed the *Knyaz* and *Knyaginya*, and men, women and children, monks, nuns and priests, some by fire, some by the sword, and violated nuns, priests' wives, good women and girls in the presence of their mothers and sisters.[151]

The *Chronicle of Novgorod* is akin to the Eastern sources reviewed so far in its laconic descriptions and lack of explicit references to cruelty. Yet there are some differences in emphases. More than in any of the other types of

---

147. Simon de Saint-Quentin, *Historia Tartarorum*, 38–39 (this episode is repeated twice more: *Historia Tartarorum*, 46, 54); Bar Hebraeus, *Chronography*, 1:398; and Juvaini, *History of the World-Conqueror*, 1:195, 270.

148. Bar Hebraeus, *Chronography*, 1:376.

149. Ibn al-'Ibrī, *Mukhtaṣar ta'rīkh al-duwal*, ed. Anton Salhani (Beirut, 1890).

150. Other Russian sources (except one short excerpt given later) were inaccessible to me because they do not exist in translation.

151. *The Chronicle of Novgorod 1016–1471*, trans. Robert Michell and Nevill Forbes (Camden third series 25) (London, 1914), 81, 82, respectively. For other such accounts, see, for instance, *s.a.* 1224 and 1236 (61, 81).

sources reviewed here regarding the Mongols, it presents the events in the biblical mode, recalling in more than one aspect the early Western chronicles dealing with the Vikings. The idea that the Mongols are a god-sent punishment for the sins of the Christians is often repeated. This instrumental view of the Mongols is most apparent in a sermon-like paragraph in which the writer mentions them as one option chosen by God from a series of possible calamities.[152] The comparison of the Mongols to locusts is likewise part of the biblical representation of the "other," and so is their characterization as godless or pagans. The references to the actions of the Mongols are laconic and without explicit references to cruelty. The actions attributed to the Mongols are mainly massacres, rape, and violence against religion.[153]

The Eastern Christian accounts are, on the whole, quite uniform in their treatment of cruelty.[154] They are part of the tradition reflected in the Muslim accounts. Thus, the difference between the Western and the Muslim sources is part of a West-East divide and does not reflect a basic difference between Christianity and Islam. The emergence of cruelty as an important cultural issue in the Western accounts of the Mongols is, of course, not only part of an intellectual process. The historical reality—that is, the unprecedented extent of the Mongol violence—also had its ample share.[155] But much of the difference between East and West in this respect lies in the

152. "And who, brothers, fathers, and children, seeing this, God's infliction on the whole Russian Land, does not lament? God let the pagans on us for our sins. God brings foreigners on to the land in his wrath, and thus crushed by them they [the Russian people] will be reminded of God. . . . And any land which has sinned God punishes with death or famine, or with the infliction of pagans, or with drought, or with heavy rain, or with other punishment, to see whether we will repent and live as God bids. . . . and the invasion of armed men, too, we accept at God's command; as punishment for our sins" (s.a. 1238, ibid., 84).

153. See s.a. 1236 (ibid., 81); on violence against religion see s.a. 1238 and 1410 (ibid., 83, 180).

154. In some respects, Armenian sources are an exception to this generalization. They concur with all other sources in presenting the Mongols as extremely violent, but some sources resemble Western ones in their affective tone and explicit references to the Mongols' cruelty and cannibalism. The main Armenian sources concerning the Mongols are Der Nersessian, "The Armenian Chronicle of the Constable Smpad"; Grigor of Akanc', *History of the Nation of the Archers*; Hayton, *La flor des estoires de la terre d'orient, Recueil des historiens des croisades, documents arméniens* 2:113–253; and the chronicle of Kirakos of Gandzak, excerpts from which are translated in E. Dulaurier, "Les Mongols d'après les historiens arméniens," *Journal Asiatique* 11 (1858): 192–255, 426–73, 481–508.

155. As in the case of the Norsemen, there are claims that the Mongols were not more cruel than other peoples. See, for instance, Charles J. Halperin, *The Tatar Yoke* (Columbus, Ohio, 1985), 16: "the Mongols were not more cruel than their neighbors."

fact that in the West, unlike in the East, there was already an earlier discourse of cruelty, even if it was little used. The convergence of these cultural developments and the shock experienced at the Mongol atrocities resulted in a massive incorporation of this discourse in the historical accounts referring to them. The lack of such a discourse did not lead the Eastern chroniclers to develop it ex nihilo in reaction to the Mongol conquests but merely to stretch the existing categories used for describing and thinking about these events.

What are the factors behind this attitude toward the issue of cruelty that are unique to the medieval West from the central Middle Ages onward? The examination of Western and Eastern accounts relating to the Mongols indicates that the historical reality is *not* one of these factors. Any difference between the Western and Eastern accounts should have been in the other direction, if at all: Because the West suffered much less from the violence of the Mongols, Western texts should have placed less emphasis on the cruelty of the Mongols, not more. The difference, then, should be sought in cultural factors. Among such factors that can account for this difference, the diffusion of Latin classical culture seems the most influential. Thus, the classical revival of the central Middle Ages provided many of the building blocks for creating this construct of cruelty, mainly in terms of themes and imagery. The insistence on presenting the Mongols as cannibals is perhaps the best example of the pervasiveness of classical matter related to cruelty. In a purely Christian context, the predominantly Latin, rather than Greek, preoccupation with cruelty has already been observed in the comparison of Eusebius's *Historia ecclesiastica* with its Latin translation by Rufinus of Aquileia. Rufinus's text probably reflects an already existing difference between the Greek and Latin parts of the Empire regarding cruelty. Rufinus's influence in the West has much to do with the perpetuation of this difference.[156]

This comparative excursus brings into focus the intercultural differences reflected in the various accounts relating to the Mongol conquests. It brings into relief the culture-specific treatment of cruelty, particularly because otherwise there are many points of similarity between the sources dealing with the Mongols. The Western sources turn out to be unique in their detailed and affective references to cruelty. Muslim sources, as well as Eastern Christian ones, report similar events but ignore the issue of cruelty.

These intercultural differences are highlighted by the only exception to this factual similarity. Only in the Western sources is cannibalism a key element of the representation of the Mongols. This divergence originates in

156. See Chapter 2, 43–46.

the renewal of the classical image of the "other," the Scythians, who are traditionally described as cannibals. The significant influence of this image reflects the role of cultural constructs in the representation and perception of cruelty. It also points to the particular role of Latin classical culture in shaping the attitudes to cruelty in the central Middle Ages. The absence of this influence in Eastern Christian ambiance accounts in part for the differences between Western and Eastern Christian sources, which are significant in spite of a common religion.

The treatment of cruelty in Western sources of the central Middle Ages stands out not only in relation to other cultures. The level of preoccupation with the subject in the twelfth century is extraordinary in the medieval West when compared with the preceding centuries. Nevertheless, the transformation is incomplete: Some of the causes that contributed to the neglect of the issue until the twelfth century continue to influence the treatment of cruelty until the end of the medieval period.[157]

A number of processes that transformed Western medieval society at that period contributed to the revival of interest in the issue of cruelty. The renewed preoccupation with ethics in the twelfth century and, in particular, the focus on "ethics of intention" provided an essential basis for dealing with this issue. The yearning for apostolic Christianity—an aspect of the Church reform—was reflected also in the increasing preoccupation with the passion of Christ, which spurred the rise of the child martyrs allegedly killed by the Jews. Finally, the Renaissance of Latin culture created wide circulation of relevant works such as the writings of Seneca and Ovid.

The greater attention to cruelty is reflected in the tendency to individualize the perpetrators of cruelty. This applies to the Jews in the martyrdom of William of Norwich as well as to the heretics in the chronicles relating to the Albigensians crusade. They are no longer merely generic and stereotypical figures, even when their characterization *is* shaped by stereotypes: They are named and localized. This applies, in a way, to the Mongols as well. Even though they are perceived as an incarnation of the barbarian invaders of the past, there is a sincere effort to trace an accurate anthropological profile.

These developments culminate in the accounts of the Mongol incursions. The violence that accompanied them, unlike that attributed to the Jews or Albigensians, was real and unprecedented in recent history. It

157. Cruelty does not appear as one of the main vices in treatises or dramatic personalizations of virtues and vices until the sixteenth century despite a few marginal references in this type of literature. Likewise, *saevitia* as grounds for divorce does not figure in canonical legislation but rather is a practical legal solution developed in the late Middle Ages in a context that is itself marginal to a Catholic society that prohibits divorce.

brought the discourse of cruelty as a descriptive tool to the peak of its development in the Middle Ages. From the thirteenth century onward, this descriptive discourse assumes an ever-increasing political and social role, to such a degree that its descriptive role would no longer be separable from its manipulative political role. The details of the Mongol violence already have the characteristics associated with the cruelty of the "other" until the modern period: indiscriminate massacres, sexual cruelty, and cannibalism.

CHAPTER FIVE
THE LATE MIDDLE AGES— MANIPULATED IMAGES AND STRUCTURED EMOTIONS

From the fourteenth century onward, there is a significant intensification of the tendencies outlined in the preceding chapters. Cruelty increasingly becomes an important cultural issue: It is represented in numerous sources, and the representations become lengthier and more affective. The main contexts within which cruelty is represented do not change; they are the cruelty of the "other," cruelty in the legal-political sphere, and martyrdom. Yet there are changes in the specific manifestations of cruelty in these contexts. Representations of cruelty become more and more manipulative rather than descriptive, and the various categories of cruelty are used with an eye toward the desired rhetorical and propagandist effect rather than toward what fits best the actual circumstances and events.[1]

This manipulation is particularly pertinent to the type of cruelty associated with the "other" in previous centuries—that is, with external barbarians such as Vikings or Mongols. At the end of the thirteenth century, after the disappearance of the Mongol threat and the violent extirpation of the popular heretical movements in southern France, there remained few external or internal "others" who posed a general or even major threat to Catholic Christendom. The Muslims in Spain were a local problem, not a problem of the whole of Christendom as they were two centuries earlier or as the Turks were to become later. Yet types of cruelty traditionally attributed to the "other" are represented frequently in sources of the period, but they are internalized: Their perpetrators are no longer external peoples but internal groups within the medieval West.

---

1. A related issue, the idea of "exceptional crime," was also similarly manipulated, increasingly so in the late medieval period; see Edward M. Peters, "*Crimen exceptum*: The History of an Idea," in *Proceedings of the Tenth International Congress of Medieval Canon Law* (Vatican City, 2001), 137–94.

The internalization of the "other" affected the mode of representation. There is a noticeable discrepancy between reality and rhetoric that derives from the manipulative purpose of the reference to cruelty. Assigning this type of cruelty to internal groups, which are not true "others," had the purpose of delegitimizing these groups and justifying violence against them. The greater sentimentality of the narration and the gravity of the violence represented are part of an effort to argue that these groups are indeed as bad as or even worse than those external "others" of past centuries.

The emergence of cruelty as a subject that had sentimental attributes reflects its growing importance. Issues that are considered ordinary do not evoke emotional response. But the process is cyclical: The new status of the subject also served as a catalyst for its manipulative use. The partial overlap between the concepts of cruelty and tyranny led to the exploitation of cruelty as a tool for political delegitimization. The claim that a ruler was cruel implied that he was a tyrant. In conjunction with the discussions on tyrannicide by political thinkers such as John of Salisbury and Thomas Aquinas, an accusation of cruelty could have had real political repercussions.

But cruelty as a cultural topic was not manipulated for political purposes alone. A type of mysticism centered on the passion of Christ appeared in the thirteenth century and became increasingly influential in the centuries that followed. In the writings of authors who belong to this trend, the *physical* suffering of Christ and the cruelty inflicted on him play a central role. The issue of cruelty is thus developed and manipulated with the purpose of achieving a religious end.

In tracing these developments, I focus on three main examples. The internalization of the cruelty of the "other" is reflected in the accounts of the Jacquerie, in which all sides in the conflict describe their opponents in terms that were formerly reserved for external "others." The purely political manipulation of the concept is evident in the sources dealing with Pedro I, king of Castile, who came to be known as "Pedro the Cruel." And finally, the religious manipulation of the emotional aspects of cruelty stands out in the works of mystical writers of the late Middle Ages such as Heinrich Suso and Julian of Norwich.

THE JACQUERIE

In the second half of the fourteenth century, a series of peasant, or anti-aristocratic, revolts took place in Western Europe.[2] The most famous of these, known as the Jacquerie, broke out in France in 1358. Both sides in the conflict extensively used imagery of the "other" to portray their opponents.[3] Writers identified with the nobility portrayed their opponents as violent peasants with animal characteristics and linked them to well-established "others" such as Muslims and Jews. The non-nobles painted the nobles in very similar colors, using almost identical topoi and imagery. A series of less partisan sources brings out the gaps between representation and reality and points to the exaggeration and manipulation of the issue of cruelty by both sides.

Whereas accounts of the Mongols support each other in portraying their violence as exceptional, the examination of a wide range of sources concerning the Jacquerie reveals the manipulative nature of the partisan sources. The most numerous and most obviously distorted representations come from the writers siding with the nobles; an outcome of the fact that losers, especially peasants and non-nobles, had less access to posterity. I examine how the peasants' cruelty is represented from the nobles' point of view and vice versa. Then I examine how these violent events were represented by less partisan writers.

Unlike previous conflicts with external invaders or internal heretics, this conflict involved no ethnic or religious diversity. In fact, even the social distance between the groups is questionable at best. Raymond Cazelles cites carefully collected evidence to counter the opinion that the Jacquerie was a war of peasants versus nobles. He shows, in fact, that artisans, merchants, bourgeois, royal officers, and perhaps even some nobles participated on the side of the rebels.[4] The characterization of the non-nobles as peasants was part of the effort to differentiate them and characterize them as "others."

Differentiating and de-humanizing the non-nobles was a first step in establishing their cruelty. Bestial images of peasants were common from the twelfth century and were a topos in romance literature. Violence as part of this animal imagery was an attribute of the *vilain* already in the works of Chrétien de Troyes.[5] Characterizing the peasants as cruel was an extension of this topos and

2. See Paul Freedman, *Images of the Medieval Peasant* (Stanford, Calif., 1999), 257–88.

3. A similar episode of violence in which "otherness" was defined according to social criteria was analyzed in Robert Darnton, *The Great Cat Massacre and Other Episodes in French Cultural History* (New York, 1984), 75–104. The episode analyzed in this source is on a microscopic scale as compared to the Jacquerie, but it is interesting with regard to the way "otherness" is characterized and used by both sides involved in the conflict.

4. Raymond Cazelles, "La Jacquerie fut-elle un mouvement paysan?" *Comptes rendus de l'Academie des Inscriptions et Belles-lettres* (1978): 654–66.

5. Freedman, *Images of the Medieval Peasant*, 133–56, 300–2; Paul Freedman, "The Medieval 'Other': The Middle Ages as 'Other,'" in *Marvels, Monsters, and Miracles: Studies in the Medieval and Early Modern Imagination*, ed. Timothy S. Jones and David A. Sprunger (Kalamazoo, Mich., 1999), 1–24. For the relation between fourteenth-century historiography and the genre of romance, see Denys Hay, *Annalists and Historians* (London, 1977), 75; Ernst Breisach, *Historiography* (Chicago, 1983), 150; and William J. Brandt, *The Shape of Medieval History* (New Haven, Conn., 1966), 106–46.

not a drastic development. From the nobles' perspective, it was necessary, especially in retrospect, for justifying the extremely violent repression of this revolt.

Jean Froissart (ca. 1333?–ca. 1404) provides one of the earliest and most detailed accounts of the Jacquerie. Froissart was one of the most influential historians of the later Middle Ages, and his influence was not limited to France alone.[6] His version of the events is based on earlier sources, and the relation between his narrative to these sources shall be discussed later. His account is considered first on account of its wide influence.

Froissart presents a very clear-cut picture: The nobles are victims, and the peasants are bestialized victimizers. Hence the blame and condemnation belong all to one side. He consistently refers to the non-nobles as *meschans gens* (wicked people). He unfolds instances of the peasants' cruelty in episodes of ascending gravity. In the first one, the peasants kill a knight and his wife and children. They then burn his castle. The second episode adds the element of sexual violence. The peasants rape a knight's pregnant wife and daughter while the knight is forced to watch, and only after that do they kill all three. In the third episode, another element, forced cannibalism, is added. The non-nobles kill a knight, roast him on a skewer, then 10 or 12 people rape his wife, try to make her eat the roasted body of her husband, and then kill her in a way defined by Froissart as *male mort* (bad death).

The main attributes of the cruelty that Froissart attributes to the peasants are sexual cruelty and cannibalism—the same that characterized the cruelty of external "others" such as the Mongols. Froissart presents sexual violence as the main danger of the peasant insurrection, claiming that he does not even "dare to write the horrible things they [the peasants] did to ladies." All the noblewomen who did not want to be raped and murdered afterward had to flee to Meaux, according to Froissart. It is in this context of sexual cruelty that Froissart aims to distance the peasants from human society. He calls them *chiens esragiés* ("mad dogs") and claims that their madness is such that it is not practiced among Christians, not even by Saracens. In this manner, he associates them with peoples who are already traditionally defined as cruel "others." It is also significant that Froissart emphasizes the irrational aspect of the peasants' cruelty.

As with the Mongols, the other prominent aspect of the peasants' cruelty is cannibalism. The peasants roast a knight and try to force his wife to eat from the body. In later recountings of this event, the cruelty of the peasants

6. For a brief survey of Froissart's influence, see John J. N. Palmer, Introduction to *Froissart: Historian*, ed. John J. N. Palmer (Woodbridge, Suffolk, 1981), 1–5; see also Hay, *Annalists and Historians*, 75–77.

is further emphasized. The way in which this story is told strongly echoes the classical stories, such as the Procne episode from Ovid's *Metamorphoses* and Seneca's *Thyestes*, in which family members are made to eat their relatives. The existence of this connection does not necessarily imply that the tale is fictional. Classical influence may have worked both ways: It may have set the emphases of Froissart's narrative, but the wide diffusion of the stories may have also influenced, even indirectly, the actual types of violence practiced.[7] Violence did not erupt because of classical influence, but its forms might have been influenced by it. Notwithstanding the differences, the actual influence of these classical motifs may be likened to the impact of movies such as Oliver Stone's *Natural Born Killers* on actual violence in the United States.[8]

Even more than in the accounts of the Mongols, the peasants' cruelty is represented in terms of "compounds" of violent actions, defined previously as acts that simultaneously combine several types of cruelty. The most violent episode mentioned here contains rape in the presence of family members, murder, and cannibalism. The narration itself is affective: The deeds of the peasants are "horrible" or such that "no human creature should even think about," and they kill the nobles "without pity or mercy."

The importance of the representations of cruelty in the accounts of the Jacquerie is reflected in their rapid intensification and expansion. Whereas in the chronicles of the Vikings this process took centuries, here significant changes can be observed in three interrelated texts that were produced within a short time. Appendix 6 contains a passage referring to the violence of the Jacques, including the episode of the knight roasted on a skewer. The earliest is by Jean le Bel (d. 1370), who was Froissart's source; the second is by Froissart; and the third by Raoul Tainguy is a later variant of Froissart's text found in one of the manuscripts of his *Chroniques*.

The differences between the versions of Jean le Bel and Froissart are subtle but consistent in the means of de-humanizing the peasants. Jean le Bel portrays them as a rabble without a leader. Froissart enhances this image, specifying that they lacked armor as well, thus evoking the image of the *vilain* with the stick from the romance genre.[9] Froissart also adds to

7. The case of Ugolino of Pisa, rendered famous by Dante and Chaucer, may reflect—besides the preoccupation with cannibalism—the way in which images affect reality. Ugolino was locked away in a tower in 1288 together with his sons and nephews, perhaps with a view of producing such an instance of "forced cannibalism."

8. See, for instance, David W. Chen, "Man Is Guilty in the Killing, for Sport, of a Firefighter," *The New York Times*, 7 October 1998.

9. See, for instance, Chrétien de Troyes, *Le Chevalier au Lion (Yvain)*, ll. 286–302, ed. Mario L. Roques (Paris, 1960), 9–10, and note 5, above.

Jean le Bel's version the comparison of the peasants to mad dogs. In addition, Froissart's language is more hyperbolic: Whereas Jean le Bel writes about the murder of noblemen and the rape of women and virgins, Froissart refers to the killing of *all* nobles and to the rape of *all* women.

The differences between Froissart's version and that of Tainguy are even more significant. Jean le Bel and Froissart remark that such actions are not committed by Christians and not even by Saracens. Tainguy completes the process of rendering the peasants "other" by omitting the Christians from the comparison and substituting them with Jews. Thus the reference is to two external groups, both traditionally known as cruel "others." Jean le Bel and Froissart declare that they refuse to tell the exact deeds committed by the *vilains* against women. This silence is in itself a strong rhetorical device because it is selective, thus implying that the untold is even worse than what was already disclosed. Tainguy, however, does disclose more and claims that the peasants committed sodomitic and other types of "disorderly" rape ["sodomitement et desordoneement"].[10] In the most violent episode relating to the knight who was roasted on a skewer, Tainguy elaborates even more freely. He claims that the people who roasted the knight were in their turn also forced to eat from the corpse (to make them more prone to commit such cruelties, as Tainguy explains). When they refused, they were killed by their comrades. Tainguy effects here a dramatic inversion—the victimizers are turned into victims. This inversion has the effect of revealing that these victimizers, who just a moment before seemed the incarnation of cruelty, are mere tools at the hands of their comrades who are even more cruel and who try to use these actions as a training in cruelty.[11]

The primary characteristics of the peasants' cruelty, according to Jean le Bel and Froissart, are murder of women and children, sexual cruelty, and cannibalism. More prominent than in the accounts of the Mongols is the aspect of the pleasure derived from cruelty, reflected in the erotic-sadistic element present in the various sexual assaults on the noble women. The aspect of pleasure appears also in the calculated inventiveness of the tor-

10. This reference to sodomitic rape concurs with John Boswell's observation that homosexuality becomes a graver crime in the later Middle Ages (*Christianity, Social Tolerance, and Homosexuality* [Chicago, 1980], 269ff).

11. Jean le Bel, *Chroniques*, ed. Jules Viard and Eugène Déprez (Paris, 1895), 257; Froissart, *Chroniques* 1:413, ed. Siméon Luce (Paris, 1874), 5:100. Froissart incorporated segments from the Chronicle of Jean le Bel into his own chronicle (see Hay, *Annalists and Historians*, 75); Raoul Tainguy's version is cited in an appendix to Siméon Luce, *Histoire de la Jacquerie* (Paris, 1894), 338–42 (from University of Leiden, fonds Vossius, French manuscript no. 9, ff. 228–29).

tures to which the noble families were subjected. The game-like inventiveness in devising new modes of torture had been considered a sign of cruelty long before the Middle Ages; it is one of the characteristics assigned to the persecutors of the early Christians.[12] Here this ingenuity is manifested in the ability to inflict the maximum physical and psychological torment on the greatest number of victims. This is achieved through the combination of severe physical tortures that end in long and painful deaths with the additional twist of compelling family members to watch while violence is done to other family members. The events are represented as progressively cruel in each recycling of Jean le Bel's text by the addition of aggravating details. The manner of narration enhances the role of cruelty within it: The detailed descriptions of violence, the affective comments, and the rhetorical interjections turn cruelty into the main theme of these accounts of the Jacquerie. The focus on cruelty, as earlier medieval sources show, is far from natural or necessary. The insurrection could be presented—similar to the incursions of the Vikings—through the destruction of churches or primarily as an instance of disobedience and treason.[13]

Cruelty in the Jacquerie was not one sided; the violence of the nonnobles was repressed in an extremely brutal manner. Thus, in the final stage of the battle at Meaux the nobles burnt the city with its (non-noble) inhabitants, because they sympathized with the Jacquerie. How did the nonnobles represent the cruelty of the nobles toward them? One of the few documents explicitly representing the non-nobles' point of view was written by Étienne Marcel, provost of the Parisian merchants and in actual control of Paris at the time. In a letter to the cities of Flanders, he describes the nobles' violence in the repression of the Jacquerie as almost identical to the nobles' descriptions of the peasants' violence:

12. See, for instance, *The Letter of Phileas*, in *Musurillo*, 323; and *Passio Sanctorum Mariani et Iacobi*, *Musurillo*, 200–201. It is also a recurring motif in pre-Christian classical culture (in stories such as the bull of Phalaris or of the deeds of first-century Roman emperors such as Nero or Caligula).

13. Marie-Thérèse de Medeiros presents Froissart's version as a "romance" version of Jean le Bel's text. The differences between the texts are seen in terms of the literary characteristics of the medieval romance. In this context, the exaggeration of violence is seen not as a real enhancement of the threat but, to the contrary, as a stylistic move whose effect is reducing the threat by pointing to its literary nature. According to de Medeiros, whereas le Bel deals with actual rape, in Froissart rape becomes "virtual" (*Jacques et chroniqueurs* [Paris, 1979], 25–67, esp. 63–64). My analysis runs counter to de Medeiros's argument: Froissart's references seem to be part of the contemporary discourse of cruelty. Froissart refers to real rape and cannibalism, the main elements of the discourse of cruelty since the descriptions of the Mongols. These elements become even more tangible and real in Raoul Tainguy's version, which is more elaborate on both issues (see Appendix 6).

We think that you have well heard the talk about how a very great multitude of nobles . . . in the way nobles [act] universally against non-nobles, without making any distinction between the guilty and the not-guilty, between good or bad . . . burnt the cities, killed the good people of the country without any pity or mercy, robbed and pillaged all that they have found. They tortured cruelly women, children, priests, [and] monks, for learning about the property of people and taking and robbing it; and many of those they killed with tortures. They robbed churches . . . corrupted young girls [virgins] and raped women in the presence of their husbands. And, briefly, committed more evil deeds more cruelly and more inhumanly than any [committed by] the Wandres [sic] or the Saracens.[14]

Similar to the aristocratic writers, Marcel emphasizes the undiscriminating character of the slaughter, the violence done to women, the fact that family members were compelled to watch their relatives tortured, and the comparison to the actions of "others" (here, too, the Saracens, who serve as a measuring rod for cruelty). An additional type of violence emphasized by Marcel is violence aimed at churches; in another passage, he describes in detail the defilement of churches, of the Eucharist, and of other holy objects by the nobles. These descriptions may be an appeal to the more traditional types of actions attributed to the "other," the purpose of which is to establish the "otherness" of the nobles beyond dispute.[15]

The basic similarity between the noble and non-noble accounts is significant. It indicates that cruelty at this period is an important issue across a wide spectrum of medieval society. It is not an esoteric issue dealt with only by intellectuals and is not limited to a specific social milieu. Moreover, this uniformity indicates that the medieval discourse of cruelty that emerged in the previous century was by now well established and diffused.

Froissart and Jean le Bel unreservedly represent the nobles' point of view, which is not surprising: Throughout his career Froissart (like Jean le Bel before him) had noble patrons, and his works—historical as well as literary—are committed to the celebration of chivalry.[16] Étienne Marcel's account naturally brings forth the position of the non-nobles. There is, however, another group of chronicles whose writers were less personally involved and thus present a third, alternative, view of the events. Chronicles such as the *Chronique des quatre premiers Valois*, *Chronographia regum*

14. Cited in François T. Perrens, *Étienne Marcel* [Paris, 1874], 280. It is unclear what "Wandres" refers to.

15. The recourse to a more traditional theme may also indicate that the discourse on cruelty evolves in aristocratic circles, and the non-nobles are lagging behind in its adoption.

16. Denys Hay defines Froissart's writings as "chivalrous historiography" and refers to him and to Jean le Bel as courtiers (*Annalists and Historians*, 75–76).

Francorum, and the Norman Chronicle offer a more complex view of the events and refrain from using the discourse of cruelty used by the two sides of the conflict.[17] They do condemn the peasants' violence, but they do not dwell on it. Moreover, some of them attribute the outbreak of the Jacquerie to the mistreatment of the non-nobles by the nobles, sanctioned by the permission given to the nobles to take provisions at their need.[18] The *Chronographia regum Francorum* states that "many of [the nobles] took very excessively from the goods of their men. This was the cause that the citizens of Beauvais rose at once."[19] The Norman chronicle concurs with this causal chain, which holds the nobles responsible for the outbreak of violence.[20] These texts also offer a more critical view of the violent repression of the Jacquerie.

The existence of sources that present less partisan views points to the manipulative use of cruelty made by the two sides of the conflict. Unlike the accounts of the Mongol incursions, the reference to cruelty was not inherent in the actual events. The balanced attribution of responsibility in the third group of sources does not imply that this is a case of implicit representation of cruelty (that is, unlike the sources relating to the Vikings). The discourse of cruelty is used by the nobles and the non-nobles as part of a propaganda war intended to elicit sympathy and support from their respective audiences, as well as to justify their use of violence against the other side.[21]

17. *Chronique des quatre premiers Valois*, ed. Siméon Luce (Paris, 1862), 71; *Chronographia regum Francorum*, ed. Henri Moranville (Paris, 1903), 270; *Chronique normande du XIVe siècle*, ed. Auguste Molinier and Emile Molinier (Paris, 1882), 128.

18. On a related issue, the legitimacy of peasant anger (not specifically relating to the Jacquerie), see Paul Freedman, "Peasant Anger in the Late Middle Ages," in *Anger's Past: The Social Uses of an Emotion in the Middle Ages*, ed. Barbara H. Rosenwein (Ithaca, 1998), 171–88.

19. *Chronographia regum Francorum*, 270.

20. *Chronique normande du XIVe siècle*, 127–28.

21. These tensions between nobles and peasants (or non-nobles) were not limited to France, and the conceptual tools used for dealing with these problems were similar wherever they occurred; see Paul Freedman, *The Origins of the Peasant Servitude in Medieval Catalonia* (Cambridge, 1991), 200. For a comparative study of peasant insurrections in Hungary and Catalonia, see Paul Freedman, "The Evolution of Servile Peasants in Hungary and in Catalonia: A Comparison," *Anuario de Estudios Medievales* 26 (1996): 909–32. Also related is the appearance of various aristocratic justifications for violence against peasants. See Kathryn Gradval, "Chrétien de Troyes, Gratian, and the Medieval Romance of Sexual Violence," *Signs* 17:3 (1992): 558–85, on the romances' attitude toward the rape of peasant women (a reply article: William D. Paden, "Rape in the Pastourelle," *Romanic Review* 80:3 [1989]: 331–49). On the theme of the utility of violence against peasants in German literature, see Gadi Algazi, "The Social Use of Private War: Some Late Medieval Views Reviewed," in *Tel Aviver Jahrbuch für deutsche Geschichte* 22 (1993): 253–73.

In addition to revealing the changing cultural role of cruelty, the manipulation of cruelty is instructive with respect to its perception by contemporaries. When the status of a person as cruel is not self-evident to contemporaries, those who wish to portray him as such make a conscious effort by attributing to him the "classic," or stereotypical, aspects of cruelty. The internal power struggle in Castile, almost contemporary to the Jacquerie, provides an instance of such a manipulation of the issue of cruelty for political purposes.

Pedro I, the son of Alfonso XI of Castile, was during his whole reign involved in a civil war against his half brother, Enrique of Trastámara. This civil war included most of the Castilian nobility, and in its course, both sides sought the aid of external forces: Aragonese and French on Enrique's part, Muslim (from Granada) and English on Pedro's. Toward the end of his reign, most of Pedro's supporters deserted him, and he was finally killed by Enrique in 1369.

Pedro had two nicknames, "the cruel" and "the just," one given to him by his opponents and the other by his supporters. The endurance of the "cruel" is due to Pedro's being on the losers' side. Getting a less biased picture of his time on the throne is almost impossible because the chronicler of his reign, Pedro López de Ayala, who served in his court, defected to Enrique's side toward the end of Pedro's reign and wrote the chronicle only after Pedro's death.

But even without having a balanced historical picture, the terminology used in the conflict is telling. Thus, the duality of *cruel* versus *just* points, once more, to the dominance of the legal aspect among medieval perceptions of cruelty. The most common medieval definition of cruelty is the excessive application of judicial violence. In the case of Pedro, the debated issue is his use of violence to maintain his rule: Did he or did he not overstep the legitimate use of force conceded to a legitimate king for the preservation of his rule? To a considerable extent, the conflict was about words—how to represent Pedro in order to justify these epithets.

For his supporters, Pedro was evidently "just" in legal terms because he was the legitimate heir to the throne of Castile, fighting against a usurper who was a bastard son of the former king. But for his opponents, defining Pedro as cruel was critical. Cruelty had been an important attribute of tyranny since late antiquity. Calling Pedro cruel implied that he was a tyrant, and therefore the struggle against him was justified. Thus, the legitimacy of Pedro's rule depended on the validity of his definition as just, and his opponents manipulated the issue of Pedro's cruelty to establish their legitimacy.

Before coming to Ayala's text, which is equivocal in respect to Pedro, I examine how the events in Spain crystallized in sources that are more chronologically and geographically distant to produce the image of Pedro the Cruel. This more distant picture reflects the final contours of Pedro's image as they emerged after his death, and they enable us to trace the way in which his opponents constructed this image.

Froissart sets the stage for Pedro's discrediting by introducing him at the outset as someone "extremely rebellious towards all the commandments and ordinances of the Church" and claiming that he harassed his good Catholic neighbors.[22] Then Froissart portrays Pedro as a cruel and hard-hearted tyrant who persecuted the Church, murdered and exiled noblemen, killed his wife, and was on friendly terms with Spanish Muslim rulers who were the "enemies of God."[23] Froissart describes Pedro as excluding himself from ever-narrowing circles. He repudiated his religion by persecuting the Church and associating himself with infidels; he became an outsider to his social class, which he actively tried to eliminate; and even his own family fell prey to his cruelty. Severing all human bonds, explicitly depicted as cruel, Pedro is presented as nonhuman, a total "other." The term "systematic differentiation" applies in full to his characterization, because Pedro is represented as standing against everything that he should have stood for: religion, class, and family.[24]

Froissart's account of Pedro's cruelty contains elements that truly belong to tyranny: the murder and exile of nobles and the oppression of the Church. Other details are less relevant to the political legitimacy of Pedro's

22. ... estoit durement rebelles à tous commandemens et ordenances de l'Eglise ... et voloit sousmettre tous ses voisins crestiiens, especialment le roy d'Arragon qui s'appelloit Pierre, liquelz estoit bons et [vrais] catholikes (Froissart, *Chroniques* 1:547, 6:185).

23. "Cilz rois dans Pières, si com fames couroit, avoit fait morir la mère de ces enfans *moult diversement*: de quoi il lor en desplaisoit, c'estoit bien raisons. Avoech tout ce, ossi [avoit] fait morir et exilliet pluiseurs haus barons dou royaume de Castille, et estoit si *crueulz* et si plains d'erreur et de *austerité* que tout si homme le cremoient et ressongnoient et le haoient, se moustrer li osaissent" (italics mine). Froissart adds that he kept the prelates of his realm in prison "par manière de tirannisie" (*Chroniques* 1:547, 6:186).

24. Another outsider who referred to Pedro's rule is the great Islamic scholar Ibn Khaldūn. He consistently refers to Pedro as *ṭāghiya*, a term denoting someone who exceeds the proper, or just, limit and therefore signifies a tyrant in some instances. But because the term has been used as the title of Christian kings in general and Ibn Khaldūn does not pass explicit judgment on Pedro, it is difficult to know whether in this case the epithet functions as a cliché or as a translation of Pedro's title the Cruel. See Ibn Khaldūn, *Ta'rif*, ed. Muhammad Ibn Tawit al-Tanji (Cairo, 1951), 84–85; and Thomas B. Irving, "Peter the Cruel and Ibn Khaldūn," *Islamic Literature* 11 (1959): 5–17, esp. 9.

rule: his relations with Muslims and his family relations. In the debate between justice and cruelty, one would expect the accusation of cruelty to be justified on legal and political grounds. Yet references to Pedro's rule by Spanish authors deal even less than Froissart with his cruelty in the political sphere, focusing instead on cruelty in his personal life. The manipulative use of cruelty in Pedro's case consists precisely of this gap: The building blocks for his portrayal as a cruel tyrant are mostly accounts of his cruelty in the personal and family sphere, not of his cruelty as a ruler.

One such episode is the murder of Pedro's half-brother Fadrique, as described by Ayala, the main chronicler of Pedro's reign. Ayala describes the event as a fratricide that was accomplished by trickery.[25] Ayala's report is unsettling in its detail. He asserts that the murder was committed according to Pedro's orders and in his presence. Ayala tells that after Fadrique was struck and left on the floor, Pedro noticed that he was not yet dead and ordered him to be finished off. The climax of the scene is the account that Pedro then sat down to eat overlooking Fadrique's corpse.[26]

But the chronicles are perhaps the mildest among medieval sources dealing with Pedro.[27] His entrance into posterity as "the Cruel" is recorded even better in a series of popular romances, which besides attesting to Pedro's reputation at the time of their composition, had their ample share in perpetuating this image. It is difficult to date these romances. They can be found in compilations that were printed at the end of the sixteenth century—a testimony to their popularity—but were probably composed not more than several decades after the events.

The legal and political arguments over the foggy borderline separating justice from cruelty have their echoes in these romances. They are succinctly summed up in a ballad named after Pedro's opponent *A los pies de Don Henrique* (At the Feet of Don Henry):

25. The title of the chapter preceding the murder is *"Como el Rey don Pedro dixo al Infante Don Juan su primo que queria matar al Maestre Don Fadrique su hermano."* The reference to Fadrique as *su hermano* is repeated in the text.

26. É desque fué muerto Sancho Ruiz de Villegas, tornóse el Rey dó yacia el Maestre [Fadrique], é fallóle que aún non era muerto; é sacó el Rey una broncha que tenia en la cinta, é diola á un mozo de su cámara, é fizole matar. É desque esto fué fecho, asentóse el Rey á comer donde el Maestre yacia muerto en una quadra que dicen de los Azulejos, que es en el Alcazar . . . (Pedro López de Ayala, *Crónica del Rey Don Pedro*, ed. Cayetano Rosell [*Biblioteca de Autores Españoles* 66] [Madrid, 1953], 483).

27. Teofilo F. Ruiz also comments on the Castilian chroniclers' lack of criticism when reporting acts of violence by the authorities; see "Violence in Late Medieval Castile: The Case of the Rioja," *Revista de História* 133 (1995): 15–36, esp. 16.

Some say that he was just
Others say that he has done evil
That the king is not cruel, if he was born
In a time which made it necessary to be so.[28]

But most of these romances deal with Pedro in an unambiguous manner. In the words of one of them, relating to his death, "[thus] came out the most cruel soul / that ever lived in a Christian heart."[29] Insofar as they deal with Pedro's cruelty, these texts refer primarily to its manifestations in his personal life and to his treatment of his wife, Blanche of Bourbon, in particular.

One of these romances, charging Pedro of commissioning the murder of the queen, opens with accusations of his unjust treatment of her.[30] The actual circumstances of the case appeal to the romantic image of a princess imprisoned in a lonely tower and call for the sympathy provided to heroines of the genre.[31] It proceeds with the queen's more general accusations against Pedro:

Oh cruel unjust king
A harsh and tyrant king
how do you permit
such inhuman cruelty?[32]

The leap from the personal circumstances to branding Pedro as a cruel tyrant, as well as the conceptual link between cruelty and justice, are both evident here.

28. *Romancero General*, ed. Angel Gonzalez Palencia (Madrid, 1947), no. 293, 195–96.

29. "Salió el alma más cruel / que vivió en pecho Cristiano" (*Romancero General*, no. 602, 385).

30. "No contento el Rey don Pedro / de tener aprisionada / a doña Blanca en Sidonia / sin razon, ni justa causa . . ." This romance appears in two late fifteenth-century compilations (*Las fuentes del Romancero General*, ed. Antonio Rodriguez-Monino [Madrid, 1957], 7:383a–385b; 8:164b–166b).

31. The same leap from accusations of intramarital cruelty to accusations of cruelty and tyranny at the state level can be observed in the letter of Urraca, queen of Castile (1109–1126), concerning her husband Alfonso I of Aragon. After accusing him of physical violence against her and of apostasy (Froissart also links cruelty to apostasy when referring to Pedro), she proceeds to his crimes on the public level: "Seuus igitur Celtiberus Gallitiam furibundus intrauit et quot et quanta facinora in regione illa patrauerit, nobilium cedes militum apud Montem Rosum crudeliter occisorum castrumque dirutum et terra depopulata bonisque omnibus expoliata, ecclesiarum uiolationes earumque dehonorati sacerdotes, bone mulieres denudate, uirgines inpudenter uiolate . . ." (*Historia Compostellana* 1.64, ed. Emma Falque [*CCCM* 70] [Turnhout, 1988], 103).

32. The fate of Blanche is commemorated in other romances as well. For instance, "Doña Blanca está en Sidonia / contando su historia amarga," "En un escuro retrete / adonde del Sol los rayos," "En un retrete, que apenas / se divisan las paredes" (*Romancero General*, nos. 81, 1025, 1235, 1:61; 2:141–42, 282–83).

From one perspective, the formation of the image of Pedro the Cruel demonstrates the basic stability of the medieval categories of cruelty. The aim of presenting Pedro as cruel is political delegitimization—that is, to imply that Pedro is unfit to rule. Hence, the explicit accusations of cruelty leveled against Pedro are those that refer to the most basic medieval contexts of cruelty: the transgression of justice and tyranny.

At the same time, Pedro's case reflects the growing sophistication with which the issue of cruelty was manipulated in the later Middle Ages. Dealing with cruelty was never *exclusively* descriptive, but the emphases shift over the centuries. The main purpose of the accounts of the Mongols is descriptive, even if they are exaggerated. In the case of the blood libel accusations against the Jews, the ideological overtones are more pronounced, but even there, a major objective was to *describe* the cruelty of the Jews, which many of the authors believed to be real and constant. The balance tilts with the references to the cruelty of the Albigensians, in which there is a gap between the actions ascribed to the heretics and the labels they are assigned. This gap widens in the late Middle Ages in the accounts of the Jacquerie and even more so in the case of Pedro.

This gap in Pedro's case consists of the use of the two types of cruelty: Pedro is accused of cruelty in the political context of tyranny, but most of the actions that are described belong to the realm of cruelty of the "other" in the sense that the examples of his cruelty are those that create a systematic differentiation and present him as a nonhuman barbarian. Pedro is cruel to his family and to his peers. Similar to the Jacques in Froissart's account, Pedro is associated with Muslims, who are well-established "others." This association extends the Muslims' "otherness" to the non-Muslims related to them.

In this way, the sources dealing with Pedro cleverly separate their *telling* and their *showing*. The explicit references to cruelty claim tyranny and injustice, but most of the examples used to prove the case implicitly *show* Pedro as a complete "other." This technique demonstrates how authors of the later Middle Ages manage to construct a manipulative and effective image of cruelty by using the traditional building blocks of cruelty. Such a procedure would have been inconceivable in earlier periods in which cruelty was referred to by these same categories.

CRUELTY AND MYSTICISM — THE PASSION OF CHRIST

The issue of cruelty and the newly acquired technique of manipulating it were not used solely for justifying violence. Representations of cruelty and suffering had a central role in a new type of mysticism that emerged in the second half of the thirteenth century and focused on the passion of Christ. This type of spirituality started to evolve in the twelfth and thirteenth centuries and reached its zenith with figures such as Heinrich Suso and Julian of Norwich.

The focus on the passion of Christ is part of a larger process of yearning for apostolic Christianity. It goes back to the twelfth century and is reflected in the martyrological activity of the central Middle Ages, much of which, in turn, consists of reprocessing ancient martyrdom accounts. The *Legenda aurea* and parts of the *Speculum historiale* of Vincent of Beauvais are examples of this trend. The coincidence of this preoccupation with the ancient Christian roots of the medieval West and of the rise of cruelty as a cultural issue is evident in these compilations, which are quite explicit in their representations of cruelty. The accusations against the Jews of ritual murders of Christian children, which are presented as a re-enactment of Christ's passion, are also to a considerable extent the result of the meeting of these two processes. Consequently, the return to the passion of Christ seems thus a natural part of these tendencies.

The most influential precursor of the genre of meditations on the passion is the *Meditationes vitae Christi* of pseudo-Bonaventure, written in the second half of the thirteenth century. In the section dealing with the passion, pseudo-Bonaventure describes the scourging of Christ in the following manner: "The royal blood flows all about, from all parts of His body. Again and again, repeatedly, closer and closer, it is done, bruise upon bruise, and cut upon cut, until not only the torturers but also the spectators are tired."[33] The intense torture that tires the torturers is a stock motif of martyrdom accounts. Nevertheless, the mode of representation is new. The writer concentrates on the *details* of each blow or wound received by Christ. The affective tone is created by the details, the repetitions, and by the narrator's interjections, such as "who was the most audacious one who scourged you so cruelly?"[34]

The role of pseudo-Bonaventure in the formation of the genre of meditations on the passion is evident in the numerous fourteenth-century versions and adaptations of it in which the passion scene appears as an independent work. Seven different translations into English were made in the fourteenth century alone. One of these versions, the *Privity of the Passion*, adds significant details to pseudo-Bonaventure's account of the nailing of Christ to the cross. It tells that the holes in the crucifix were designed so that Christ's feet would not reach them, and that he was stretched with

33. *Meditationes vitae Christi* 76; *Meditations on the Life of Christ*, trans. Isa Ragusa (Princeton, N.J., 1961), 328.

34. Ibid., 329.

ropes, "with gret violence," to bring his feet to the holes. Afterward "they reysede vpe þe crosse one Ende . . . & lett it falle downe in to a mortase of stone . . . and In this hevy fallynge all þe Ioyntes & cenowes of his blesside body braste in-sondire."[35]

Whereas in earlier accounts Christ suffers mainly from physical violence, later writers developed the theme with more finesse into a veritable synesthesia of suffering. Thus, Richard Rolle's (1300–1349) *Meditations on the Passion* mentions Christ's suffering from the smell of carrion in the place of crucifixion.[36] These tendencies reached their full development, however, in the writings of two mystics spanning the fourteenth century, Heinrich Suso (1295–1366) and Julian of Norwich (b. ca. 1343).

Suso was a key figure in the evolution of the mysticism centered on the suffering of Christ both in terms of developing earlier trends and in terms of his influence. Suso's *Meditations* on the passion form the last chapter of the German version of his *Little Book of Eternal Wisdom*. The hundred meditations are a mystical exercise, and Suso urges that they be repeated every day. Physical suffering figures prominently in the *Meditations*. The intense unease produced by the descriptions of Christ's suffering is achieved by a systematic breakup of the experience of the passion. Thus, Suso enumerates how Christ suffered in each of his five senses.[37] Christ's nailing is envisioned almost in slow motion: "(1) Beloved Lord, your right hand was pierced by the nail. (2) Your left hand was transfixed . . . (3) Your left arm was painfully dislocated," and so on.[38]

The visions of Julian of Norwich—*showings*, in her terminology—are even more detailed. Julian was most likely a nun or recluse in one of the religious establishments in the region of Norwich. When she was 30 years old, she fell ill, almost to the point of death. During this illness, she had a series of mystical visions. Her writings clearly show that mystical writing is not a spontaneous outpouring of feeling but a process of meticulous composition. The elaboration of the first version of the *Showings* into a longer second version points to the self-conscious creation of an artifact. The descriptions of physi-

35. *Privity of the Passion*, ed. Carl Horstman in *Yorkshire Writers: Richard Rolle of Hampole and his Followers* (London, 1895), 1:205–6.

36. Richard Rolle, *Meditations on the Passion*, in *Yorkshire Writers*, 1:87.

37. (1) Beloved Lord, on the high branch of the cross your clear eyes were dimmed, distorted . . . (4) Your sweet mouth was offended by a bitter potion. (5) Your delicate sense of touch was offended by hard blows (*The Little Book of Eternal Wisdom*, chap. 25 in *The Exemplar: Life and Writings of Blessed Henry Suso, O.P.*, trans. M. A. Edward [Dubuque, Iowa, 1962], 2:118).

38. Ibid., 2:119.

cal suffering are expanded in this second version, thus pointing once more to the central role of cruelty and pain in this mystical tradition.[39]

The realism of her descriptions considerably surpasses the more stereotypical accounts of pseudo-Bonaventure and the earlier English versions, and even those of Suso. Julian's descriptions of the dying Christ shift continually between the external point of view to the internal. Thus, in the eighth *Showing* Julian describes the changes of color in Christ's face: "I saw the swete face as it were drye and blodeles with pale dyeng and deede pale, langhuryng and than turned more deede in to blew, and after in browne blew, as the flessch turned more depe dede."[40] Then she carefully observes the changes in the lips and nostrils and the drying up of the body. Elsewhere, she describes with excruciating detail Christ's thirst on the cross and the agonies of the dying Christ.[41] The extraordinary force of these reconstructions lies in the detail: the changes in the color of the body, the shriveling of the skin, and the terrible cold of the dying body augmented by the strong blowing wind.

Breaking down physical violence into its individual components is an essential aspect of these mystical writings. The identification with the suffering Christ is accomplished through the small details. The reason for this was concisely summed up by Leonato in Shakespeare's *Much Ado about Nothing*: "There was neuer yet Philosopher, that could endure the toothake patiently, how euer they haue writ the stile of gods, And made a push at chance and sufferance."[42] Pain is essentially a subjective and private experience that cannot be shared. Therefore the pain of the crucifixion itself is quite incomprehensible and inexpressible. Yet one *can* identify with the smaller details: the thirst, the smell of carrion, and the cold. By identifying with these, a certain amount of identification with the larger experience *is* achieved. Beyond that, identification with the minor aspects of the crucifixion has a rhetorical effect: The resulting unease only emphasizes the magnitude of the other, unfathomable, part of Christ's suffering.

39. Esther Cohen has noticed an increased awareness to physical pain in general in the late Middle Ages; see "Towards a History of European Physical Sensibility: Pain in the Later Middle Ages," *Science in Context* 8:1 (1995): 47–74.

40. *A Book of Showings* 16 [the long text], ed. Edmund Colledge and James Walsh (Toronto, 1978), 2:357. The concentration on the more macabre aspects of the passion is reflected in the plastic arts as well. This tendency is particularly prominent in Hans Holbein's painting, *The Body of the Dead Christ in the Tomb*, 1521 or 1522 (Basel, Öffentliche Kunstsammlung, Kunstmuseum). See also Denise N. Baker, *Julian of Norwich's 'Showings'* (Princeton, N.J., 1994), 44–51.

41. *A Book of Showings* 17, 360–65.

42. Shakespeare, *Much Ado about Nothing* 5.1. On the subjective nature of pain, see Elaine Scarry, *The Body in Pain* (New York, 1985).

The mystical accounts or meditations on the passion refer explicitly to the issue of cruelty. Pseudo-Bonaventure mentions the cruelty of the Jews in their decision to crucify Christ.[43] Julian of Norwich mentions the cruel way in which the garland of thorns was applied to Christ's head.[44] Suso also condemns the cruelty of Christ's tormentors.[45] Even though such references are not numerous, the link between the passion mysticism and the issue of cruelty in general was made by contemporaries and is not just a modern scholarly construct. Thus, Margery Kempe, an English mystic who received spiritual advice from Julian, relates in a revealing passage that "sumtyme, whan sche saw the crucyfyx, er yf sche sey a man had a wownde er a best . . . er yyf a man bett a childe befor hir er smet an hors er another best wyth a whippe . . . hir thowt sche saw owyr Lord be betyn er wowndyd lyk as sche saw in the man er in the best."[46] This passage also points to the mutual influence between the growing sensitivity to cruelty and the preoccupation with the passion: The sensitivity to cruelty led to a focus on Christ's passion, but the awareness of Christ's suffering also increased the sensitivity to cruelty in general.

Aside from the longing for apostolic Christianity, other late medieval cultural processes and historical events were at the roots of this mystical movement. The emphasis on intentions in the dominant ethical system favored this type of spiritual identification with the passion of Christ. The Western Church was always wary of physical asceticism. The appearance, in the late Middle Ages, of various flagellant groups who sought to physically re-enact Christ's suffering was not viewed favorably, rendering spiritual meditation on the passion a more acceptable alternative. This type of mysticism did not completely replace physical asceticism: Many of the more famous mystics—St. Francis of Assisi, Clare of Assisi, and Heinrich Suso—combined their spiritual meditations with some form of physical asceticism.[47] Nevertheless, this spiritual movement marginalized physical asceticism to a considerable extent.

43. *Meditationes vitae Christi* 77; *Meditations on the Life of Christ*, 330.

44. *A Book of Showings* 17, 362.

45. O *saevitia* ac *duritia* immensa tam enormiter te torquentium. Qualiter o *cruentae* bestiae, leonibus *ferociores*, lupis rapacibus *saeviores*, agnum illum mansuetissimum, speciosumque forma pare filiis hominum, nobilem et delicatum, pium ac mansuetum sic *crudeliter* torquere potuistis? (*Horologium sapientiae* 1.15, ed. P. Künzle [Freiburg, 1977], 500).

46. Margery Kempe, *The Book of Margery Kempe*, chap. 28, ll. 1585–89, ed. Lynn Staley (Kalamazoo, Mich., 1996), http://www.lib.rochester.edu/camelot/teams/kempe2.htm (accessed 8/8/02).

47. Suso, for instance, made a wooden cross with protruding nails, and used to carry it on his naked body for eight hours, sometimes also lashing himself, so that the nails would stick into his flesh, "in honor of Christ's wounds" (*Life and Writings of Blessed Henry Suso*, chap. 16, 1:39).

Among contemporary historical events related to this surge of affective mysticism, the Black Death was certainly one of the events that made physical suffering familiar and an imminent threat. Another surge of affective mysticism in the sixteenth century, one that coincided with the wars of religion, seems to corroborate this linkage. Events such as these provided an impetus to locate human suffering in a meaningful spiritual context. The mysticism centered on the passion was *one* possible solution to this problem.

Representations of the passion were also closely linked to the late medieval penal system. Mitchell B. Merback has studied late medieval and early modern paintings of the crucifixion. He has shown the bi-directional influence between the representation of the two thieves and contemporary penal practices. The execution of the two thieves, whose iconography was less bound by tradition than was that of the crucifixion of Jesus, mirrors the way in which real executions were performed. At the same time, however, the incorporation of this legal reality into the crucifixion scene lent it theological significance.[48] Thus, the preoccupation with the cruelty of the passion in the late medieval period is not an isolated phenomenon. It is related to the emphasis on pain and suffering in the iconography of the crucifixion as well as to actual legal practices.

Nevertheless, the link to contemporary trends should not obscure the significance of the appearance of this type of mysticism. Cruelty and mysticism are both potentially subversive: Medieval mystics, and particularly women mystics, were perceived as treading the thin line between orthodoxy and heresy. The issue of cruelty was dangerously close to the question of legitimacy or illegitimacy of power. It seems that the conjunction of cruelty and mysticism in this movement of spirituality centered on the passion lent legitimacy to the preoccupation with both issues. But the change in the status of cruelty involved here is such that cruelty does not merely become a legitimate issue for discussion and representation. In this type of spirituality, the issue of cruelty becomes a tool for the attainment of the mystical experience. And despite the links between the mysticism of the passion and other contemporary trends, the appearance of this type of mysticism is not a natural or necessary development. It touches on problematic theological issues. In late antiquity and in the early Middle Ages, the issue of theodicy led to a marginalization of the role of cruelty in the accounts of the passion

48. Mitchell B. Merback, *The Thief, the Cross and the Wheel* (Chicago, 1999). I have generally avoided reference to iconographic sources because by their nature they belong exclusively to the mode of showing. Whereas in written sources there is a semantic field that points explicitly to cruelty, in iconographic sources it is even more difficult to distinguish between violence and cruelty.

of Christ and of other martyrs. The late medieval developments run counter to this tradition.

Preoccupation with the issue of cruelty increases in the late Middle Ages as reflected in the existence of theoretical discussions, such as that of Antoninus of Florence, that develop the themes taken up by previous thinkers.[49] Representations of cruelty also continue trends that had begun to develop in the central Middle Ages. Descriptions of cruelty become more explicit, more detailed, and more affective. But the change in respect to earlier periods is not just an incremental development. The issue of cruelty becomes an object for manipulation—that is, the representation of cruelty has purposes beyond a simple description of the events. Moreover, the manipulation is set to structure the emotions of its audience to achieve an effect that would have been impossible using a detached, or factual, description of the events.

In the Jacquerie, both sides of the conflict, nobles and non-nobles, exploit images of the cruelty of the "other" to delegitimize their opponents, directing fear and rage at the rival and inducing identification with the victims, primarily through an affective description of their suffering. The extent of the manipulation is underlined by the comparison between more and less partisan accounts. The ulterior purpose of the preoccupation with cruelty in the case of Pedro the Cruel is even clearer: delegitimizing a legitimate monarch by portraying him as cruel and, hence, a tyrant. In this instance, the manipulation is apparent on account of the gap between the accusations of tyranny and the concrete examples of his cruelty, most of which are not from the political realm. The importance of cruelty as a cultural issue and the ability to manipulate it are even more visible when the manipulation is not done with the purpose of presenting someone as cruel. Representations of Christ's passion reflect how the issue of cruelty was exploited for purely religious purposes: the attainment of the mystical experience.

49. See Chapter 1, 23–24.

CHAPTER SIX
THE EARLY MODERN PERIOD —
CRUELTY TRANSFORMED

Between the middle of the fifteenth century and the middle of the sixteenth century, a momentous change took place in the cultural role of cruelty, a change that cannot be seen only in terms of continuity with the medieval developments examined in the previous chapters. Most notable is the sheer quantity and range of cultural preoccupation with cruelty: It becomes more of a significant cultural issue at the turn of the sixteenth century than it ever was before, despite its increasing importance since the thirteenth century. In addition, the attitudes toward cruelty and the modes in which it is represented also undergo major changes. These developments are directly linked to the historical events of this period: the atrocities committed during the wars of religion by both Catholics and Protestants and the violence accompanying the conquest of the New World.

The magnitude of these events made cruelty an issue that could not be ignored. The violence involved had essentially new aspects when compared with medieval violence. Internal violence was an integral part of medieval life, but it was localized socially and geographically. Moreover, it was perceived as local in the eyes of the people involved in the violence, whether as victims or victimizers. Thus the peasant rebellions of the late medieval period were perceived as local events and not as a large-scale war between peasants and nobles raging all over Europe.[1] In contrast, the wars of religion were a more wide-ranging phenomenon that affected the whole of Western Europe, and the local violence in each particular place was perceived as part of a larger context. The conquest of the New World did not directly affect as many people in the West as the wars of religion, but nevertheless, it was also seen as an endeavor in which the "Old World" as an entity was involved. In addition, the settlement of the New World and the treatment of the native population were perceived as directly related to the wars of religion.

---

1. Étienne Marcel's comments (see Chapter 5, 129–30) are the exception. Moreover, Marcel cannot be taken as a representative peasant.

These developments in turn affected the way in which cruelty was treated. The medieval mode of reference to cruelty did not, of course, disappear suddenly. In certain respects, early modern texts appear as the outcome of an accelerated development of medieval tendencies. But even those continuous processes change their meaning as they reach their peak. Thus, for instance, early modern texts use the same late medieval building blocks for representing cruelty: massacres, sexual cruelty, and cannibalism. But their meanings and functions within the narrative change because the whole cultural context of cruelty is transformed.

In this chapter, I begin by tracing the areas in which the early modern processing and development of medieval material is most visible. Pointing to the similarities with the medieval period also brings into relief the dissimilar aspects and the changing contexts. Thus, the blood libel accusations against the Jews crystallize in the story of Simon, allegedly martyred by the Jews of Trent in 1475. The account of his martyrdom, written by Giovanni Mattia Tiberino, a doctor, develops the thematic elements of older cases—for example, William of Norwich and Hugh of Lincoln—and combines them with the late medieval affective spirituality that centered on the passion of Christ. The affective strain becomes almost grotesque in the sentimentality of texts such as the *Vita di Caterina Vergine* by Pietro Aretino. The line separating these phenomena from their medieval parallels is fuzzy, but it exists: Tiberino turns the cruelty of the Jews into the main theme of his account, unlike its medieval predecessors in which cruelty had an important but auxiliary role. The historical context also changed: Unlike any of his medieval predecessors, Simon of Trent was canonized. Similarly, Sebastian Münster's *Cosmographia* is based almost exclusively on medieval texts, yet it emphasizes cruelty much more than those sources.

The transition to a new mode in the perception and representation of cruelty was noticed by contemporaries, some of whom reacted against it by holding to the older, medieval modes of handling the issue. The English writer John Lydgate (1370?–1451?), for instance, rejected the new emphasis on irrational cruelty and the increasingly explicit representation of sexual cruelty. Adapting Boccaccio's *De casibus*, a neo-humanist text, he re-medievalized it by omitting parts of the original and by imposing medieval hermeneutic paradigms on other parts. A reluctance to adopt the new discourse is evident as well in the writings of William Allen, who used strictly legalistic medieval notions of cruelty to distinguish between Catholic persecution of Protestants and Protestant persecution of Catholics.

Later texts, written after the outbreak of the wars of religion, complete the separation from the medieval mode of reference to cruelty. In their form, Protestant martyrologies—for example, those of Jean Crespin and John Foxe—abandon demonstratively the path set by late medieval Catholic martyrdom accounts. Instead, they look back to compilations such as Eusebius's *Historia ecclesiastica* in their factual, unsentimental tone and the detailed *acta*-like documentation they supply.

Moreover, an even more significant break with tradition is undertaken in these martyrologies and to an even greater extent in Jean de Léry's *Histoire d'un voyage en terre de Brésil*. Cruelty ceases to be an absolute ethical entity as these works adopt a quantitative and comparative approach. Cruelty is measured and rated according to various criteria, such as the severity of the actions committed and the number of the victims. The quantitative treatment of cruelty involves a comparative outlook on the issue, including a comparison between Catholics and Protestants, between natives of the Americas and their conquerors, and between the Turks and any of the previous groups. The implications of this approach were complex: It signaled a more relativistic attitude to the issue of cruelty in general, but the measurement of cruelty led also to the positioning of absolute quantitative boundaries beyond which pain and violence were always cruel, regardless of any justification. This relativistic approach to cruelty, together with the intensive preoccupation with the subject itself, are the main innovative, even revolutionary, aspects of the early modern treatment of cruelty.

In 1475, a missing Christian child (probably about two or three years old) was discovered dead in Trent.[2] The bare facts of the case are quite similar to those of the medieval children martyrs. There were, allegedly, obvious indicators pointing to the guilt of the local Jews. The importance of this particular martyrdom in its time is reflected in the rapid development of a cult of Simon, which culminated in his canonization.

The events concerning the death of Simon of Trent have been discussed extensively in recent years.[3] Blood libel accusations against the Jews and the

2. The account states that he could not speak yet he could call "mother."

3. See: Ronnie Po-Chia Hsia, *The Myth of Ritual Murder* (New Haven, Conn., 1998), 43–50; and Ronnie Po-Chia Hsia, *Trent 1475* (New Haven, Conn., 1992). The increasing prominence of these charges of infanticide against the Jews are evident also in another work of the same period, Alfonso de Espina's *Fortalicium fidei*. He devotes a long section (book 3, *consideratio* 7) to a collection of various instances that reflect the cruelty of the Jews (*incipit consideratio septima de iudeorum crudelitatibus*); most of this section is devoted to stories of Christian children murdered by the Jews in various countries of Europe (Alfonso de Espina, *Fortalicium fidei contra iudeos saracenos aliisque christiane fidei inimicos* [Nuremberg, 1494], 141r–51r). On Alfonso de Espina and his work, see Alisa Meyuhas-Ginio, "'The Fortress of Faith' at the End of the West: Alonso de Espina and his *Fortalitium Fidei*," in *Proceedings of the Tenth World Congress of Jewish Studies* (Jerusalem, 1989), Division B, 1:101–8 [in Hebrew]; and Alisa Meyuhas-Ginio, "The Expulsion of the Jews from the Kingdom of France in the Fourteenth Century and its Significance as Viewed by Alonso (Alfonso) de Espina, Author of *Fortalitium fidei*," *Michael* 12 (1991): 67–82 [in Hebrew].

efforts to have the murdered children recognized as martyrs were originally a medieval genre. From this perspective, the case of Simon is part of this medieval tradition. Yet some aspects of the account of his death and the role of cruelty in it are essentially new. Also new is the reaction of the official Church: Although it did not recognize any of the medieval children martyrs, Simon was canonized in 1588.[4]

Giovanni Mattia Tiberino, the doctor who examined Simon's body soon after the event, has written the most extensive account of this case. Tiberino's account was one of the influential factors in launching the fury against the Jews, as his account benefited from the invention of the printing press and achieved wide circulation.[5] Tiberino's account, in the form of a letter to the people of his native city Brescia, is written in a florid style. At the outset, Tiberino claims that he is writing of "a matter of the utmost importance, which no age from the passion of the Lord until these times has heard." He urges his audience to "hear . . . of the unheard of crime," and proceeds to his subject. The Jews, writes Tiberino, are like vipers nurtured at the breasts of the Christians.[6] And from implicit connotations of cruelty evoked by the animal imagery, Tiberino passes at once, in the same sentence, to explicit accusations: The Jews are cruel (*crudeles iudei*[7]) not only because they are usurers but because "they feed of the live blood of our sons," whom they atrociously torture in their synagogues and kill as they killed Christ.[8] The danger posed by the Jews is driven home by the use of the first person ("our sons").

In this short prologue, before any fact of the case has been disclosed, Tiberino has established the cruelty of the Jews, their animal qualities, and their cannibalistic characteristics. Concerning this last issue, it is to be noted, Tiberino exceeds even the alleged facts of the specific case, because he presents the Jews as feeding on blood as a dietary habit (which was attributed in the past to the Mongols), not just making ritual use of it. In the following narrative, Tiberino switches between these three strands of imagery—human cruelty, animal-like characteristics, and cannibalism. The tone of narration varies as well, from affective descriptions of the suffering of Simon to a purportedly factual tone in the references to the Jews.

4. Hsia, *Trent 1475*, 132.

5. For the importance of the invention of print in the diffusion of this account, see ibid., 57–60. Tiberino's account was published in Frumenzio Ghetta, *Fra Bernardino Tomitano da Feltre e gli ebrei di Trento nel 1475* (Trent, 1986), 40–45.

6. In sinu proprio viperas nutriunt (ibid., 41).

7. Ghetta's edition has *crudeles indei*, evidently erroneous.

8. Filiorum nostrorum vivo *sanguine depascuntur*, quos *atroci* in sinagogis suis affligunt supplicio, et instar Christi *crudeli* funere iugulant (ibid., 41; italics mine).

Tiberino develops the cannibalistic imagery, vividly describing the Jews of Trent sitting at their Passover dinner, one of them declaring, "we have an abundance of meats and fish, only one thing is missing."[9] According to Tiberino, all the Jews present understood the "missing thing" as referring to a Christian child, whom "they kill atrociously in contempt of our Lord Jesus Christ."[10] Thus Tiberino again insinuates that dead Christians are a dietary preference for the Jews, and only then does he mention the ritual use of blood for the Passover bread. Thus in fact, Tiberino establishes three motives for the killing of Christian children: dietary cannibalism, ritual cannibalism, and hate of Christians. When Simon arrives, Tiberino describes the Jews as wild animals howling in anticipation of Christian blood.[11] The narrative switches to the affective mode whenever Tiberino moves from the Jews to Simon. Describing Simon's abduction, for instance, Tiberino writes: "The child, looking back, started, with tears, to raise childish cries, and to invoke the sweet name of mother."[12]

These elements combine in the culminating scene of Simon's martyrdom. The diabolical character of the Jews is insinuated implicitly in the statement that the deed was done at a time when both men and animals slept.[13] The torture is depicted vividly, a task probably facilitated by Tiberino's profession.[14] Twice during this scene he refers explicitly to the cruelty of the Jews.[15] Tiberino relates affectively how the Jews continue to torture the already half-dead child (*semimortuum infantem*). Describing the moment of death, Tiberino gathers up all his literary talents, showing Simon dying as he inclines his bloody head like a poppy falling under heavy rain.[16] Tiberino later sums up by referring sentimentally to Simon as "the glorious Simon, virgin, martyr and innocent, hardly weaned, and whose tongue did not yet unravel human speech."[17]

Most of the characteristics assigned by Tiberino to the Jews exist in previous medieval representations of cruelty. Tiberino's novelty consists of two

9. Et carnes et pisces abunde nobis sunt; unum tamtum nobis deest (ibid.).

10. Quem in contemptum domini nostri Iesu Christi mactant atrociter (ibid.).

11. Ululabant siccis faucibus super christianum sanguinem (ibid., 42).

12. Ibid.

13. Tempus erat quo . . . quiscebant voces hominumque canumque (ibid., 43).

14. Vivam carnem vivo cum sanguine lacerabant (ibid.).

15. "Atrocissimis iudeis" and "sevissimus ille senex tanti sceleris caput" (ibid.).

16. Iam plus quam per horam miserandus puer terribili duraverat in supplicio et interdicto spiritu colapsis viribus deficiebat, attollens graves oculos in celum superos advocare videbatur in testes, et inclinato capite sanctum Domino reddidit spiritum. Purpureus veluti cum flos succisus aratro languescit moriens lapsaque papavera collo dimisere caput pluvie cum forte gravant (ibid.).

17. Ibid., 44.

features. First, Tiberino combines the imagery of the cruelty of the "other" with the affectivity of the late medieval mysticism of the passion. The result is highly effective, more than the simple sum of its components. Second, and even more significant, is the shift from the traditional purpose of martyrdom accounts. Depicting the cruelty of the Jews is an end in itself in Tiberino's account, whereas in earlier martyrdom accounts the representation of cruelty was instrumental for praising the martyr by demonstrating his fortitude in withstanding the tortures. Tiberino makes cruelty the subject of his text, as he declares explicitly at the beginning of his account: "Hear you who rule peoples . . . and awaken the inhabitants of the earth so that they shall see what vipers they nourish in their bosoms, the cruel Jews . . . who over our very heads conspire destruction, and feed on the live blood of our sons."[18] This warning is a general one against the cruelty of the Jews, and the specific case of Simon is, as it were, only an exemplum.

As mentioned earlier, the successful portrayal of the cruelty of the Jews was aided by the technological innovation of the printing press. It assured wide circulation of Tiberino's text and, perhaps more significantly for the actual impact of the story, a pictorial representation of Simon's martyrdom appeared as an engraving in the Chronicle of Hartmann Schedel, published in 1493.[19] The picture shows Simon tortured by a group of Jews while he stands on a table. One Jew inflicts a cut on his penis, probably intended to represent a circumcision, while another collects the blood in a bowl. All of the Jews in the image are named, thus increasing the verisimilitude of the illustration.[20]

The alleged cruelty of the Jews supplied an implicit justification for excessive judicial violence against them, which later caused Pope Sixtus IV to order a thorough review of the investigation itself. This combination was probably a major factor in the unprecedented canonization of Simon in 1588. Another singular aspect of this case, the significance of which is discussed later, is the fact that the account that set the whole process in motion was the initiative of a doctor, not a cleric. This origin points to the need to

18. Audite qui regitis populos inauditum scelus, et pastorum more fidelium vestris populis invigilate, expergiscantur habitantes terram et videant quales in sinu proprio viperas nutriunt, *crudeles* iudei non solum christianorum res rabiosa usurarum fame consumunt sed in capita nostra perniciemque coniurati filiorum nostrorum vivo sanguine depascuntur, quos *atroci* in sinagogis suis affligunt supplicio, et instar Christi *crudeli* funere iugulant (ibid., 41).

19. Hartmann Schedel, *Liber cronicarum cum figuris et ymaginibus ab initio mundi* (Nuremberg, 1493), f. 254v. The printing press provided easier access to the visualization of cruelty, as was also the case of the Mongols in Sebastian Münster's *Cosmographia* (see below, 151).

20. For an interpretation of this illustration, see Hsia, *Myth of Ritual Murder*, 43–50; and Hsia, *Trent 1475*, 57–60.

famucıqʒ moobıas vırauıs moyıes fırabel aıʒ mayeı aıı fynagoga teıı eı — peeeıeı ....— ... — ..... .— p—
mū nevagıre poffet fudarıolū appofuerūt ʒ ertenfıs brachıjs pmo papulū forpıcıb⁹. moɾ genā derteɾā p
cıdentes. Inde ɖfqʒ forpıce carnē ɔuellıt. Sudıb⁹ ɖeınde pacuɾ pupugere. cū ılle manus alter plantas cō
tınet crudelıteɾ fanguıne collecto bymonos coɾ moɾe canetes. addıt mınıs ɣba. accıpıas fufpēfe ıbefu. fe
cere fıc olım maıoɾes nɾı. fıc pfundanɾ celo terra marıqʒ ɾpıcole. fıc caput eıus ınter vlnas cecıdıt ʒ vıta lı
bera ad fuperos fecıt ıter. ınde ad cenas pperarūt aʒımas ɖe fanguıne eıus ın ɾpı ɖeɖec⁹ ederūt. coqʒ moɾ
tuo ftatım corpus ın pınquū domus coɾ flumen pıecerūt ʒ pafca cū gaudıo celebrarūt. Querētes ɖeıɴ
de anɾıı parētes gnatū paruulū. poftrıdıe eū ın fluıⱶıo ınuenerūt. ɖ ıllıco vɾbıs ptoɾı fcelus ɖenūcıarūt. Is
ptoɾ ıobānes ɖe falıs nobılıs brıⱶıenfıū cıuıs legū doctoɾ vıfo puero erboɾruıt facın⁹ ʒ pfeftım vɾbıs ıuɪ
deos ɔpbendıt ʒ eculeo eos fıgıllatım ımponēs toɾmētıs aftrıctı eo ordıne crımē retulerūt. ɖ dılıgētı erⱶ
amınatıone cognıto ıudeos ɔdıgnıs fupplıcıjs extermınauıt. pɾeful eo tpe vɾbıs Jo. bınderbach colleⱶ
gıt ertıctū corp⁹ ʒ fepulchɾo mādat. multıs eueftıgıo cepıt floɾere mıracul. Inde er oī ɾpıano oɾbe ppfoɾ
ɔcurfus ad fcī huıus paruulı fepulchɾū eft factus vt etıā vrbs ıpa cū mıraculıs ʒ opıbus multıs fıt aucta
Coɾpoɾı ɣo ıpıus puerı trıdentını cıues bafılıcam pulchɾam ererere 1475.

Ofımıle etıā fcel⁹ apɖ motā oppıɖū qɖ ē ı fınıb⁹ agrı foɾı tulıɴ p⁹ ɖnquēnıū ıudeı pegeɾt. Nā etıā alıⱶ
um pueɾū fılı mō mactauerūt. p ɖ tres coɾ captıuı venetıjs mıffı fueɾt ʒ atrocı fupplıcıo ɔerematı ſt.
Iterū thurchı ınferıoɾem ıngreffı mıſıam magna cede fternunf. Debınc magnā genuenfıum vɾbe caⱶ
pbam quā ad meotıdem adbuc poffıdebant. Genuenfes erpugnant. cıuıtas populofa, ʒ mercatoɾıbuf
plurımū apta tuıt hoc anno cıue genueofı eā pɾodente ın turcboɾ man. ɖeuenıt ın lıttoɾe eurını marıs fıta.

FIGURE 3. The Martyrdom of Simon of Trent (Hartmann Schedel). *Liber cronicarum cum figuris et ymaginibus ab initio mundi* (Nuremberg, 1493), f. 254v.

subject cruelty to objective criteria. Thus, regarding physical violence, the account of a doctor carries professional weight.

In the account of the martyrdom of Simon of Trent, we have seen how medieval elements are used to create a narrative of cruelty relating to contemporary events. The introduction of cruelty into re-tellings of ancient and medieval history is perhaps even more indicative of the increasing cultural importance of the issue of cruelty. Sebastian Münster (1489–1552), a Renaissance scholar, published his *Cosmographia* in 1544.[21] This work is, in a different sense than Tiberino's narrative, a combination of old and new. In the *Cosmographia*, Münster attempts to sum up the geographical and historical knowledge relating to the Old and New Worlds. Münster's accounts of medieval "others" reflect the way in which the medieval sources were interpreted in the sixteenth century.[22]

The process by which later accounts of the Vikings become more and more preoccupied with cruelty, both in *showing* and in *telling*, has been observed in the transition from the early medieval accounts to the chronicles of the twelfth and thirteenth centuries. In the chronicles of the central Middle Ages, the additions to the early medieval accounts have been subtle. In the chronicle of Matthew Paris, for instance, there is no correlation between the representation of the cruelty of the Vikings and that of the Mongols: The latter is presented in much greater detail and more explicitly and has different characteristics. Münster, however, attributes to the Vikings almost every possible type of cruelty except cannibalism and uses numerous lexical references to cruelty. His summary of these incursions is entitled "The cruelty of the Normans" (*Crudelitas Nortmannorum*)[23] and describes the Vikings as devastating every place "with sword and fire," burning monasteries, raping, murdering, and most of all, enjoying themselves. He writes about one of their leaders that "booty which was not rendered agreeable by blood displeased him," thus presenting the pleasure taken in the violence as the *main* driving force behind the Vikings' cruelty (unlike older chronicles, which assign equal share, if not a greater one, to greed).[24] The description of the Vikings' actions is much more affective due to the richer use of adjectives

21. Münster was a true "Renaissance man": he was a mathematician, cartographer, and Hebraist.

22. The popularity and influence of this work in the sixteenth century enable us to assume that Münster's presentation is representative. The mere circulation of the *Cosmographia* would have made his interpretation of the medieval events a widely accepted one.

23. This paragraph heading appears on the margins in the 1550 edition.

24. Quo tempore [circa annum Christi 800] Nortmanni seu Nordwegi cum Danis excursiones & depopulationes horrendas fecerunt in Saxonia, Frisia, Scotia, Gallia, Aquitania, & c. omnia loca igne & ferro deuastantes. . . . Fuit autem inter alios *crudeles* duces, Haddingus regio sanguine cretus, uir feroci animo, ad arma natus, qui fortem exercitum exposuit in Galliam, praedabundus incedens quocunque se uerteret. Ecclesiarum incendia, matronarum stupra, puellarum raptus, uirorum neces sine numero peregit. Displicuit illi praeda, quam non sanguis commendabat. *Saeuissima* hominum *crudelitas* tantum iniecit terroris regnicolis, ut diu nemo inueniretur, qui exercitum opponeret grassabundis. Durauit ad multos annos haec *crudelium* hominum debachatio (Sebastian Münster, *Cosmographia* [Basel, 1550], 834; italics mine).

FIGURE 4. A Mongol roasting a headless man on a spit. The caption of this image at the margin reads "Anthropophagi" (man eaters; Münster, *Cosmographia*, 1060).

and adverbs, such as "inspiring horror" (*horrendas*), "most savage" (*saeuissima*), and "without number" (*sine numero*, in relation to victims).[25]

Münster's representation of the Mongols is similarly explicit and emphasizes the pleasure they take in their acts of cruelty. He dwells at large on their cannibalism, which is practiced "in order to display their cruelty and achieve their desire [*uindicandi desiderium*]."[26] As in the case of Simon of Trent, the representation of cruelty is enhanced by an illustration, which emphasizes the importance of cannibalism in the representation of cruelty.

Münster uses an illustration for another purpose, that of linking the Mongols to the Scythians, the historic "other" since the times of Herodotus. Besides specifying that they lived in the same place, the connection is suggested by the use of an identical illustration, which appears twice—once in the section on the Scythians and once in the section devoted to the Mongols—showing the habitat of the Mongols and that of the Scythians.

25. Similar tendencies can be observed in Münster's description of the Magyar incursions (ibid., 865). The Magyars are presented as raping both men and women. The attribution of sodomitic rape to the Magyars enhances their otherness, as is the case with the mention of homosexual rape in Tainguy's version of Froissart's chronicle. These references concur with Boswell's observation that homosexuality becomes a graver crime in the later Middle Ages (John Boswell, *Christianity, Social Tolerance, and Homosexuality* [Chicago, 1980], 269ff). The "modern" preoccupation with medieval cruelty is evident also in eighteenth-century interpretations of Saint Olaf's violence (Asko Timonen, "Saint Olaf's 'cruelty': Violence by the Scandinavian King Interpreted over the Centuries," *Journal of Medieval History* 22 [1996]: 285–96).

26. Münster, *Cosmographia*, 1060. In this chapter, entitled "De cibo, potu & uestimentis Tartarorum," Münster mentions also that the Tartars drink milk and do not drink wine (see Chapter 4, 103).

FIGURE 5. This drawing, presumably depicting the Mongols, also appears in the section on the Scythians, thereby establishing a visual identity between the two peoples (Münster, *Cosmographia*, 1053, 1059).

The development, to the excess, of medieval trends is reflected in the *Vita di Caterina Vergine* of Pietro Aretino (1492–1556), a contemporary of Münster who is more well known for his secular and sexually explicit works. Aretino's account of St. Catherine is almost a short novel,[27] extending far beyond the length of medieval accounts. Exaggeration is prominent, and not just in the length of the work. The work pushes the late medieval mode of representation to its limits until it becomes grotesque. Various types of cruel tortures and executions are narrated at length: cauldrons of lead and of boiling water, burial alive, crucifixions, and the unleashing of wild beasts on the martyrs, among other tortures. The description of the massacre of the Christians of Alexandria, for instance, is more than 23 paragraphs long! The narration itself is extremely sentimental, breaking into exclamations such as: "But why does this pen not weep? Why does this ink not break into tears? Why does this paper not languish? Why does the reader not sigh?"[28] Likewise, Aretino uses all the lexical range of references to cruelty to weave dense compounds such as "the cruelty of a punishment unknown in hell, more so on earth" or "cruelly cruel."[29]

"ANCIENT AND MODERNS" — CONTESTING DISCOURSES OF CRUELTY

The shift from old to new modes of reference to cruelty was not swift and unidirectional. An example of the resistance to the new attitudes toward

27. Pietro Aretino, "La vita di Caterina Vergine," in *Le vite dei santi*, ed. Flavia Santin (Rome, 1977). In this edition, the martyrdom extends over 147 pages.

28. *Vita di Caterina Vergine*, 3.153, *Le vite dei santi*, 150.

29. *Vita di Caterina Vergine*, 1.154, 3.159, *Le vite dei santi*, 68 and 151, respectively. See also, 3.220, *Le vite dei santi*, 161: "Egli deveria bastare, a chi vole permaner crudele, lo esser crudo, senza cercare di aggiungere crudeltá a crudeltá."

cruelty is the writing of John Lydgate, an important fifteenth-century author and translator who did much for the diffusion of neo-humanist and early Renaissance texts in England. Lydgate's writings display a repulsion from the new emphasis on the irrational and sexual aspects of cruelty. This reactionary position is reflected in his adaptation of Boccaccio's *De casibus*, a neo-humanist text that highlights the new aspects of the representation of cruelty. Lydgate translated into English Laurent de Premierfait's French translation of Boccaccio's Latin, but Laurent was basically faithful to the original, and the changes introduced are Lydgate's own.

The two diverging attitudes, old versus new, stand out in the representation of Nero, one of the traditional symbols of cruelty since late antiquity. Nero's reputation for cruelty rested on the events narrated by Roman historians as well as on his persecution of Christians, the most notable being the execution of Peter and Paul. Like Herod in various biblical plays, toward the end of the Middle Ages Nero's figure became an exaggerated prototype of cruelty.[30]

Boccaccio's representation of Nero is out of line with this medieval tradition. He makes the two-dimensional figure of cruelty into a three-dimensional one by emphasizing its human aspects: Nero is a weak man seduced by power rather than a demon. According to the overall design of his work—to present men abandoned by fortune—Boccaccio presents Nero's talents and good qualities, which degenerated only after he became emperor.[31] Criticism creeps in only after the first third of the chapter; in the account of Nero's degeneration into the ruthless tyrant he is remembered as. But this is the later stage of a *process*, unlike the static two-dimensional emblem of cruelty that appears in most medieval literature.

Lydgate's account of Nero in his *Fall of Princes* regresses once more into the medieval mode of representing Nero and cruelty. Lydgate introduces him by writing, "Nero the Tirant kometh next onto the ring," and characterizes him as "Most disnaturel of condicioun / Bi gret outrages of cursid cruelte, / That euere regned in Roome the cite."[32] Nero's cruelty thus becomes a static quality and not part of a psychological process.[33]

30. See Hamlet's remark to the players, "I would have such a fellow whipped for o'erdoing Termagant; it out-herods Herod" (Shakespeare, *Hamlet*, III.2).

31. Giovanni Boccaccio, *De casibus* 7:4:10 in *Tutte le opere di Giovanni Boccaccio*, ed. Vittore Branca (Rome, 1983), 9:602–4.

32. John Lydgate, *The Fall of Princes*, ed. Henry Bergen (Washington, D.C., 1923), part 3, book 7, ll. 600–4, 791.

33. The lack of actual vice in the early years is attributed by Lydgate solely to Seneca's influence, not to a lack of propensity for vice (ibid., book 7, ll. 614–27, 792).

Lydgate abbreviates much that he finds repulsive in Boccaccio's account of Nero, explaining his editorial decisions explicitly. Thus, he passes quickly over the homosexual episodes of Sporus and Onpharus, two of Nero's male lovers, one of whom was also castrated by Nero.[34] His reluctance to deal with the irrational aspects of cruelty is, likewise, explicitly spelled out. Lydgate states that he is ashamed on this account to have included Nero in his book, the only justification being that his story demonstrates the bad end of tyrants.[35]

Lydgate's reading of the story into medieval categories is best seen in his reference to Nero's rape of the Vestal virgin Rubria. Boccaccio and Laurent merely tell that Nero forced himself on her publicly. Lydgate turns Rubria into a Christian martyr. Having classified the story, he supplies some of the stock elements of female martyr stories. Thus, he tells that Nero placed Rubria in a brothel, a detail that is absent in Boccaccio and Laurent's version.[36]

Lydgate "medievalizes" the references to cruelty found in his sources, abridging or omitting episodes that reflect the new emphases on the irrational aspect of cruelty and on rape, and expanding stories that can be fitted into older categories of cruelty. These tendencies can be observed in the story of another arch-tyrant, Dionysus of Syracuse. Whereas Boccaccio refers in a general manner to his crimes, Lydgate enumerates them and fits them into the medieval categorization of the deadly sins.[37] He also considerably expands Boccaccio's references to the robbery of temples—another traditional category of cruelty—and abbreviates his references to sexual violence.

34. Be my writing men shal neuer reede / The mateer is so foul and outragous/ To be rehersed (ibid., book 7, ll. 719–21, 794).

35. Toward the end of the section on Nero, Lydgate writes, "Of whos [Nero's] woodnesse good heed when I took / I was ashamed to sette hym in this book" (ibid., book 7, ll. 738–39, 794). In Lenvoye, Lydgate's final comments, he unwrites, as it were, the whole story: "Yif that I myhte, I wolde race his name / Out of this book . . . let no wiht take[n] heede / For to remembre so many a cruel deede / Sauf onli this, to thynken in substaunce, / How eueri tiraunt eendith with mischaunce" (ibid., book 7, ll. 782–88, 796).

36. Boccaccio, De casibus, 7:4:27, 608; Laurent de Premierfait, De Casibus (Bruges, 1476); Fall of Princes, book 7, ll. 707–18, 794. Another way in which Lydgate transforms Boccaccio's representation of Nero was noted by Henry A. Kelly, who points out that Lydgate turns Nero from a writer of tragedies (as Boccaccio would have him) into a comedian, probably because he could not think of Nero as worthy enough to compose tragedies (Henry A. Kelly, Chaucerian Tragedy [Cambridge, 1997], 173–75).

37. "Becuse he was, with al his gret outrage, / Ful of alle vices, pride and lecherie, / Of auarice, of ire and of envie" (Fall of Princes, book 4, ll. 808–10, 496. Boccaccio has "Sed quid veterum primordia queram hominis scelestarum turpitudinum omnium fedati?" [De casibus 4:4:1, 294]).

Another type of "reactionary" attitude toward cruelty is expressed by the Catholic William Allen, writing against the persecution of Catholics in England. In his *True, Sincere, and Modest Defense of English Catholics*, he points to the difference between Queen Mary's persecutions of the Protestants and the Protestant persecution of Catholics in his own day. Allen explains that "Queen Mary against the Protestants executed only the old laws of our country and of all Christendom," and therefore her actions fall under the category of justice. The Protestants, conversely, cannot claim that because they abolished the laws for heresy and, moreover, they pervert the law by allegedly condemning Catholics for heresy while in fact they are being persecuted for their faith.[38] This strictly legalistic argument looks back to medieval approaches to cruelty rather than to modern ones.

But these reactionary responses to the new discourse were not very effective. Late medieval literature is increasingly preoccupied with detailed representations of violence, some of it explicitly labeled as cruelty. The subject matter of many of these works is of classical origin and deals precisely with the types of violence that Lydgate found so repugnant. Seneca's tragedies are distinguished by the high level of violence represented in them, which was noted with approval (and imitation) or disapproval by all readers.[39] Their reception reflects the phenomenon of a late medieval attraction to the subject of cruelty, accompanied by a repulsion from some of its aspects, as was evident in the philosophical discussions of cruelty from this period. Seneca's tragedies reappear at about the same time as the renewed theoretical interest in the issue of cruelty but do not make their full impact, however, until the Renaissance. The repulsion from the tragedies is reflected in the issue of the two Senecas: the dramatist (*Seneca tragoedus*) and the "moral" philosopher (*Seneca moralis*). The debate in the fourteenth century among Italian humanists on this matter encompassed many areas: philological, literary, historical, as well as moral. There seems to have been disapproval of some of the moral aspects of the tragedies. Even Petrarch, who upheld the theory of a single Seneca, commented that distinguishing between two Senecas would enhance the philosopher's moral stature but would detract from his fame as a genius.[40]

38. William Allen, *A True, Sincere, and Modest Defense of English Catholics*, ed. Robert M. Kingdon (Ithaca, 1965), 93.

39. See E. F. Watling, Introduction to *Seneca - Four Tragedies and Octavia* (Harmondsworth, 1966), 7–39. For a criticism on this aspect of the tragedies, see the remarks of Schlegel quoted there (11).

40. ". . . Ita quantum morum demitur infamie, tantundem ingenii fame detrahi oportet" (*Familiari* 24:5:17, cited in Guido Martellotti, "La questione dei due Seneca da Petrarca a Benvenuto," *Italia medioevale e umanistica* 15 [1972]: 149–69, esp. 153). Martellotti mentions other classical authors who were "divided" into two on philological grounds, but in Seneca's case the moral discrepancy seems to have been an important consideration (150).

Late medieval literature clearly displays Senecan and Ovidian influence in the representation of cruelty, providing numerous combinations of rape and cannibalism. The Italian Albertino Mussato composed in 1314–1315 a tragedy named *Ecerinis*, presenting the career of the tyrannical ruler of Padua. Ecerinus was born after the devil, in the form of a bull, raped his mother. Ecerinus himself is amused by mutilations of a sexual nature, such as cutting children's genitals and women's breasts.[41] Gregorio Corraro composed in 1428–1429 a Latin play retelling the Ovidian story of Procne in which she kills her son and prepares him as a meal for her husband Tereus as punishment for raping her sister, Philomela. Tereus himself is also related to the theme of cannibalism, as he is reputed to have fed his horses human flesh.[42]

Renaissance drama, especially the English genre of "revenge tragedy," is a further development of these graphic displays of violence, in which classical influence is once more evident. The extreme violence represented in some of these Elizabethan tragedies is striking even for modern readers.[43] Seneca's particular influence was recognized and acknowledged by Renaissance writers. Praising the revenge tragedy *Gorboduc*, Sidney writes that it is "clyming to the height of *Seneca* his stile."[44] In Kyd's *Spanish Tragedy*, Hieronimo pledges himself to vengeance while quoting from three different plays by Seneca.[45]

THE WARS OF RELIGION AND THE CONQUEST OF THE NEW WORLD

Two sets of events, both characterized by cataclysmic violence, mark the transition into the modern period and into an essentially different attitude

41. Albertino Mussato, *Ecerinis*, ll. 266–69, in *Mussato's Ecerinis and Loschi's Achilles*, ed. Luigi Padrin and Joseph R. Berrigan (Munich, 1975), 44–45; see Henry A. Kelly, *Ideas and Forms of Tragedy from Aristotle to the Middle Ages* (Cambridge, 1993), 134–37.

42. Gregorio Corraro, *Progne*, ed. Ulrike de Vries (Heidelberg, 1987); see Kelly, *Ideas and Forms of Tragedy*, 187–91.

43. Antonin Artaud, the founder of the modern Theater of Cruelty, refers to a play by John Ford as a source of inspiration; see Carol C. Rosen, "The Language of Cruelty in Ford's '*Tis Pity She's a Whore*,'" in *Drama in the Renaissance*, ed. Clifford Davidson, C. J. Gianakaris, and John H. Stroupe (New York, 1986), 315–27. On the relations between Elizabethan drama and the modern Theater of Cruelty, see also William L. Stull, "'This Metamorphosde Tragoedie': Thomas Kyd, Cyril Tourneur, and the Jacobean Theatre of Cruelty," *Ariel* 14 (1983): 35–49. On the extent of Seneca's influence on this aspect of Renaissance drama, see Robert S. Miola, *Shakespeare and Classical Tragedy* (Oxford, 1992), 3–10.

44. Cited in Miola, *Shakespeare and Classical Tragedy*, 11.

45. Thomas Kyd, *The Spanish Tragedy*, III, xiii, ed. James R. Murlyne (New York, 1970), 85–87 (the references to Seneca in this scene are mentioned by Miola, *Shakespeare and Classical Tragedy*, 11). Murlyne notes Senecan influence in the fact that Kyd "shares with Seneca a certain interest in bloodshed and various kinds of horror" (xvii).

toward the issue of cruelty: the conquest of the New World and the wars of religion. Historically, the violence in America preceded that of the wars in Europe, and it is likely that there is a direct link between the violence practiced in these two contexts. The paganism and alleged cannibalism of the Indians justified higher levels of violence against them. These norms of violence were probably imported to Europe later when the wars of religion erupted. In fact, it seems unlikely that two distinct norms for violence—one for unbelievers across the seas and a different one for European unbelievers—could be kept even if this was the intention.

In fact, the cruelty of the conquistadores versus the cruelty imputed to the native population becomes a hotly debated issue only after it becomes enmeshed in the struggle between Catholics and Protestants. The reasons for this chronological reversal are discussed in more detail later. Nevertheless, briefly put, it seems only natural that violence close to home would be more preoccupying than violence at the other end of the world. The way in which the problem of cruelty in the New World is introduced into sixteenth-century culture is also telling; it is mentioned mainly by Protestants as an objective proof, as it were, to the cruelty of the Catholic Spaniards.

The sudden increase in actual violence that accompanied the wars of religion had repercussions on contemporary culture. Violence was naturally a major topic in sources that reported the events, such as chronicles or martyrdom accounts. But it was also amply represented in cultural products that were not directly related to the events, such as the visual arts and literature. The nature of these events made cruelty specifically, and not merely the more general concept of violence, a central issue. Since the "renaissance of cruelty" in the thirteenth century, cruelty was not only a philosophical or descriptive issue. The concept was used as a label, the purpose of which was to undermine the legitimacy of rulers, minorities, and social and religious groups that were considered subversive. The religious conflict of the sixteenth century raged precisely around these topics: Was the Pope's position as the head of Christendom legitimate, or was he a self-proclaimed usurper? Were the Protestants rebels, heretics, or the true guardians of Christianity? These religious issues were intertwined with social issues that were a source of violence even before the outbreak of the wars, such as the status of peasants in various regions.[46] Because there could not be a swift and decisive outcome to this conflict, a massive propaganda effort was waged on both sides, and cruelty had a central role in it, serving three purposes: discredit-

46. See: Stephen J. Greenblatt, "Murdering Peasants: Status, Genre, and the Representation of Rebellion," in *Representing the English Renaissance*, ed. Stephen J. Greenblatt (Berkeley, Calif., 1988), 1–29; and Paul H. Freedman, *Images of the Medieval Peasant* (Stanford, Calif., 1999), 257–88.

ing the other side, rallying supporters to prevent further acts of cruelty and to avenge past ones, and justifying the use of one's own violence.

Because the wars focused on questions of faith, violence would be mostly seen either through the prism of martyrdom or through that of heresy. Martyrdom provides a context in which violence is almost invariably perceived as cruelty by the victims. And Protestant texts do indeed provide detailed accounts of the massacres, tortures, and executions committed by Catholics. Yet in describing their fellow martyrs, Protestant authors had two problems. The first was doctrinal: One of the principal arguments of reformed theologians against the Roman Catholic Church concerned its cult of the saints. How then could Protestants celebrate their own martyrs? And, in fact, Jean Crespin's martyrology was approved for publication by the Council of Geneva only on condition that the words *martyr* and *saint* be deleted. Yet the need for martyrs and for works celebrating them had the upper hand, and later editions included the forbidden words in their title.[47] The second problem was how to represent the cruelty of the Catholics. This issue was troublesome given that the existing hagiographic discourse of cruelty was primarily Catholic and characterized by sentimental excesses that were also repugnant to Protestant tastes.

The solutions worked out were not as far from their Catholic origins as Protestant authors might have wished. Yet they *are* different from the late medieval and early modern martyrdom accounts examined thus far. I look into two of the most popular and influential Protestant martyrologies: the English *Book of martyrs* by John Foxe (1516–1587) and the French *Histoire des martyrs* by Jean Crespin (1520–1572). Despite some significant differences, the two works share a basic approach to the issue of cruelty that has two prominent characteristics. First, the narration shifts between two modes: A basically factual, *acta*-like, style is interrupted by episodes that are affective and contain numerous explicit references to cruelty. Second, cruelty is presented within a comparative context whose purpose is to create "otherness" in places where it is not self-evident. These stylistic and thematic features point to the problems surrounding the representation of cruelty and to some of the solutions worked out in the early modern period.

Foxe's book, *Acts and Monuments of the Christian Martyrs* in its full name, is a voluminous compilation of martyrdom accounts from the beginning of Christianity to his own day. The first of twelve books deals with the persecutions against early Christians (until Constantine). Foxe's account of the early persecutions is quite straightforward. He follows the ancient Church

47. Leon-Ernst Halkin, "Hagiographie protestante," *Analecta Bollandiana* 68 (1950): 457–58. The approved title was "Recueil de plusieurs personnes qui ont constamment enduré la mort pour le nom de Nostre Seigneur Jésus Christ."

historians, mainly Eusebius, quite closely. This adherence to the sources applies to the issue of cruelty as well.[48] And, similar to the ancient authors, he links cruelty to tyranny.[49]

Opening the work with the early martyrs is essential to Foxe's large underlying argument and is not merely a lip service to tradition. This importance becomes clear from the subject that follows, which is a digression in terms of the traditional martyrological genre. Foxe supplies a brief "History of the Turks," in which he concentrates mainly on demonstrating their cruelty.[50] In the introductory remarks to this section, Foxe states that the Christians are punished by the Turks because they are no better themselves. He does not accuse the Catholics directly, apparently speaking on behalf of all Christians. Yet the implicit accusation is clear.[51] After completing his sketch of Turkish history, Foxe is more systematic and sets before the reader the outline of his argument and the structural function of the pagan and Turkish persecutions within it: The "heathen emperors," the "proud pope," and the "barbarous Turk" are the "the three principal and capital enemies of the church of Christ, signified in the Apocalypse." Their cruelty "against Christ's people hath been such, that to judge which of them did most exceed in cruelty of persecution, it is hard to say."[52] The pagans and the Turks then are the measuring rods of cruelty—two control groups in modern terms—and the cruelty of the Catholics should be appraised within this comparative structure.

How does Foxe depict the cruelty of the Turks in this long and systematic prologue? His relation of the capture of Buda in 1529 is representative and deserves to be quoted at length. It fulfills the dramatic role of a pistol that is seen in the first act of a play and shoots in the last. Foxe proceeds from the Turks to the persecution of Protestants in England, to the

48. Infrequently, Foxe adds some derisive adjectives to his references to the persecutors—for example, "the *outrageous* cruelty of Dioclesian" (Foxe, *Acts and Monuments*, ed. Stephen R. Cattley [London, 1891], 1:224).

49. For instance, "And thus far continued wicked Valerian in his tyranny against the saints of Christ. But as all the tyrants before" (ibid., 1:215).

50. The denomination "brief" is perhaps misleading; it occupies about one hundred pages in the cited edition, but it is brief in relation to the size of the whole work.

51. We fight against a persecutor, being no less persecutors ourselves. We wrestle against a bloody tyrant, and our hands be full of blood as his. He killeth Christ's people with the sword, and we burn them with fire . . . The Turk has prevailed so mightily not because Christ is weak, but because Christians be wicked, and their doctrine impure. Our temples with images, our hearts with idolatry are polluted (Foxe, *Acts and Monuments*, 4:19).

52. Ibid., 4:79. Foxe does not explicitly declare here that he considers the Catholic Church more cruel; yet he proceeds to prove that the Pope is more likely to be the Antichrist than the Turks.

persecutions in the Continent, and to the isle of Guernsey, where the significance of the following passage on the Turks will finally become apparent:

> The Turk . . . recovering again the city of Buda . . . removed his army into Austria . . . showing many examples of great cruelty and tyranny most lamentable to hear and understand. For of some he put out their eyes, some he cut off their hands, of some their ears and noses; and their children he shamefully mutilated. The maidens he corrupted, the matrons had their breasts cut off, and such as were with child were ripped, and their children cast into the fire. And these examples of horrible and barbarous tyranny this wretched Turk perpetrated by the way coming toward Vienna . . . besides the captives which he took by the way and led into servitude most miserable, amounting to the number of thirty thousand.[53]

Foxe refers explicitly and affectively to the cruelty of the Turks. Having by now established his comparative scheme, he does not have to refer explicitly to the cruelty of the English persecutors. With the logic of a syllogism, if what the Turks do is cruel, and what the English do is similar to what the Turks or the pagans do (or worse), then what the English do is also cruel.

Adopting this solution to the problem of style, Foxe can use a factual and detached narration for the *Acts* of his English martyrs. The word *acts*, which came to be part of the book's title, is apt because the stories of the persecuted Englishmen resemble the ancient *acta* of the early martyrs. Foxe's *Acts* contain protocols, letters, and other documents.[54] This similarity is also part of Foxe's structure and is related to his scheme of comparative cruelty. By establishing that the acts are similar to those of the ancient martyrs, he implies that the martyrs themselves are similar to their ancestors and that their persecutors are similar to the pagan persecutors.

The second act of Foxe's narrative of cruelty[55] describes the persecutions against the English Protestants. References to cruelty are not a significant component of these accounts. Thus, Foxe factually describes how the

---

53. Ibid., 4:54.

54. Documents were inserted into early Christian martyrdom accounts. See, for instance, the "Letter of the Churches of Lyons and Vienne" and the "Letter of Phileas" incorporated in Eusebius's *Historia ecclesiastica* and the account purportedly written by Perpetua herself and incorporated in *The Martyrdom of Perpetua and Felicitas*. On Foxe's ideologically oriented editing of the original documents written by the English martyrs, see Susan Wabuda, "Henry Bull, Miles Coverdale, and the Making of Foxe's *Book of Martyrs*," in *Martyrs and Martyrologies*, ed. Diana Wood (*Studies in Church History* 30) (Oxford, 1993), 245–58.

55. As distinguished from his chronological narrative.

daughter of William Tylsworth "was compelled with her own hands to set fire to her dear father; and at the same time her husband John Clerk did penance at her father's burning, and bare a faggot."[56] Even when explicit lexical references to cruelty exist, their number is insignificant in relation to the length of the account.[57] Foxe does not dwell in general on the physical violence attending martyrdom. In a polemic defending one of his martyrs' eligibility for the title, he remarks, "the cause be it, and not the pain, that maketh a martyr," thus emphasizing intentions rather than actions.

Yet the instances in which Foxe deviates from this mode of narration are significant because they shed light on how he perceived the relation between cruelty and the "other," and they present a more explicit form of representing cruelty. Thus, for instance, he describes the martyrdom of John Clerk, who was executed in Metz by being dismembered while still alive and then burnt.[58] Foxe quotes from an account by Johannes Oecolampadius (1482–1531) relating the execution of a priest in Germany, which ends with an appraisal: "This is the truth of this most cruel act, which a Turk would scarcely have committed against his mortal enemy."[59] Many detailed instances of cruelty, which are explicitly labeled as such, can be found in Foxe's rendering of a French account entitled *A notable history of the persecution and destruction of the people of Merindol and Cabriers, in the country of Provence: where not a few persons, but whole villages and townships, with the most part of all the aforesaid country, both men, women, and children, were put to all kinds of cruelty, and suffered martyrdom for the profession of the gospel.*[60] The cruelty practiced against the Protestants is described in terms of the cruelty of the "other": As ordered by the Pope's legate, the soldiers massacred indiscriminately, raped, killed babies, and cut the mothers' breasts so that babies who were still alive would die of hunger. Foxe explicitly compares the cruelty of the Catholics to that of the Turks: "no otherwise than the infidels and cruel Turks have dealt with the Christians, as before in the story of the Turks you may read. For as the papists and Turks are alike in their religion; so are the papists like, or rather exceed them in all kinds of cruelty than can be devised."[61] Foxe links the cruelty of the Catholics to the inval-

56. Foxe, *Acts and Monuments*, 4:123.

57. The account devoted to Richard Hun, for instance, is twenty-two pages long in the edition cited here (ibid., 4:183–205); it contains references to cruel laws, the clergy's cruel tyranny, cruelly, cruel murderers, and cruelly oppressed (4:183, 183, 185, 197, 198, respectively).

58. Ibid., 4:361.

59. Ibid., 4:366.

60. Ibid., 4:474–507; note the length of this account.

61. Ibid., 4:500.

idity of their religion and sums up by characterizing their cruelty as tyranny, another delegitimizing move.

There seems to be a system underlying Foxe's stylistic fluctuations. The more explicit accounts—in relation to cruelty—refer to action that takes place on the Continent, not in England. But although this tendency is quite consistent, it is nevertheless puzzling, because his subject is the persecution in England. There may be several explanations for this anomaly. On the factual level, the persecutions in England may have been less violent than those on the Continent in the sense that the victims were executed according to the law without the "extras" of torture, mutilation, massacres, and the like. In England, unlike other regions of Western Europe, there was no geographical division between the two religions, and therefore wholesale massacres of towns or villages were not practiced. Foxe's reserve in demonizing the persecutors of the English martyrs may have also been influenced to some degree by the Protestants' tendency to present themselves as loyal subjects and their reluctance to be seen as traitors, a tendency that may have tempered their criticism of the authorities.[62] In any case, raising the issue of tyranny, which Foxe did, was subversive enough in itself, and political prudence may have been the cause for his relative lack of elaboration concerning cruelty.

However, in accounting for this dual mode of representation, I focus on Foxe's perception of cruelty as a quality of the "other." In addition to the factors enumerated above—as in the accounts of the Merovingian martyrs and the martyrs of Cordova—the everyday familiarity with the persecutors was an obstacle to presenting them as "other." Thus, the extent to which cruelty is represented depends on the degree of "otherness" that can be attributed to its perpetrator. This attribution, in turn, is determined by Foxe's (or the reader's) cultural and geographic distance from the perpetrators of cruelty.

The important role of "otherness" in Foxe's accounts of cruelty can be observed when he deals with an incident that occurs literally on the border—that is, on the isle of Guernsey. Here we have finally reached the final act of Foxe's presentation, which looks back to the account of the Turkish massacre in Buda. When he introduces the case, Foxe once more places cruelty in a comparative scheme:

> Amongst all and singular histories touched in this book before, as there be
> many pitiful, divers lamentable, some horrible and tragical; so is there none
> almost either in cruelty to be compared, or so far off from all compassion

62. See David Loades, "John Foxe and the Traitors: The Politics of the Marian Persecution," in *Martyrs and Martyrologies*, 231–44.

and sense of humanity, as this merciless fact of the papists, done in the Isle of Guernsey.[63]

Three women, one of whom was pregnant, were accused of heresy and consequently burned at the stake. The pregnant woman, who was in a late stage of her pregnancy, fell down and gave birth to a male baby. He was removed from the place and sent to the provost and then to the bailiff. The latter ordered him to be placed back in the fire

> where it was burnt with the silly[64] mother, grandmother, and aunt, very pitiful to behold. And so the infant baptized in his own blood, to fill up the number of God's innocent saints, was both born and died a martyr, leaving behind to the world, which it never saw, a spectacle wherein the whole world may see the *Herodian cruelty* of this graceless generation of catholic tormentors, ad perpetuam rei infamiam.[65]

This account is one of the rare instances in which cruelty is described and discussed to that length and in such an explicit manner concerning an English martyr. The peculiar aspect of this incident, however, is that it does not really occur in England: It takes place on the border. The liminal status of the island between "us" and the "other" is reflected in Foxe's taking the trouble to explain that "the isle of Guernsey . . . is a member of England" and in his statement that some of the eyewitness accounts were in English and some in French.[66] The comparative frame in which Foxe places his work presents an analogy to this incident: In the section devoted to the Turks, Foxe reported that during the conquest of Buda "such [matrons] as were with child were ripped, and their children cast into the fire." The link may have not been necessarily intended but probably did lie in the back of Foxe's mind when he wrote about the cruelty of the Turks.

Central to Foxe's representation of cruelty is the comparative scheme and its use for projecting "otherness." Foxe cannot represent the English Catholics as "other," and for reasons already mentioned does not necessarily want to use an affective and explicit mode of reference to cruelty in rela-

63. Foxe, *Acts and Monuments*, 4:226. The title also refers to the cruelty of the event: "A tragical, Lamentable, and Pitiful History, full of most Cruel and Tyrannical Murder, done by the pretensed catholics upon three women and an infant; to wit, the mother, her two daughters, and the child, in the Isle of Guernsey, for Christ's true religion, July 18, the year of our Lord 1556." Note that the title links, once more, cruelty and tyranny.

64. The word *silly* here has the sense of "worthy of pity, compassion" or "helpless" [Oxford English Dictionary (Oxford, 1961[1933]), 9, 50–51].

65. Foxe, *Acts and Monuments*, 8:226, 230 (italics mine).

66. Ibid., 8:226, 230.

tion to them. But, nevertheless, he does want to make the point that they are as cruel as pagan, Turkish, or Continental Catholic persecutors. The comparative scheme he has drawn at the outset projects this "otherness" on the English Catholics, and the similarity is reinforced through analogous incidents. Thus it is true that there are gradations of "otherness," but nevertheless the point of Foxe's structure is to state or to prove that as persecutors, the English Catholics are as bad as any in the past or in the present. In his description of "real others," Foxe continues the late medieval tradition of representing cruelty. But the context of this tradition changes: It is no more the default option but one choice among others that are used in a more complex comparative structure. In this way, a factual narrative may have its explicitly cruel counterpart pages, and even volumes, apart.

Jean Crespin's *Histoire des martyrs* is nearly contemporary to Foxe's work. Similar to Foxe's work, it was published in several editions over a great number of years before it attained its final form. The first edition was published in 1554, the last in 1619. The structure and scope of the two works is similar: Crespin also starts with the martyrs of the early Church and then proceeds through a brief summary of Muslim history to the Turks. The pagans and the Turks have the same function as in Foxe's martyrology. Crespin is much briefer in these sections but is blunter as to their purpose. He stresses the conformity of the later martyrs to those of the early Church, and immediately after the section on the Turks, he switches to the "last persecution started and continued by the popes," stating that "the persecution of the Popes accompanies that of the Turks. It is much more dangerous . . . and much more cruel, since it is exercised by those who should have been the most peaceful and most sincere in their Christian faith."[67]

Crespin is much more explicit in his representations of the French Catholics' cruelty. His lexical references to cruelty are more numerous, his tone is more affective, and he emphasizes much more than Foxe that the Catholics enjoy their cruelty. Besides the numerous references to cruelty in the text, many of Crespin's titles, subtitles, and margin headings refer to cruelty, thus pointing to the importance of the issue.[68] The difference between Crespin and Foxe, as was suggested earlier, is related to the greater violence

67. Jean Crespin, *Histoire des martyrs* (1619 edition), ed. D. Benoit (Paris, 1885–1889), 1:37.

68. Crespin has titles such as "Histoire memorable des cruautez enormes commises en la personne d'Antoine de Richieud, Seigneur de Mouvans, et autres notables personnages persecutez et cruellement meurtris en la haute Provence, pour la Parole de Dieu" (*Histoire des martyrs*, 2:765); see also 2:263. On cruelty in the text, see for instance 3:267–72.

used against Protestants in France (as compared with England). Most of the martyrs whom Foxe celebrates were executed following an orderly judicial process, and the amount of physical violence used in their interrogations and executions does not seem extraordinary. Torture was not introduced into the English legal procedure at the time that it was adopted on the Continent—that is, in the central Middle Ages. It *was* introduced in the sixteenth and seventeenth centuries but even then only rarely, mainly in cases of political crimes such as treason or sedition.[69] Foxe's leaning toward the technique of *showing* (whereas Crespin favors more explicit *telling*) also determines the relative significance of the Turks in the two narratives. They are central to Foxe because of his choice of narrative technique: The comparison to the Turks is the most effective pointer to the cruelty of the English Catholics.

The Catholics' enjoyment of their cruelty is central to the way Crespin portrays them. The introductory sonnet of the 1564 edition opens with these verses: "O beautiful subject of new cruelty / for those which take pleasure only in cruelty" and ends by referring to the wish to torture the martyrs even more severely "so that now you will have what to content yourself with."[70] Describing the gradual dismemberment of Bertrand le Blas of Tournay, Crespin remarks that the persecutors gloried in this "cruel spectacle."[71] Another aspect of cruelty is the reference to the perpetrators of cruelty as Scythians and cannibals.[72]

Crespin's overall tone is more affective than Foxe's. He relates that after the massacre of Protestants in Meaux the Catholics also destroyed the bridge "for fear that the stones themselves will testify to their cruelty . . . bloodied by the blood of innocents."[73] This tendency is even more evident when he describes in detail a specific incident, such as the massacre of the Protestant community of Brossardière by Catholic soldiers during the Sunday prayers of August 13, 1595. Crespin emphasizes the premeditated aspect of this incident, claiming that the soldiers resolved to massacre even

---

69. Edward Peters, *Torture* (New York, 1985), 58–59, 70, 79–80.

70. Crespin seems to be ironic here, referring both to people who actually enjoy the torture of the martyrs and people who like to read about it, who are probably Protestants: "O beau suiect de cruauté nouuelle / Pour ceux qui n'ont qu'en cruauté plaisir. . . . Que vous voudriez . . . plus fort les tourmenter / Or auez vous de quoy vous contenter / Les rebruslans tous vivans dans ce liure." (*Histoire des martyrs*, 3:899).

71. Ibid., 2:315. Foxe has only an abridged account of this martyrdom, which therefore cannot be compared to Crespin's. Yet he does not refer explicitly to the cruelty of Bertrand's execution.

72. "Scythes barbares," "ces Scythes," and "anthropophages" (Crespin, *Histoire des martyrs*, 3:897).

73. Ibid., 3:272.

the little children before they reached Brossardière.[74] Concerning the massacre itself he writes,

> . . .without any remorse, and without being touched by any pity, commiseration and natural affection, which even brute beasts have, they killed and cruelly murdered with blows of the sword, all men and children which they could find, and of any age and condition, this in presence of a good number of maidens, bourgeois women, and other women and maidens.[75]

The affective character of the passage is created by the repetitions of expressions or words with similar meaning, which are in themselves phrased hyperbolically (by the use of the adjective *any* [*aucun*]). Similar expressions are scattered throughout the narrative: for example, "vn si piteux & deplorable massacres," "telle cruauté & barbarie," "pour n'obmettre aucune sorte de cruauté." The authenticity of the account relating to Brossardière is enhanced by containing a detailed list of all the victims under categories such as "The names of those which were massacred outside the assembly place" or "The names of the wounded women."

It is Crespin's terminology more than his general thematic focus and imagery, however, that points to new aspects in the early modern treatment of cruelty. First, Crespin implicitly posits *humanity* and *cruelty* as a set of antonyms by using *inhumanity* as a synonym for cruelty.[76] This lexical choice is characteristically early modern: Ficino, for instance, sets in one of his Latin letters *humanitas* (humanity) as the opposite of *crudelitas*. Legal tracts, such as the *Tractatus de indiciis & tortura* (*Treatise on evidence and torture*) published in 1493 by Francesco Bruni, reflect the same spirit. This adaptation of the medieval *Tractatus de tormentis* (*Treatise on Tortures*) speaks at greater length than its predecessors on the judge's duty to act with moderation rather than "without restraint and inhumanely [*inhumane*]."[77] This development is linked to processes described in more detail in Chapter 1, mainly the rising importance of the body and of the physical aspects of existence and the way they were related to the issue of cruelty in the early modern period.[78]

74. Ibid., 3:885.
75. Ibid., 3:885.
76. For the interchangeable use of these terms see, for instance, ibid., 1:251 (on the execution of a German priest); 1:385 (the Turks characterized as cruel and inhuman); and 3:887, 889 (the list of victims in Brossardière, and the presumed murder of the priest there).
77. See Chapter 1, 27.
78. A corollary to that is the relatively minor place of *inhumanitas* as a synonym for cruelty in the medieval period. *Inhumanitas* (as a noun) appears in the *Patrologia Latina* 144 times. In comparison, *crudelitas* appears 2,936 times; *saevitia* appears 1,261 times; *ferocitas* appears 470 times; and *atrocitas* appears 315 times.

The other prominent aspect of Crespin's terminology is his frequent use of the plural form of cruelty (*cruautez* [cruelties]).[79] The reference to cruelty in plural was relatively rare in the Middle Ages, and Crespin's use of it was part of what seems to have been a general increase in the frequency of its use in the early modern period. Thus, for instance, the section on the Jews in Alfonso de Espina's *Fortalicium fidei* (*Fortress of Faith*) is entitled "On the cruelties of the Jews" [*de iudeorum crudelitatibus*].[80] The main purpose of the use of this form is to indicate that more than one kind of cruelty was practiced.[81] The invention of new modes of torture and variation of several types of torture were, since late antiquity, a sign that judicial violence had turned into cruelty. In this sense, the plural form emphasizes the cruelty of the Catholics and links the present martyrdoms to those of antiquity. But beyond that, it seems to be part of an effort, similar to the list of victims, to make cruelty less abstract and indicate that it consisted of a variety of different actions.

Moreover, in the sources examined thus far, from Tiberino to Crespin, one can detect as an undercurrent the most revolutionary aspect of the early modern approach, even if it is not yet openly manifest. This is a tendency to reify cruelty by making it an objective category and by quantifying it. Thus it does not seem accidental that the promoter of Simon of Trent to sainthood was a doctor. His voice was influential because it was the opinion of a professional on a matter in his field—that is, examining a victim of physical violence. The comparative scheme set by Foxe and Crespin for examining cruelty is another way of objectifying cruelty and making its examination scientific. Likewise, the lists of victims and the use of *cruelties* (in the plural) serve the same purpose of making the representation of cruelty less abstract and more tangible.

The most drastic steps in the direction of objectifying cruelty were taken by two people: Michel de Montaigne and Jean de Léry. Montaigne, as we have seen, reifies cruelty in several ways. He attributes this quality to himself and associates it also with more mundane everyday activities, such as hunting,

79. "Cruautez & oppressions tyranniques" (preface to the 1554 edition, Crespin, *Histoire des martyrs*, 1:xxxiii); "les cruautez, vilenies, & meschancetez" (1:35); "telles cruautez" (1:37); "cruautez & tyrannies" (1:417); "vne cruauté non vsitee" (1:418); "cruautez enormes" (2:765); "infinies cruautez" (3:267); "cruautez" (3:268); "leurs cruautez" (3:272); "se soumist à toutes leurs felonnies & cruautez" (3:891).

80. De Espina, *Fortalicium fidei*, 141r.

81. For instance, "pour n'obmettre aucune sorte de cruauté," "quelque espece de cruauté," "toute sorte de cruauté," and "pour comble de leurs cruautez" (all taken from the account of the massacre at Brossardière, Crespin, *Histoire des martyrs*, 3:885–89).

and not only with large-scale massacres. He, too, discusses cruelty in a comparative context. But most of all, it is Montaigne's ethical framework, which is based primarily on the judgment of actual action and not solely on intention, that turns cruelty into a less abstract issue. Cruelty is set by Montaigne as an objective entity. Medieval approaches to cruelty were much more relativistic and open to manipulation: Violence prompted by commendable intentions was not cruelty; only violence that could not be justified in this manner was defined as cruelty.

In an appendix to his *Histoire d'un voyage en terre de Brésil* (*History of a Voyage to the Land of Brazil*), Jean de Léry (1534–1613) unites the thematic strands discussed thus far. Léry refers both to the Europeans' treatment of the natives in the New World and to the wars of religion, and moreover, he explicitly links the two. Léry, a Calvinist, writes about both issues from personal experience: He spent more than two years in a Protestant colony near present-day Rio de Janeiro and in 1558 returned from the New World to Geneva. His account was first published in 1578.

The fifteenth chapter of Léry's account is entitled "How the Americans treat their prisoners taken at war, and the ceremonies which they observe both for killing them and for eating them." In the third edition of 1585, Léry enlarged this chapter to include accounts of cruelty from the Old World. In the fourth edition of 1599, this comparative section was given a more prominent place as a separate appendix entitled "On the cruelties exercised by the Turks and other people: and namely by the Spaniards, much more barbarous than even the savages [of the New World]."[82]

The novelty of this text when compared with medieval representations of cruelty is striking, despite the many points of similarity that are highlighted below. There is no parallel medieval text whose declared subject is cruelty and that piles up various deeds of cruelty at such length.[83] The purpose of this catalogue of atrocities is also novel, a comparative examination of cruelty per se. This is evidently not a detached scientific study, and its author had ulterior purposes that are discussed later, but it is a study nonetheless. Léry himself points out the comparative structure of his text:

> . . . finally, making a comparison between cruelty and cruelty, let us make now three pictures each joined to the other. In the first our Brazilian savages

82. "Des cruautez exercées par les Turcs, et autres peuples: et nommément par les Espagnols, beaucoup plus barbares que les Sauvages mesmes" (Jean de Léry, *Histoire d'un voyage en terre de Brésil*, ed. Frank Lestringant [Paris, 1994], 571 [hereafter cited as *Voyage en terre de Brésil*]).

83. Twenty-five pages (571–95) in the edition cited here.

are vividly represented . . . In the second [picture] are portrayed Turacan with his turban, ordering the building of his pyramid of human heads . . . Then a third [picture] where you will see the furious bedevilled French, breaking all the laws of nature.[84]

Léry dealt with the cruelty of the natives of Brazil in a previous chapter (chap. 15), presenting it as an aggravated form of cannibalism. The natives eat the flesh of their enemies and do not spare even little children.[85] The comparison with the two other groups, the Turks and the French, is likewise made in the context of war. Many of the characteristics of cruelty as depicted by Léry are identical to the medieval descriptions of cruelty in the same contexts. Léry emphasizes repeatedly, both for the Turks and for the French in the wars of religion, excessive violence that is manifested in the massacre of women and children.[86] Similar to Montaigne, Léry considers anything beyond a straightforward execution as cruelty and supplies instances of elaborate executions committed by the Turks.[87]

In addition to the excessive nature of the violence committed, the victimizers' pleasure is also emphasized by Léry. This emphasis is manifested in the artful invention of new modes of torture and execution. Some of the Turks derive aesthetic satisfaction from their actions: "Turacan" decapitates his prisoners and arranges the bodies in the form of a pyramid; "Amurat" buys 600 of the most beautiful Greek prisoners for a ritual sacrifice.

Cruelty in the context of tyranny is also attributed to the Turks, and it is exemplified by the career of Uladus, the ruler of Moldavia, and his ways of doing away with his real or suspected enemies. The characteristics of this type of cruelty are similar to those of cruelty in the context of war, however, with one aggravating circumstance: that it is directed against the ruler's own subjects and not against his enemies.[88]

Having arranged the section on the Turks in order of ascending cruelty, Léry concludes that the Turks are more cruel than the native Brazilians.

84. *Voyage en terre de Brésil*, 584–85.

85. Ibid., 369–70.

86. "Jusques aux femmes et petit enfans," "jusques aux femmes et petit enfans qui estoyent encores dans le berceau," "car il y avoit jusques à des petites creatures executées, mesmes aux mammelles de leurs meres où elles avoyent esté estranglées," "Mais, ô choses du tout espouvantables, les petis enfants n'ont-ils pas esté rostis. . ." (ibid., 575, 576, 576, 582, respectively).

87. Léry introduces one of Emperor Mechmet's acts of cruelty in the following manner: ". . . n'estant pas content de faire passer au fil de glaive tous ceux de la pluspart des villes et chasteaux qu'il prenoit. . ." (ibid., 573). For Montaigne, see Chapter 1, 25.

88. . . . le carnage qu'Uladus avoit fait de ses propres subjects (*Voyage en terre de Brésil*, 576).

What makes them so? The inventiveness in devising the acts of cruelty, the pleasure derived from them, and the fact that they are not addressed only at the enemy. In addition, it is implied that the large scale of the atrocities is also one of the characteristics of the Turkish cruelty, which makes it worse than that of the Brazilians.

Léry concludes the section on the Turks with the comment that perhaps one should not expect the "unnatural" Turks to be better than the Brazilian cannibals. This statement serves as a convenient bridge to his next subject: "What happens between us that call ourselves Christians?"[89]

Cruelty in the wars of religion, claims Léry, referring of course to cruelty committed by the Catholics, is even worse than the cruelty of the Turks. It is similar in the large scale of the carnage and in its indiscriminate nature, not sparing women and children.[90] It has, however, two additional aspects that make it infinitely worse than the cruelty of the Turks. One is the widespread practice of cannibalism, reflected in instances of eating the heart and liver of the enemies and roasting little children "like suckling piglets."[91] Thus the cruelty of the wars of religion combines the cruelty of the Turks and that of the Brazilians. But its second and worse aspect is its internal nature; it is not directed against an enemy nation. The Frenchmen do not commit these acts against an enemy nation but "bathe in the blood of their relatives, neighbors, and compatriots."[92]

Léry concludes his declared threefold structure with an additional element, which he adds to his comparative scheme (of Brazilians, Turks, and Catholics). In this section, Léry presents what he considers the purest form of cruelty, which he attributes to the Spaniards. The rhetorical effect of this fourth section is due, in part, to the fact that its appearance is a surprise. Léry carefully presents the outline of his discussion at the beginning of this appendix but describes it as tripartite.[93] This unexpected fourth category brings about a dramatic reversal because its victims are the villains of the first picture: the natives of America. In this manner, Léry emphasizes the magnitude of the Spaniards' cruelty, which is perpetrated with no apparent reason aside from the pleasure they derive from it. This cruelty is not even the outcome of rage or war but is a result of a total dehumanization of the natives; they are treated by the Spanish as objects or livestock—that is, food for their dogs. Léry relates how the Spaniards used to joke, saying "lend me

89. Ibid., 578.
90. Some of the descriptions recall accounts of the Jacquerie, particularly the torture of women in front of their children.
91. Comme couchons de laict (*Voyage en terre de Brésil*, 586).
92. Ibid., 587.
93. See above, 168–69.

a quarter of your Viellaco [native] . . . to give to my dog, and when I kill one of my own, I will return the like to you."[94] Feeding dogs with people is presented as an even lower moral degree than cannibalism, thus contrasting again the Spaniards with the Brazilians. These accusations recall similar ones against the Mongols: Matthew Paris claimed that the less beautiful captive women were treated by the Mongols as livestock; the Armenian chronicler Grigor of Akanc' reported that the Mongols fed their dogs with prisoners.

In fact, most of the materials used by Léry exist already in medieval representations of cruelty: pleasure from cruelty; tyranny; and excess, manifested in the torture and murder of women and children. Even the images used are medieval.[95] Likewise, the comparison of the rival with the other is also a medieval technique, noted already in the context of the Jacquerie.

Yet when one compares Léry's text with medieval representations of cruelty, it is evident that a drastic change has taken place. Most apparently, cruelty emerges as a subject worthy of discussion and, moreover, is incorporated in a quasi-scientific comparative context. Both aspects of this change are unparalleled in the Middle Ages. The medieval references and comparisons to the cruelty of the "other" are different in nature. Cruelty is one of the attributes assigned to the enemy, and although it may be an important one, it is not the main subject of discussion; it is always a by-product of the religious or ideological rivalry. Comparisons are essentially simple when they are made. Usually they are bipolar, between the virtuous "us" and the cruel "other." At most, they are tripolar, and even then the comparison is made only as a rhetorical device whose aim is to present the rival as even worse than a dreaded "other."[96] In the rare comparisons made by medieval authors between the cruelty of the ingroup and that of an outgroup, the purpose of the comparison is purely apologetic—that is, to claim that the actions of the ingroup are *not* cruelty. Foxe and Crespin are closer to Léry in their comparative treatment of cruelty, but neither of them makes this comparison per se on the declarative level, and it is on a much more limited scope than Léry's discussion.

Léry presents a novel and elaborate tripartite comparison and supplies numerous details to back up his claims of cruelty. Moreover, he reveals the

94. *Voyage en terre de Brésil*, 592. Montaigne, too, had an ambivalent view of the cannibal natives, especially when compared with the behavior of the Europeans in America; see Michel de Certeau, "Le lieu de l'autre. Montaigne: 'Des Cannibales,'" in *Le racisme: mythes et sciences*, ed. Maurice Olender (Brussels, 1981), 187–200.

95. Wishing to emphasize that the cruelty of the wars of religion is worse than any preceding it, Léry quotes the following rhyme with its list of stock medieval figures of cruelty "Riez Pharaon / Achab, et Neron / Herodes aussi / Vostre Barbarie / Est ensevelie / Par ce faict ici" (*Voyage en terre de Brésil*, 587).

96. Such is the case in the accounts of the Jacquerie in which both sides accused each other of being worse than the Saracens.

scale and the criteria that are the basis of his presentation. In his comparative endeavor, Léry breaks cruelty down into its single components and
enumerates which of them is present for each of the societies he analyzes.
Thus, it is easily understandable why the cruelty of the Catholic French is
worse than that of the native Brazilians; it combines the cruelty of the Turks
with that of the Brazilians and, furthermore, is directed inwardly.

In this manner, Léry provides a scale for the *quantification* of cruelty. The
number of victims is an important aspect of this quantification. Thus he
writes that the Spaniards "have depopulated in the Western Indies more
countries than Europe contains, having already killed more than fifteen
million souls before the abovementioned author left [for the New World],
which was around 1542."[97] Léry is careful here to present detailed facts
about the magnitude of the massacre of the native population in America by
the Spanish, which is a central element in his claim that Spanish cruelty is
the worst form of cruelty. He is careful to state the number of victims and the
year to which this figure holds true, and he provides a scale for comparison
with Europe.

The quantification of cruelty, which is perhaps the single most important
element in the new mode of reference to cruelty, enables Léry to deal directly
with accusations that the Protestants also committed atrocities: "But someone
of the Roman Catholic Church may say: you accuse our [people] of everything, without dealing at all with those of your religion. How is that? Were
they angels while they had arms in their fists?"[98] Léry's response to this is
mainly quantitative: The Protestants *were* less cruel than their rivals, and he
proceeds to explain why. They were less cruel, and thus morally superior to
the Catholics when the conflict started; they degenerated only at a later stage
as a reaction to Catholic cruelty. In addition, he attributes cruelty only to
individual Protestants, not to the Protestants as a group. This way, he quanti-
fies cruelty by limiting the number of its perpetrators.[99] The fourth picture,
depicting the cruelty of the Spaniards, renders the cruelty of the Protestants
insignificant. The figures supplied by Léry regarding the victims of Spaniards
make it impossible for Protestants to match their feat.

The quantification of cruelty is linked to the early modern tendency to
reify and objectify cruelty, a tendency that has been observed in other types
of reference to the subject.[100] But quantification directly influences impor-

97. *Voyage en terre de Brésil*, 593.
98. Ibid., 587.
99. . . . je ne veux pas nier que plusieurs incorrigibles ne soyent devenues comme
Diables (ibid., 587–8). Admitting one's own guilt, as Denis Crouzet remarks in relation
to Léry's account of the siege of Sancerre, lends credibility to accusations against the
other side (*Les guerriers de Dieu* [Paris, 1990], 2:162).

tant aspects of the treatment and representation of cruelty. Cruelty becomes much more physical and detailed. The medieval concern for intentions is only a minor consideration when cruelty has to be measured; the specific actions and figures are much more important. Quantification is almost meaningless when one considers intentions: From this point of view, it does not matter if the torturer exercises his art on one person, on ten, or on a thousand. That is also the reason that practically all of Léry's examples involve masses of victims. Thus, intentions are marginal to Léry's reference to Protestant cruelty (Léry uses the expression "such a good cause managed badly").[101]

This process is closely related to other fifteenth- and sixteenth-century developments. Accurate and detailed descriptions of cruelty are part of the general tendency toward a closer observation of natural phenomena, which existed in the sciences and in the plastic arts. The idea of quantification, however, is even more closely related to mathematical developments that occurred in the late sixteenth and early seventeenth centuries. Quantification is related to the development of arithmetic and especially of probability, a science based on sampling and concerned with concepts such as evidence and degrees of belief. These concepts are also central to this new, relativistic perception of cruelty. This relationship between mathematical developments and contemporary cultural concepts has been studied by Ian Hacking and Barbara Shapiro.[102] Likewise, the diffusion of this quantitative mode of thinking has been noticed also in the assessment of legal evidence, where "accumulation" of evidence was sometimes considered sufficient even if "full proof" was lacking.[103]

It is significant that some characteristics of Léry's treatment of cruelty were shared by Montaigne, who was Catholic. In Montaigne's writings, we find the same focus on the physical, the view that the worst kind of cruelty is that committed for pleasure, and the focus on the actions themselves rather than on intentions. These common premises lead the two writers to similar conclusions—for example, to consider as cruelty anything beyond a "straightforward" execution.[104] In the context of opposition between old

100. See above, 167.

101. "Une si bonne cause mal menée" (*Voyage en terre de Brésil*, 588).

102. Ian Hacking, *The Emergence of Probability* (Cambridge, 1975), 1–48; Ian Hacking, "From the Emergence of Probability to the Erosion of Determinism," in *Probabilistic Thinking, Thermodynamics and the Interaction of the History and Philosophy of Science*, ed. Jaakko Hintikka, David C. Gruender, and Evandro Agazzi (Dordrecht, 1981) 2:105–23; and Barbara J. Shapiro, *Probability and Certainty in Seventeenth-Century England* (Princeton, N.J., 1983), 105ff. (on moral probabilism).

103. Anders Hald, *A History of Probability and Statistics and Their Applications before 1750* (New York, 1990), 32.

and new paradigms of cruelty, it is worth noting that the Roman censor who read Montaigne's essays found this particular point objectionable.[105] The source of the objection was probably not so much the effort to limit the violence but the setting of an absolute, nonrelative limit.

Nevertheless, the agreement between Montaigne and Léry, despite their cultural and religious differences, shows that the new mode of reference to cruelty prevailed. It indicates that these characteristics are indeed the pivotal points of reference in the reworking of medieval materials (sometimes by reversal) into a new mode of representing and thinking about cruelty in the early modern period.

The move to make the concept of cruelty more objective, reified, and less abstract is perhaps the most significant shift away from the medieval conceptions of cruelty. Now, cruelty could be graded: Some actions, historical situations, persons, or social groups could be characterized as more, or less, cruel than others. This ranking was achieved by quantifying cruelty according to different criteria: comparative, numerical, or other. A closely related phenomenon is the increasing dominance of actions (rather than intentions) in early modern ethics. From the point of view of an intentions-oriented ethic, it does not matter if a murderer kills one person or a hundred; from the perspective of an action-oriented ethic, it makes all the difference.

These developments did not simply transform cruelty from an absolute concept to a relative one, however. In a sense, the opposite is true. Although from a medieval perspective killing even one person for pleasure is cruel, killing a hundred people because they are heretics is not. Thus, paradoxically, the apparent relativization of cruelty had the effect of setting some absolute categories. When violence reached a critical mass, it would be considered invariably cruel, which is what enables Léry and Montaigne to conclude, independently, that any execution that is not swift and straightforward is cruel.

This process had more mundane and less theoretical aspects. Late medieval and early modern representations of cruelty became increasingly and unsettlingly detailed. This change is evident in all the types of sources examined here. This tendency can be observed in iconographic sources as well. The detailed representations of judiciary violence in the late Middle

104. See note 87, above.

105. Montaigne, *Journal de voyage en Italie*, in *Oeuvres complètes*, ed. Albert Thibaudet and Maurice Rat (Paris, 1962), 1229; English translation: *The Complete Works of Montaigne*, trans. Donald M. Frame (Stanford, Calif., 1943), 955. This episode is mentioned in Maryanne C. Horowitz, *Seeds of Virtue and Knowledge* (Princeton, N.J., 1998), 220.

Ages and early Renaissance have been noted by Samuel Y. Edgerton.[106] This change in representation was no doubt due in part to the increasing realism of painting in general, and not only to changes in the perception of cruelty. But the new iconographic mode of reference to cruelty is even clearer in the representation of Jews and of Roman soldiers in scenes related to the Crucifixion or to the Massacre of the Innocents. In Ruth Mellinkoff's study of the representation of the "other" in late medieval painting, there are several examples that emphasize the pleasure of the victimizers by representing them smiling or grinning. This pleasure is particularly evident in the portrayal of the smiling Jews in the *Crucifixion* of Conrad Laib (ca. 1449) and of the soldier transfixing a baby in the *Murder of the Innocents* from the St. Lawrence Church in Nuremberg (ca. 1460–1465).[107]

Cannibalism as a manifestation of cruelty starts to figure significantly in thirteenth century sources, mainly those that refer to the Mongols. In the early modern period, cannibalism plays an increasingly significant role in textual and iconographic representations of cruelty. The image of cannibalism is an important aspect of the Latin classical culture revived in the late Middle Ages, mainly Ovid's *Metamorphoses* and Seneca's tragedies. This development cannot be attributed solely to cultural processes, however. The preoccupation with cannibalism in the fifteenth and sixteenth centuries is partly the result of the discovery that some of the New World peoples were cannibals. It is also linked to the violence practiced in the wars of religion. Actual cannibalism seems to have been more common in those wars than it was in the Jacquerie, for instance. It is difficult to assign causal relationship here: whether actual cannibalism was more common because the cultural image of cannibalism was more current, or whether culture had only a mimetic function in this case. It seems plausible to assume a two-way relationship between the cultural images and historical events. Such a linkage appears to be vivid enough three centuries later, in a case that shows how the image of cannibalism persists much beyond its actual practice. Alain Corbin studied the murder case of a young French nobleman for allegedly voicing republican sentiments in the village of Hautefoye in 1870. The villagers used cannibalistic imagery to describe the killing and mutilation, even though no cannibalism was involved. The authorities, in turn, projected backward such imagery to turn the villagers into nineteenth-century Jacques.[108]

106. Samuel Y. Edgerton, Jr., *Pictures and Punishment* (Ithaca, 1985).

107. Ruth Mellinkoff, *Outcasts: Signs of Otherness in Northern European Art of the Late Middle Ages* (Berkeley, Calif., 1993), 2:plates III.37 and IV.17, respectively; see also plates I.49, I.71, and II.26.

108. Alain Corbin, *Le village des cannibals* (Paris, 1990).

Cannibalism in early modern sources is often linked to sexual cruelty. The link itself has classical origins, as reflected in contemporary literary works. But it is present in various other sources, in which it appears as the type of cruelty attributed to people or groups that are characterized as "other." The preoccupation with sexual cruelty may be related to a more explicit treatment of sexual issues in general, as evident in secular literature. Incidentally, the link between cruelty, cannibalism, and sex seems to persist to our own times in films such as *The Silence of the Lambs* (1991).

What was the role of cruelty in the relationship between author and audience? In the realm of Renaissance drama, it is evident that violence and cruelty were part of the mainstream discourse: The explicit violence represented by the authors was matched by the audience's interest in it, a process that could be seen in economic terms of supply and demand. In other early modern texts, the role of cruelty is more complex. Thus, in the context of martyrdom, for instance, cruelty had the role of asserting the martyr's status as such. The martyr's suffering and the forms it took created a parallel between him and the early martyrs or Christ. The insistence on cruelty and the explicit links to early, uncontested martyrs indicate a sense of insecurity: The authors were unsure how the events would be interpreted and wished to dispel any doubt as to "their" martyr's sainthood. This uncertainty is true in particular of the martyrs of the early Reformation, in whose case the whole issue of their martyrdom was part of a polemical argument.

This observation also indicates that the issue of cruelty is subversive. The potential dangers of referring to cruelty may be one of the reasons for the overall preference for the cults of contemporary saints from the central Middle Ages to the end of the Middle Ages and the relatively low popularity of the cults of martyrs. The actions of the inquisitors, when viewed apart from the justifying ideological context, could seem cruel as well as dangerously similar to the actions of the ancient persecutors. The return to these issues in the Protestant martyrologies, which is an explicit attempt to draw the parallel between the Catholics and the pagan persecutors, only shows that this concern was well founded.

The subversiveness of cruelty had an effect on the ways in which it was represented. The interest in cruelty was an active one, but as the reactions against the new discourse of cruelty indicate, it may have been at least frowned on. Detailed representations of violence, particularly those interspersed with affective and condemning comments, served as a countermeasure to the subversive pleasure of dealing with the subject. The author of such descriptions acknowledges by these explicit and disapproving references that the issue is, in fact, subversive, while absolving himself of complicity in this illicit activity.

CONCLUSION

Having reached the end of this book, we can go back to the opening example of Simon of Monfort's actions during the Albigensian crusade. In the light of the preceding chapters, does this account by Peter of Vaux-de-Cernay confirm the image, set forth by Elias and others, of the cruel "dark ages?" The answer to this question is not simply "yes" or "no" but is, nevertheless, closer to "no."

There is a relation between the incidence of actual violence—such as killing and rape, especially on a mass scale—and sensitivity to cruelty. In this sense, "there is no smoke without fire." That is, preoccupation with cruelty or sensitivity to this issue is not just the result of theoretic speculation. Nevertheless, reports of violence and cruelty cannot be interpreted as indicative of the level of actual cruelty, and, moreover, can indicate the existence of a counterreaction to what is perceived as cruelty. Thus, Peter of Vaux-de-Cernay's account of Simon undoubtedly indicates that Simon committed violent actions. But the apologetic manner of report suggests the existence of an undercurrent of repulsion from such actions. Thus, Peter's account may suggest a lightening of the horizon of the "dark ages" rather than its further darkening.

The treatment of cruelty is, more than anything, a cultural issue; cultural preoccupation with it varies between periods and cultures much more than does the actual practice of violence. It is affected by a mixture of cultural, religious, social, and political factors. Hence, the presence or absence of explicit references to cruelty varies from culture to culture as well as across different periods within the same cultural context.

Cruelty was an important cultural issue in Imperial Rome of the first centuries A.D. The way in which cruelty was treated in this period had lasting effects on the ways in which it was handled until the sixteenth century. The philosophical and dramatic writings of Seneca were of particular significance. Whenever the issue was discussed as a subject per se in subsequent periods, the relevant passages from Seneca's essays were cited as the basic text. His dramatic works, together with Ovid's *Metamorphoses*, deeply influenced the representation of cruelty from the central Middle

Ages onward. Other Roman authors also dealt with this subject: Valerius Maximus devoted a chapter to cruelty in his compilation of historical examples of various virtues and vices. Cruelty was also amply represented in the writings of Roman historians, such as Tacitus and Ammianus Marcelinus.

The transition to Christianity seems to mark a declining interest in the issue of cruelty. Cruelty is no longer a topic for theoretical speculation. Thinkers like Augustine or Jerome did not discuss cruelty as a subject per se. Christian chroniclers and hagiographers did refer explicitly to cruelty but with different emphases than their pagan contemporaries. The reluctance to deal with this subject was related to Christians' view of cruelty as an innate aspect of paganism. Consequently, dealing with cruelty or representing it was either irrelevant or outright repulsive for Christian authors. Interest in this issue was affected even further by the anti-classical backlash of Christian late antiquity. In addition, disparaging attitudes toward the body were held by some of the most influential Christian thinkers, such as Augustine. This contributed its share to the reluctance of Christian authors to deal with the issue.

The shift to the early medieval period is even more abrupt insofar as cruelty is concerned. Cruelty disappears almost completely: There are no theoretical discussions of the subject, and even more surprising is the absence of references to cruelty in contemporary chronicles that reflect a very violent historical reality. The Muslim conquests, the incursions of Magyars and Vikings, and the high level of internal violence are generally reported in a brief and factual manner, without any reference to the cruelty of these agents of violence. Nevertheless, a minority of hagiographic sources do refer to the cruelty of the Vikings, and the manner in which they do so shows that the discourse of cruelty as it evolved in late antiquity was not lost. Hence, the majority of early medieval sources does not deal explicitly with cruelty as a result of a cultural choice.

This attitude begins to change in the twelfth century. Thus, chroniclers who use earlier materials interpolate references to cruelty in the texts they cite. The relative importance of cruelty rises also in martyrdom accounts written at this period, especially those dealing with children allegedly killed by the Jews. The cultural role of cruelty increases in the thirteenth century. For the first time in the Middle Ages, cruelty is treated as a suitable topic for philosophical discussion in Thomas Aquinas's *Summa theologiae*. In conjunction with historical events, mainly the unprecedented violence practiced by the Mongols, thirteenth-century chronicles reporting these incidents turn cruelty into an anthropological category: It becomes the primary characteristic of the invading "other," whose most recent incarnation is the Mongols. A necessary and active component of these developments is the Renaissance of Latin classical culture and of Seneca's writings in particular, which accelerated in the thirteenth century.

The cultural role of cruelty further increases in its importance in the late Middle Ages, but its essence changes as well. In the central Middle Ages, cruelty has mainly been either the object of speculation or of representation for descriptive purposes. In the cases of Thomas Becket and of the Albigensians, one can see the beginning of the manipulation of cruelty for political purposes. In the late Middle Ages, cruelty increasingly becomes an object of manipulation for social, political, and religious purposes. Constructs of the cruelty of the invading "other," which evolved in response to the Mongol threat, were adapted and applied to internal marginalized groups, such as heretics or peasants. Cruelty served as a delegitimizing label: It justified violence against marginalized social groups. In the political sphere, this label associated a ruler with tyranny and hence was used by other contenders to power. An altogether different type of manipulation emerges in the late medieval spirituality focused on the passion of Christ. Painfully minute and affective reconstructions of the cruelty suffered by Christ were the primary tool used by mystics for achieving the mystical experience.

Some of these trends continue to evolve in the early modern period. But by and large, the sixteenth century presents a break from the medieval treatment of cruelty. Whereas the rise in the fortunes of cruelty as a cultural issue has been gradual from the central Middle Ages onward, in the sixteenth century there is an explosion of references to the subject in most areas of culture: philosophy, literature, historiography, and hagiography.

The unprecedented role of cruelty in early modern culture cannot be seen as a continuation of medieval processes: It was enabled by changes in the same factors that limited the role of cruelty in medieval culture. Of particular significance was the shift away from the medieval ethical system that emphasized intentions to one that focused on actions. Cruelty became a reified, objective category that could be quantified; thus, it became possible to scale and compare cruelty. People or groups no longer belonged to the binary categories of "cruel" or "not cruel"; they could be more cruel than some, less cruel than others. The reduced role of intentions in the ethical outlook also led to the resurgence of the irrational aspects of cruelty that were mostly ignored during the Middle Ages. The importance accorded in the Renaissance to the body and to the physical aspects of existence further increased the relevance of cruelty.

The intense preoccupation with cruelty in the early modern period also highlights the question, "What is the relative share of cultural processes versus historical events in determining the cultural treatment of cruelty?"

The interest in cruelty in the early modern period was largely due to the extremely high levels of violence that accompanied the wars of religion and the conquest of the New World. Judicial punishments also became much more violent than they were during the medieval period. The renewed interest in cruelty in the thirteenth century was also due in part to historical events—primarily the Mongol conquests.

Nevertheless, as an intercultural comparison shows, cruelty is a cultural issue only in the medieval West. Historical events such as the Mongol conquests did not render cruelty an important topic in Islamic culture or in the culture of the Eastern Christians, who were afflicted by Mongol violence even more severely than Christians in the medieval West. Historical events served in the West as triggers that kindled interest in the subject, but this happened only against a peculiar cultural background.

The Latin Roman legacy of medieval culture seems to have been a key factor in the way cruelty was treated. The Western mode of reference to cruelty evolved in Imperial Rome; it was not inherited from Greek culture. The reasons for the Roman interest in the issue are beyond the scope of this study and remain open questions. The effect of Latin classical influence on the treatment of cruelty was more profound than that of religious differences, such as those that existed between Christianity and Islam. This effect is reflected in the diverging attitudes of Greek and Latin Christianity in late antiquity as well as in the basically similar attitude of Islamic and Eastern Christian sources in later periods.

"It was just to see them falling into the pit which they had dug and drink from the cup which they had so often made others drink." Thus, as an ordained retaliation, Peter of Vaux-de-Cernay justifies the mutilation of the Albigensians by Simon of Monfort. Ironically, one may say, a similar thing happened to the civilization of the medieval West. The complex cultural construct of cruelty developed as an increasingly manipulative tool for describing people and groups as the "other." With the transition into the modern period, however, this construct was turned against the medieval civilization that created it and gave birth to the image—turned topos—of the "cruel Middle Ages."

APPENDIX ONE
LEXICAL AND BIBLICAL
CONTEXTS OF CRUELTY

Lexical references to cruelty supply the basic words and meanings associated with the concept. Identifying the lexical field of references to cruelty is also important because the words associated with cruelty serve as labels, indicating that the context of cruelty is evoked and supplying part of its meaning.

Early dictionaries and glossaries provide adequate information about the various contexts of cruelty. Isidore of Seville's *Etymologiae* is by far the most influential of early medieval lexical aids. Isidore explains *crudelis* in the following manner: "Cruel [*crudelis*], this is raw [*crudus*], which the Greeks call *omón* in translation, as if uncooked and impossible to eat. It is also harsh hard."[1] Isidore, then, links cruelty to the physical concept of raw meat and then proceeds to two human qualities, whose basic meaning in this context is hardness of heart.

In an eighth-century Latin glossary, cruelty is linked with two nexuses of meaning. The word *atrox* is explained by four words: *inmaturus, crudelis, malus,* and *sevus.* The first nexus is linked to the idea of rawness, mentioned by Isidore. *Malus* is a much more general term implying evil. *Sevus* implies the savagery of wild beasts and is one of the more common medieval synonyms for cruelty. *Atrox* also implies relentlessness, with connotations of beastly behavior and lack of rational restraint. The other nexus of terms is legal: The adjective *severus* is defined as *iratus, crudelis.* The noun *severitas* is defined as *integritas judicii. Severitas,* in its turn, is given as the meaning of *austeritas.* Thus, an irrational aspect of cruelty is indicated by the following chain: *atrox—crudelis—sevus—iratus.* In addition, a legal context emerges from the chain formed by these lexical linkages: *crudelis—severus—severitas—austeritas—integritas judicii.*[2] The two chains are linked, as we can see

1. *Isidori Hispalensis episcopi etymologiarum sive originum libri XX,* 10.48, ed. Wallace M. Lindsay (Oxford, 1989[1911]).
2. *The Corpus Glossary,* ed. Wallace M. Lindsay (Cambridge, 1921).

because the word *crudelis* appears in both of them. The connection established between cruelty and severity in judgment is not new: Once established explicitly, it can be searched backward and found in the *Etymologiae*, under the entry *severus*.[3]

Anglo-Saxon glossaries of the ninth and tenth centuries reveal a similar web of Latin terms: *crudelis—saevus—asper—durus—ferox—severus*. The Anglo-Saxon terms used for the translation are mainly *welhriou, unhere, stiþ*, and *reþe*.[4] They convey similar meanings and relate to similar contexts: a quality appertaining to barbarians, blood-shedding, hard-heartedness, and ferocity. It is significant that the legal context in which cruelty marks the upper limit of justifiable severity is present in the use of the Anglo-Saxon term (*reþe*), as used in other Anglo-Saxon texts: It appears in relation to God's judgment in the case of the flood, for instance.[5]

Papias (fl. ca. 1050), an eleventh-century grammarian, compiled a dictionary (*Elementarium doctrinae rudimentum*) that was widely diffused and influential in the later Middle Ages. Papias places cruelty in similar contexts. He defines *crudelis* in the context of perverted human relations: "Cruel [*crudelis*] to inferiors: haughty to equals, defiant to superiors, ungrateful to a friend, undutiful to parents." This definition is related to the legal context of cruelty in defining cruel as an excess in the exercise of power or authority toward people located lower on the social scale (while not denying that they deserve treatment as inferiors). The other links viewed so far also exist; Papias defines *atrox* as *crudelis, immisericors*. In another entry on *crudelis*, cruelty is linked to raw meat and blood, as in Isidore's *Etymologiae*. The links to animal savagery and irrational fury are made in the entries on *saevitia*:

> *Saeua iniqua: mala: crudelis, saeuientes irae.*
> *Saeuit furit irascitur insanit.*
> *Saeuitia furor crudelitas iracundia.*[6]

A fifteenth-century English gloss supplies the following web of cross-references to cruelty:

3. Severus, quasi saevus verus; tenet enim sine pietate iustitiam (*Isidori Hispalensis episcopi etymologiarum sive originum libri XX*, 10.250).

4. *Anglo-Saxon and Old English Vocabularies*, ed. Thomas Wright and R. P. Wülcker, (Leipzig, 1884[1857]).

5. For references, see Joseph Bosworth and Thomas N. Toller, *An Anglo-Saxon Dictionary* (London, 1898), 793.

6. Papias, *Elementarium*, ed. Violetta de Angelis (Milan, 1977); see Gernot Wieland, "Papias" in *Dictionary of the Middle Ages* (New York, 1987), 9:391.

crudelis—cruell.
seueo, be cruell.
sevus, cruel.
crudelis, cruel or spytuose
immanis . . . ferus, cruel.
crudeliter, cruely.
ferox, crudelis, trux, atrox, seuus, seuerus, cruell.[7]

This entry shows that, in fact, all these terms form a nexus whose general meaning is cruelty. Moreover, it shows that in the passage to the vernacular, the internal variety in nuances among the Latin terms is blurred, and all words are explained in English by *cruel* and its derivatives.

This survey of lexical references to cruelty from the seventh to the fifteenth centuries reflects the basic stability of the lexical and semantic field of cruelty. Three main contexts related to cruelty stand out:

1. The etymological relation to raw meat and blood.
2. The irrational aspect of cruelty related to beastly behavior and fury.
3. The legal aspect of cruelty. In this context, unlike the preceding ones, cruelty is an aspect of human relations and, thus, characteristically a human quality.

BIBLICAL FIELD OF REFERENCE

A purely lexical approach is insufficient, however. Scriptures and biblical images were a basic element in constructing the ways in which medieval people thought and expressed themselves. It is thus necessary to review the scriptural references to cruelty and the manner in which they were interpreted. Words denoting cruelty are rare both in the Hebrew version of the Old Testament and in the Latin *Vulgata*. In the *Vulgata*, the words denoting cruelty are distributed as follows: *crudelis* (25 appearances), *saevus* (10), *ferox* (7), *atrox* (1).[8] This frequency also mirrors, roughly, the situation in medieval texts in general: The most common words for cruelty are those derived from *crudelis* and *saevus*; after these, most common are words derived from *ferox* and *atrox*.[9] Of the 43 appearances of words derived from these adjectives, only two appear in the New Testament. The distribution according to

---

7. The last entry, which is the most detailed, is the most significant because it is part of a list of human qualities (*English Glosses from British Library Additional Manuscript 37075*, ed. Thomas W. Ross and Edward Brooks, Jr. [Norman, Okla., 1984]).

8. These figures include all the words derived from the four adjectives.

9. See Chapter 6, note 78.

books is uneven, a fact that helps in locating the major contexts: Twelve out of the forty-three entries (28 percent) are from 2 Maccabees; eight (19 percent) from the books of Wisdom attributed to Solomon (Proverbs and the Wisdom of Solomon); seven (16 percent) from the major prophets (Isaiah, Jeremiah, Ezechiel); and four (9 percent) from the Book of Esther.

The explicit scriptural references to cruelty, in the manner in which they were interpreted in the Middle Ages, fall into four principal categories:

1. *Cruelty as a human quality (in the context of inter-personal relations):*
   a. The disregard of the "natural" injunction to be kind to certain categories of people such as kin.[10]
   b. A type of wickedness[11]—The relevant verse was interpreted in the Middle Ages as cruelty toward subjects and inferiors.[12]
   c. Cruelty in war—The prophet Oded condemns the cruelty of the people of Israel in a war they waged against Judah, characterizing cruelty as massacre, plunder, and the taking of captives.[13]

2. *Tyranny (in a politico-religious context):* Most entries in the Book of Maccabees refer to Antiochus's cruelty, as reflected in his religious persecution of the Jews. The principal episode that has established Antiochus's reputation as cruelty incarnate is the execution of a woman and her seven sons. This scene was considered in the Middle Ages as a prefiguration of Christian martyrdom, thus regarding Antiochus as the precursor of later persecutors.[14] In general, cruelty in the Book of Maccabees applies to the actions of people associated with the rule of Antiochus.[15]

   The references to the cruelty of other persecutors of the Jews, such as Haman and Holophernes, also come under this heading.[16]

10. Prov. 11:17.

11. Prov. 12:10.

12. Bede interprets, "Viscera autem impiorum crudelia, qui non solum non compatiuntur subditis sed etiam iuxta hoc quod dominus ait: Percutiunt pueros et ancillas dicentes: Moram facit dominus meus venire" (*In Proverbia Salomonis libri III*, ed. David Hurst, in *Bedae Venerabilis opera* part 2, [CCSL 119b] [Turnhout, 1983], 2b:76). Rabanus Maurus offers the same interpretation (*Expositio in proverbia Salomonis* 2.12, PL 111:720–21).

13. In the *Vulgata* version, two words from the lexical field of cruelty appear in his speech: *atrociter* and *crudelitas* (2 Chron. 28:9).

14. 2 Macc. 7: Antiochus is characterized as *crudelis tyrannus* in 7:27. Other references to cruelty in this episode: 7:39, 42.

15. A massacre of the Jews by the inhabitants of Jaffa (2 Macc. 12:5); the officers of Antiochus (5:22); Menelaus, who bought the office of High Priest from Antiochus (4:25); Nicanor's followers warn him not to act *ferociter et barbare* in pursuing Judas on Sabbath (15:2).

16. Esther 4:3, 7:4, 14:11, 16:10; Jth. 3:11.

The only instance in which the cruelty is not addressed specifically to Jews is Nabuchodonosor's decree to execute the wise men of Babylon.[17]

3. *A nonhuman quality (appertaining to animals or demons):* Cruelty as a quality of wild beasts is usually described by one of the adjectival forms of *saevus*,[18] and sometimes the derivatives of *ferox*.[19] One of the two New Testament references to cruelty characterizes as *saevi* the two possessed men who come across Christ's way in Galilee, whose demons were later turned into swine.[20]

Beastly ferocity as cruelty is sometimes used metaphorically to describe the positive quality of human courage, however. This is done in the case of the warriors of David and of Judas Maccabaeus.[21]

4. *Divine justice:* Cruelty in this context is the application of the utmost severity of justice toward the wicked. Usually it refers to a collective punishment (of mankind or of the people of Israel). The prophets frequently refer to this aspect of cruelty in their descriptions of the afflictions by which God will punish his people, particularly by means of peoples such as the Assyrians and the Babylonians.[22] These references also supply the basic imagery for the medieval descriptions of the cruelty of the "other." Thus, for instance, Isaiah describes the immense slaughter made by the Babylonians: killing children in front of their parents and raping women in front of their husbands.[23]

It must be noted, however, that in the biblical passages themselves cruelty appears as part of divine justice and is not directly attributed to the people who enact it. Nor are they censured on this account; they are merely tools in the hands of God, similar to some natural calamity.[24] This position, which absolves the perpetrators of cruelty from responsibility for their deeds, is somewhat anomalous, and Christian commentators did not always adhere to it. Thus, for instance, Jerome does attribute cruelty to the Babylonians even

17. Daniel 2:15.

18. Judg. 14:5; Wisd. of Sol. 12:9, 16:5 (savage beasts as divine punishment).

19. 2 Macc. 11:9, 15:21.

20. Matt. 8:28.

21. 2 Sam. 17:8; 2 Macc. 10:35, 12:15 (ferociter).

22. Jer. 6:23, 30:14, 50:42; Isa. 14:6, 19:4 (the affliction of the Egyptians by cruel rulers); Ezech. 31:12. Sometimes, the prophet refers to a particular day of judgment (Isa. 13:9).

23. Isa. 13:15–18.

24. Conversely, in some cases the denomination of cruelty is sometimes transferred to the afflictions themselves even if they are not human beings or living persons. Such is the reference in the *Apocalypse* to *vulnus saevum* (Apoc. 16:2; Wisd. of Sol. 19:15).

though he continues to see them an instrument of divine justice for punishing the people of Israel.[25]

A minority of references place cruelty in the context of private judgment by God. Thus, in the Book of Proverbs it is mentioned that the Lord shall send a cruel angel to punish the wicked.[26] The references to cruelty in Job also pertain to aspects of divine justice.[27]

25. Illos autem abusos esse crudelitate sua, et plus imposuisse plagarum quam dei ultio lagitabat, magnumque babyloniae crudelitatis indicium est, ne senibus quidem pepercisse, quorum aetas etiam inter hostes uenerabilis est (*Commentarii in Isaiam* 13.47.4/7, ed. Marc Adriaen [*CCSL* 73a] [Turnhout, 1963], 523).

26. Prov. 17:11.

27. Job 30:21.

APPENDIX TWO
MODERN APPROACHES
TO CRUELTY

General Discussions

The most notable contemporary discussion of cruelty is the essay "Putting Cruelty First" by Judith Shklar.[1] This discussion demonstrates that the basic modern text on cruelty is still Montaigne's essay on the subject. Shklar's basic definition is concerned with physical violence: She defines cruelty as "the willful inflicting of physical pain on a weaker being in order to cause anguish and fear."[2] Later in her essay, she refines this basic definition by adding the element of injustice: An action seems more cruel the more it seems gratuitous and unjust.[3] Shklar consciously follows Montaigne in emphasizing the action rather than the intention of the actor. Thus, while still reserving an element of intentionality in the definition, she declines to consider the pleasure the victimizer derives from the act.[4] The pleasurable aspect of cruelty is cast out of philosophical discourse, presumably on account of the incompatibility between a science of reason and the most extreme example of irrationality. As Shklar points out, one does find references to this issue in psychological studies, the discourse presumably assigned to deal with irrationality.

Shklar refers also to moral cruelty, known also as mental cruelty, which she defines as "deliberate and persistent humiliation, so that the victim can eventually trust neither himself nor anyone else." For Shklar, cruelty has a prominent political aspect: It is used as an instrument to inspire paralyzing fear in its victims.[5]

---

1. Judith N. Shklar, *Ordinary Vices* (Cambridge, Mass., 1984), 7–44; the essay is the first chapter of the book.
2. Ibid., 8.
3. Ibid., 24.
4. Ibid., 43.
5. Ibid., 37.

An important addition to Shklar's general discussion of cruelty is an article by Christine McKinnon. Although in agreement with the general scope of Shklar's essay, she limits the scope of cruelty, omitting the political context. For McKinnon, cruelty is gratuitous: It is precisely the lack of any practical purpose (such as the tyrant's fear of losing his rule) that constitutes cruelty; its main characteristic is the victimizer's awareness of the suffering he inflicts, and the pleasure derived from the victim's suffering is its primary purpose.[6]

Cruelty to Animals

Most recent discussions of cruelty are held in the context of cruelty to animals. These discussions do not significantly modify the basic definition of violence toward a weaker object, either involving pleasure on the part of the actor or merely specifying its gratuitous nature.[7] The points of debate are what, if any, are the legitimate uses of animals, and what uses are illegitimate and constitute cruelty. The definition of cruelty is stretched in some instances to include also the conditions in which animals are kept, even if their use is considered legitimate. It should be noted that this topic parallels the debate on institutionalized cruelty in reference to human beings (particularly in the legal context); cruelty in this case is defined as infliction of suffering on another being beyond what is considered necessary and justified.[8] There is also a debate on

6. "We shall modify Shklar's claim somewhat so that the end [of cruelty] may be nothing more than the causing of pain (so as to produce pleasure in the oppressor)," (Christine McKinnon, "Ways of Wrong-Doing, the Vices, and Cruelty," *Journal of Value Inquiry* 23 [1989]: 319–35, esp. 330, 333). Another modern study of cruelty is Philip P. Hallie, *The Paradox of Cruelty* (Middletown, Conn., 1969). Hallie's is not a philosophical or theoretical study per se; it follows the way cruelty is represented in various artistic genres of the modern period: painting, Sade's novels, and the horror tale, among others.

7. John Passmore, "The Treatment of Animals," *Journal of the History of Ideas* 36 (1975): 195–218, esp. 195; Tom Regan, "Cruelty, Kindness, and Unnecessary Suffering," *Philosophy* 55 (1980): 532–41, esp. 534.

8. Passmore, "Treatment of Animals," 195. This point comes up in other discussions of the treatment of animals and is not always labeled explicitly as cruelty. For example, "the issue of the infliction of unnecessary and excessive pain and suffering upon animals, which is not offset by a significant long-term gain in pleasure for humans or for animals, is a matter that ought to concern" (Michael Fox, "'Animal Liberation': A Critique," *Ethics* 88 [1978]: 106–18, esp. 118; all articles in *Ethics* 88:2 [1978] deal with the treatment of animals).

whether passive cruelty—that is, indifference to the suffering of animals—should be included with active cruelty.[9]

Legal discussions of cruelty concentrate on the issue of which legal procedures should be considered as cruel and therefore illegitimate. Most discussions refer to the Eighth Amendment of the U.S. Constitution, which bans cruel and unusual punishment, and to the question of whether the amendment is applicable to the death penalty. The issue is viewed both from the retributive angle—whether it is just to punish certain offenses by death[10]—and from the utilitarian angle—whether it is useful for society to use this punishment. Even among retributivists, there is no agreement. Some claim that such punishment is just[11]; others claim that it is cruel because the amendment refers to the general precept of decency, and the death penalty denies the human dignity of its object.[12] Viewed from the utilitarian point of view, there is more agreement that the death penalty is not useful as a deterrent against crime and is therefore cruel in the sense that it is a severe step that is unnecessary, whereas milder punishments would have yielded similar results.[13] These two approaches parallel in many points the distinc-

9. Indifference to suffering (of animals) as cruelty is proposed by Tom Regan: "Some cruel people do not feel pleasure in making others suffer. Indeed, they seem not to feel anything. Their cruelty is manifested by a lack of what is judged appropriate feeling, as pity or mercy, for the plight of the individual whose suffering they cause, rather than pleasure in causing it" (Regan, "Cruelty, Kindness," 534). Passmore distinguishes between active cruelty and indifference to suffering by using the term *callousness* in reference to the latter (Passmore, "Treatment of Animals," 195).

10. All these discussions are theoretical and refer to the "ideal" case in which there is no possibility for judicial mistakes of identity, evidence, etc.

11. For a justification of capital punishment that, however, falls short of claiming its necessity, see Igor Primoratz, *Justifying Legal Punishment* (Atlantic Highlands, N.J., 1989), 158–67. The retributivist arguments justifying the death penalty are reviewed in Michael D. A. Freeman, "Retributivism and the Death Sentence," in *Law, Morality and Rights*, ed. Michael A. Stewart (Dordrecht, 1979), 406–10.

12. Thomas A. Long, "Capital Punishment—'Cruel and Unusual'?" *Ethics* 83:3 (1973): 214–23; and Robert S. Gerstein, "Capital Punishment—'Cruel and Unusual'?: A Retributivist Response," *Ethics* 85 (1974): 75–79. Similar arguments are put forth in Jeffrie G. Murphy, "Cruel and Unusual Punishments," in *Law, Morality and Rights*, 373–404; Freeman "Retributivism," in *Law, Morality and Rights*, 405–422; and John Cottingham, "Punishment and Respect for Persons," in *Law, Morality and Rights*, 423–431.

13. On the inefficacy of capital punishment as deterrent see Primoratz, *Justifying Legal Punishment*, 155–58; and Long, "Capital Punishment," 221–22.

tion applied to medieval sources between "ethics of action" and "ethics of intention." The retributive approach is closer to ethics of action—that is, weighing only the actions themselves for moral evaluation regardless of the legitimacy of the purpose (in this case, justice or deterrence). The utilitarian approach is closer to ethics of intention, as it weighs the legitimacy of actions by the legitimacy of their purpose (justice and security for society).

The phrase "cruel and unusual" was understood in the legal context to refer not only to the question of capital punishment but also to any punishment that infringes on human dignity. In the Supreme Court decision on *Trop v. Dulles* (1958), it has been written that "the basic concept underlying the Eighth Amendment is nothing less than the dignity of man."[14] The appeal to the concept of *decency* for the definition of cruelty emphasizes the supremacy of actions over intentions in this context. Actions that violate the concept of decency are cruel in themselves, regardless of their aim. This definition stands in contrast to the definition of cruelty in general philosophical discussions, which emphasize the gratuitous nature of cruelty.[15]

PSYCHOLOGICAL STUDIES

Psychological studies of cruelty deal mostly with the origins of cruel behavior. Freud considered cruelty inherent in human nature. In "Thoughts for the Times on War and Death," cruelty is presented as a basic trait of human character that is held under control by civilization and finds its expression in situations such as war, in which the controlling forces of civilization are cast aside.[16] In another place, Freud presents cruelty as a component of sexuality. Here, too, cruelty is a natural impulse; the link between cruelty and sexuality is severed by the development of the "capacity for pity."[17]

14. Another instance in which the Eighth Amendment was applied is cited in the same decision: "But when the court was confronted with a punishment of 12 years in irons at hard and painful labor imposed for the crime of falsifying public records, it did not hesitate to declare that the penalty was cruel in its excessiveness and unusual in its character" (*Weems v. United States* [1910]).

15. Long offers a definition of cruelty similar to McKinnon's in order to refute it. He claims, giving torture by secret police organizations as an example, that some forms of violence are cruelty even if they seem justified to their perpetrators (Long, "Capital Punishment," 219).

16. Sigmund Freud, "Thoughts for the Times on War and Death," in *The Standard Edition of the Complete Psychological Works of Sigmund Freud*, trans. James Strachey (London, 1957[1915]), 14:275–88.

17. Sigmund Freud, "Three Essays on the Theory of Sexuality," in *Complete Psychological Works of Sigmund Freud*, 7:157, 159, 166–67, 192–93.

This view of "natural cruelty" has been challenged by Harvey A. Hornstein, a social psychologist, who maintained that benevolent behavior is more natural to man. His work naturally deals much more with kindness rather than with cruelty.[18]

Otherwise, in current psychological research, cruelty is a marginal issue. It seems that the main concern with cruelty is still, as with Freud, its origins and its development—that is, why and how aberrant behavior develops. Thus there are numerous studies that explore the link between children's cruelty toward animals and other children and violent criminal behavior later in life. Many of the studies focus on cruelty toward "weak" groups of society, such as animals, children, and the aged.[19]

MODERN RESEARCH INDIRECTLY RELATED TO THE ISSUE OF CRUELTY

In addition to these explicit discussions of cruelty, there are a number of sociologically oriented studies that refer implicitly to the subject of cruelty by dealing with related issues. Norbert Elias, mentioned earlier, is the only one who refers directly to the Middle Ages. He does not treat cruelty per se but discusses it in the context of changes in aggressiveness, and he holds a position that is initially similar to Freud's in referring to the delegitimization of cruelty as part of what he defines as the "civilizing process."

Quincy Wright's comprehensive study of war touches on several related issues, such as the urge for war and ethical attitudes toward war. He also attempts an intercultural approach to bellicosity in various civilizations, defining cruelty as one of its main four components.[20] Other long-range

18. Harvey A. Hornstein, *Cruelty and Kindness—A New Look at Aggression and Altruism* (Englewood Cliffs, N.J., 1976).

19. A search of the PsycLit database using the keyword *cruelty* (covering publications in this field in the years 1974–1997) produced only 137 entries, most of them not in leading journals and many touching only marginally on the issue (according to the abstracts of these studies). See, for instance, Stephen R. Kellert and Alan R. Felthous, "Childhood Cruelty toward Animals among Criminals and Noncriminals," *Human Relations* 38:12 (1985): 1113–1129; O. Jarde, B. Marc, J. Dwyer, P. Fournier, et al., "Mistreatment of the Aged in the Home Environment in Northern France: A Year Survey (1990)," *Medicine and Law* 11:7–8 (1992): 641–48; Sandra L. Bloom, "Hearing the Survivor's Voice: Sundering the Wall of Denial," *Journal of Psychohistory* 21:4 (1994): 461–77 (special issue: "Cult Abuse of Children: Witch Hunt or Reality?"); Barbara W. Boat, "The Relationship between Violence to Children and Violence to Animals: An Ignored Link?" *Journal of Interpersonal Violence* 10:2 (1995): 229–35; and Carl Goldberg, "The Daimonic Development of the Malevolent Personality," *Journal of Humanistic Psychology* 35:3 (1995): 7–36.

studies that touch on this issue are Michel Foucault's investigation of the development of the Western penal system. Foucault, in a way reminiscent of Elias, also traces a type of civilizing process from the early modern period to the nineteenth century: Punishment recedes from the public scene to secluded places. It also acquires a reformatory role for the criminal in addition to the retributive purpose of older punishments.[21]

Several detailed case studies are also related to the issue of cruelty to some extent: Clifford Geertz's references to violence and cruelty in Balinese culture raise some methodological problems concerning the treatment of violence in different cultures, mainly the imposition of modern Western values when studying other cultures and the assumption of the existence of universal values. In addition, Geertz points to the ulterior motives that sometimes underlie the depiction of other cultures as cruel and as "other." Two studies that deal with legal cases related to cruelty in nineteenth-century France, one by Michel Foucault and another by Alain Corbin, reveal some of the basic elements of the medieval discourse of cruelty, especially when cruelty is discussed in relation to the "other." Thus, Foucault's edition of texts and studies related to the trial of Pierre Rivière reveals an evolutionary conception of cruelty reflected in the quest for signs of cruelty in Pierre's childhood, as well as links between cruelty and tyranny and between cruelty and the devil. Corbin's analysis of a case of peasant violence in a French village in the nineteenth century also echoes ancient characterizations of cruelty based on the dehumanization of an alleged "other," using images of cannibalism and employing the medieval image of the Jacquerie.[22]

HOW MODERN ARE MODERN APPROACHES?

This survey indicates that cruelty is not a central subject for study and speculation in modern contemporary research, whether historical or pertaining to other disciplines. It also points to the traditional character of modern

20. See Quincy Wright, *A Study of War* (Chicago, 1942), 1:122–24, 131–44, and 2:885–87. See also Raymond Aron, *Peace and War*, trans. Richard Howard and Anette Baker Fox (London, 1966[1962]), 329–30, 335–36.

21. Michel Foucault, *Surveiller et punir* (Paris, 1975). Another long-range study, which is mainly descriptive, is Eric Carlton, *Massacres: An Historical Perspective* (Aldershot, 1994).

22. Clifford Geertz, *The Interpretation of Cultures* (New York, 1973); Clifford Geertz, "Found in Translation: On the Social History of the Moral Imagination," in *Local Knowledge*, 36–54; Michel Foucault, *Moi, Pierre Rivière, ayant égorgé ma mère, ma soeur et mon frère . . .* (Paris, 1973) (especially: Jean-Pierre Peter and Jeanne Favret, "L'animal, le fou, le mort," 293–319); Alain Corbin, *Le village des cannibals* (Paris, 1990).

approaches to cruelty, which make use, sometimes inadvertently, of the ancient, medieval, and Renaissance categories and conceptions of cruelty. The general philosophical discussions are extensions of Montaigne's treatment of the issue. The application of these ideas concerning cruelty to animals *is* a new emphasis but not a revolutionary idea.[23]

The legal discussions of cruelty, which question the limit of legal punishment, use the same criterion of cruelty used by Seneca and Thomas Aquinas: Namely, cruelty is an exaggeration of legal punishment. Thus the difference between the modern and the ancient and medieval treatments of legal cruelty concern only the definition of the limit; the basic premises of the discussion are the same.

The evolutionary conception of cruelty that underlies many of the psychological references to cruelty—that is, that cruelty is a natural impulse—is prominent in Augustine's writings, including Freud's premise that cruelty is tempered and prevented from materializing by the development of empathy in the human character.

Even the more revolutionary attitudes that are not in the mainstream of Western approaches to cruelty are of doubtful novelty. Nietzsche's approach to the issue is less revolutionary than it seems on first sight. It is essentially based on the reversal of the traditional categories. His praise of violence is based on the evolutionary conception: Cruelty is indeed an earlier stage of development. But this stage is better, as it reflects an unadulterated stage of development. This positive, pristine cruelty was perverted by Judeo-Christian culture and became reflexive. Cruelty in the context of Christianity, according to Nietzsche, is the ascetic quest for spiritual self-torture. Thus, Nietzsche's conception of cruelty is strikingly similar to Bernard of Clairvaux's criticism of exaggerated monastic asceticism as an instance of reflexive spiritual cruelty. Nietzsche basically uses the traditional categories in a different manner in presenting the process of soul-searching itself as cruelty and not just its exaggerated deviations.[24]

23. On cruelty to animals, see Thomas Aquinas, *Summa theologiae* 2–1–102 (*De caeremonialium praeceptorum causis*) *art.* 6 (*r.a.* 1); Thomas refers in his discussion to Maimonides, *Guide of the Perplexed* 3:48. See also Nahmanides's commentary on Deut. 22:6 and Ibn Ezra's commentary on the same verse and on Exod. 13:19.

24. See Friedrich Nietzsche, "Beyond Good and Evil," 229, in *Basic Writings of Nietzsche*, trans. Walter Kaufmann (New York, 1966), 348–49; and Friedrich Nietzsche, *On the Genealogy of Morality, passim*, especially 2:6–7, 16, 22, and 3:20, ed. Keith Ansell-Pearson, trans. Carol Diethe (Cambridge, 1994), 45–48, 60–62, 68–69, 109–12.

APPENDIX THREE
CRUELTY IN THE LETTER OF THE CHURCHES OF LYONS AND VIENNE: EUSEBIUS'S AND RUFINUS'S VERSIONS COMPARED

[1] (5.1.5) . . . the adversary attacked us . . . practising his adherents and training them against the servants of God, so that we were not merely excluded from houses . . .

. . . congressus est inimicus . . . et per hoc institueret et informaret ministros suos adversum servos dei omne ministerium sceleris et *crudelitatis* explere, ita ut primo domorum nobis prohiberetur habitatio . . .

[2] (5.1.9) Then they were brought before the governor, and when he used all his savagery[1] against them, then intervened Vettius Epagathus . . .

in quos ille tanta *crudelitate* usus est, ut *saevitiae* eius *species singulas nemo possit exponere*. Vettius igitur Epagathus . . .

[3] (5.1.9) His [Epagathus's] character forbade him to endure the unreasonable judgment given against us . . .

. . . tam *crudelia* servis dei supplicia videret inferri *contra ius fasque* tot poenas humanis visceribus excogitari, indignitatem rei ultra non ferens poscit . . .

[4] (5.1.18) . . . took turns in torturing her [Blandina] in every way from morning until evening . . .

denique a prima luce usque ad vesperam tormenta *semper innovantes* . . .[2]

1. The word used is ὠμότης, more akin to the Latin *saevitia* (in the English translation it was translated as "cruelty").
2. Unlike other expressions that refer to the variety of tortures undergone by the martyrs, this expression is ambiguous: Besides the meaning of invention or innovation, the verb *innovare* may also have the meaning of renewal—"their tortures were constantly renewed."

[5] (5.1.20) Sanctus also himself endured nobly, beyond measure or human power, all the ill-treatment of men, for though the wicked hoped through persistence and the rigor of his tortures to wring from him something wrong, he resisted them with such constance that he did not even tell his own name or the race or the city whence he was, nor whether he was slave or free, but to all questions answered in Latin, "I am a Christian."

diaconus quoque sanctus nomine, etiam ipse supra quam dici potest et supra quam humanam fas est ferre naturam, acrius insistentibus *ministris daemonum*, quo aliquid ab eo elicere possent confessionis inlicitae, *nova* poenarum genera pertulit, et quae longe substantiam humanae condicionis excederent. at ille vir deo plenus in tantum *crudelitates* eorum risit et *ferinam* quaestione *saevitiam*, ut numquam dignatus sit vel quis esset genere, unde domo vel patria, nomen saltim suum eis fateri, sed de his singulis interrogatus nihil aliud in omnibus tormentis nisi Christianum se esse respondit: "hoc mihi nomen, hoc genus et patria est." "aliud," inquit, "omnino nihil sum quam Christianus."

[6] (5.1.23) His body was a witness to his treatment; it was all one wound and bruise, wrenched and torn out of human shape . . .

verumtamen membris omnibus martyr erat et toto corpore unum vulnus horrebat. periit in eo humanae formae agnitio, et non solum quis esset, sed et quid esset, tormentorum *crudelitas* ne agnosci posset abstulerat.

[7] (5.1.24) . . . or that by dying under torture he would put fear into the rest.

. . . aut, si in tormentis animam posuisset, terrorem *crudelitatis* et metum ceteris intentandum.

[8] (5.1.24) . . . and he regained his former appearance and the use of his limbs, so that through the grace of Christ the second torturing became not torment but cure.

. . . restitutum est in primam speciem corpus per secunda tormenta et officia membrorum, quae abstulerat prima *crudelitas*, secunda reparavit, ita ut iterata supplicia non ei iam poenam contulerint, sed medellam.

[9] (5.1.50) . . . for to please the mob the governor had given Attalus back to the beasts.

. . . quem *contra praeceptum Caesaris*, gratificari populis volens, etiam ipsum bestiis tradi iussit.

[10] (5.1.54) They exposed them to all the terrors and put them through every torture in turn, trying to make them swear, but not being able to do so.

. . . sed per omnia tormentorum genera quasi quodam eos circulo peragentes nihil deesse poenis patiebantur, quod *crudelitas* invenisset.

[11] (5.1.57–58) Not even thus was their madness and savagery[3] to the saints satisfied, for incited by a wild beast, wild and barbarous tribes could scarcely stop, and their violence began again in a new way on the bodies . . .

sed nec sic quidem satietatem aliquam capere *crudelitas* quivit. antiqui etenim serpentis virulentia concitati feri ac barbari mores mansuescere nesciebant. ex ipsa quippe sanctorum patientia *saevior* eis contentioni rabies accendebatur . . .

[12] (5.1.59–60) Then they threw out the remains left by the beasts and by the fire, torn and charred, and for many days watched with a military guard the heads of the rest, together with their trunks, all unburied. And some raged and gnashed their teeth at the remains, seeking some further vengeance from them, others laughed and jeered, glorifying their idols and ascribing to them the punishment of the Christians . . .[4]

sed si quid forte vel bestiis vel igni reliquum ex corporibus martyrum fuerat ipsaque cum truncis suis capita punitorum insepulta per custodiam militum servabantur et quaerebatur, si quid ultra posset inferre humana *crudelitas* etiam in eos, qui iam vitae huius limen excesserant, exultabant tamen gentes magnificantes simulacra sua, quorum virtute datam in illos vindictam dicebant.[5]

3. See note 1, above.

4. Eusebius, *The Ecclesiastical History*, trans. Kirsopp Lake (London, 1949), 1:409, 409, 411, 415, 415–7, 417, 419, 419, 431, 433, 435, 435, respectively.

5. Eusebius and Rufinus, *Historia ecclesiastica* 5.1.5–5.1.60, ed. T. Mommsen (Leipzig, 1903), 1:403, 405, 405, 409, 411, 411, 411, 411, 423, 425, 425, 427, respectively.

APPENDIX FOUR
CRUELTY IN THE CHRONICLES
OF THE VIKINGS

ANGLO-SAXON CHRONICLE	ASSER	HISTORIA REGUM
865 (A) In this year the heathen army encamped on Thanet and made peace with the people of Kent. And the people of Kent promised them money for that peace. And under the cover of that peace and promise of money the army stole away inland by night and ravaged all eastern Kent.	In the year of the incarnation of the Lord 864 the pagans wintered in the isle of Thanet, and made a firm pact with the people of Kent, who promised to give them money for the keeping of this pact. Meanwhile, the Danes, in the manner of foxes, broke out at night secretly from the fort. And the pact being broken, and spurning the promise of money, (They knew . . . they would attain more wealth by taking spoils by stealth than by peace), They laid waste the whole eastern region of the people of Kent.	In the year 864 the pagans wintered in an island which is called Thanet, which is surrounded on all sides by the waters of the river. They made a firm pact with the people of Kent, and promised to the people of Kent to give them money for the keeping of this pact. Meanwhile, the Danes, in the manner of foxes, broke out at night secretly from the fort. And the pact being broken, and spurning the promise of money, they appeared quiet for a few days. But, oh, a thing not to be done [sed o nefas]! They laid waste the whole eastern region of the people of Kent. They knew . . . they would attain more wealth by taking spoils by stealth than by peace, which was what was done [by them].

ANGLO-SAXON CHRONICLE	ASSER	HISTORIA REGUM
866 (A) . . . And the same year a great heathen army came into England and took up winter quarters in East Anglia; and there they were supplied with horses, and the East Angles made peace with them.[1]	In the same year, a great fleet of the pagans [coming] from the Danube came to Britain, and wintered in the reign of the Eastern Angles, which are called *Eastengle* in Saxon, and there the greatest part of the army was made [an army of] horsemen.[2]	In the same year, a great fleet of the pagans [coming] from the Danube entered the boundaries of Britain. And so they wintered in the reign of the Eastern Angles, which are called *Eastengle* in Saxon speech. There the copious army became [an army of] horsemen, raiding and running in different directions, this way and that way, taking enormous booty, not sparing neither men nor women, widows, or virgins.[3]

1. *The Anglo-Saxon Chronicle*, ed. and trans. Dorothy Whitelock (London, 1961), 45.
2. John Asser, *Life of King Alfred* (*De rebus gestis Alfredi*) 20-21, ed. W. H. Stevenson (Oxford, 1904), 18–19.
3. Simeon of Durham, *Historia regum*, ed. Thomas Arnold (*RS* 75) (London, 1885), 1:73.

APPENDIX FIVE
THE CAPTURE OF BOKHARA
AND SAMARQAND
BY THE MONGOLS

THE CAPTURE OF BOKHARA

(Nuwayrī) النويري

واحاطوا بالمسلمين فامر اصحابه ان
يقتسموهم ففعلوا ذلك

(And they surrounded the Muslims, and he ordered his companions to divide the Muslims, and they did so.)

(Ibn al-Athīr) ابن الاثير

ودخل الكفار البلد فنهبوه وقتلوا من وجدوا
فيه, واحاط بالمسلمين, فامر اصحابه ان
يقتسموهم, فاقتسموهم.

(And the unbelievers entered into the town and plundered it, and killed whoever they found inside it. And he surrounded the Muslims and ordered his companions to divide them, and they divided them.)

ـكان يومًا عظيمًا من كثرة البكاء من الرجال
ـالنساء والولدان, وتفرقوا ايدي سبا,
ـتمزقوا كل ممزق, واقتسموا النساء ايضًا,

(And this was a frightful day on account of the amount of wailing for the men, women and children, and they separated the captives and tore to pieces all that could be torn, and they divided the women as well.)

واصبحت بخارى خاوية على عروشها كأن لم
تغن بالامس, وارتكبوا من النساء العظيم,
والناس ينظرون ويكون, ولا يستطيعون ان
يدفعوا عن انفسهم شيئًا مما نزل بهم,

(And Bokhara became desolated, on her palaces, as if she were not happy only yesterday, and they did enormously evil things to the women while the men watched and cried; and they could not cast away anything from what befell them.)

و واصبحت بخارى خاوية, على عروشها,
وارتكب التتار من الفساد العظيم والناس
ينظرون اليهم ولا يستطيعون ردهم.

(And Bokhara became desolated, on her palaces, and the Tatars committed enormously wicked actions, and the people watched them and could not repel them.)

فمنهم من لم يرض بذلك, واختار الموت على
ذلك, فقاتل حتى قُتل, وممن فعل ذلك
واختار ان يُقتل ولا يرى ما نزل بالمسلمين,
الفقيه الامام ركن الدين امام زاده وولده,
فانهما لما رايا ما يُفعل بالحُرَم قاتلا حتى قُتلا.
وكذلك فعل القاضي صدر الدين خان,

(And there were among them such that were not content with that and chose death instead and fought until they were killed; and of those who did so and chose to fight and not to see what befell the Muslims was the jurist the *imam* Rukn al-Dīn Imām Zāda and his child. And when the two of them saw what was done with the women, they fought until they were killed. And the *qāḍī* Ṣadr al-Dīn Khān did likewise.)

فمن[ه]م من لم يرض بذلك واختار الموت
وقاتل حتى قتل,

(And there were among them such that were not content with that and fought until they were killed.)

ومن استلم أُخذ أسيرًا,

(And those who gave themselves up were taken as captives.)

ومنهم من استسلم وأسر.

(And there were among them who gave themselves up and were taken as captives.)

والقوا النار في البلد والمدارس والمساجد وعذبوا الناس بانواع العذاب في طلب الاموال.

(And they put the city to flames, and the *madaris* and the mosques, and tortured the people with various types of torture in their quest for money.)

والقوا النار قي البلد، والمدارس، والمساجد، وعذبوا الناس بانواع العذاب في طلب المال.

(And they put the city to flames, and the *madaris* and the mosques, and tortured the people with various types of torture in their quest for money.)

THE CAPTURE OF SAMARQAND

النويري (Nuwayrī)

فلما كان في اليوم الرابع نودي في البلد أن يخرج اهله باجمعهم ومن تأخر قتلوه، فخرج جميع من به من الرجال والنساء والصبيان، ففعلوا مع أهل سمرقند كفعلهم مع اهل بخارا من النهب والقتل والسبي والفساد، ونهبوا ما في البلد، ثم احرقوا الجامع وتركوا البلد على حاله،

(And in the fourth day it was proclaimed in town that its inhabitants should get out all, and he who delayed was killed. And all who were in it got out—men, women and boys—and they did to the people of Samarqand as they did to the people of Bokhara: plunder, killing, captivity, and corrupt actions. And they plundered what was in the city and set fire to the mosque and left the city as it was.)

ابن الاثير (Ibn al-Athīr)

فلما كان اليوم الرابع نادوا في البلد أن يخرج اهله جميعهم، ومن تأخر قتلوه، فخرج جميع الرجال والنساء والصبيان، ففعلوا مع أهل سمرقند مثل فعلهم مع اهل بخارى من النهب، والقتل، والسبي، والفساد، ودخلوا البلد فنهبوا ما فيه، واحرقوا الجامع وتركوا باقي البلد على حاله،

(And in the fourth day they called in the city that all its inhabitants should get out, and he who delayed was killed. And all the men and women and boys went out. And they did to the people of Samarqand as they did to the people of Bokhara: plunder, killing, captivity, and corrupt actions. And they entered the city and plundered what was in it and set fire to the mosque and left the rest of the city as it was.)

وافتضوا الأبكار, وعذبوا الناس بانواع
العذاب في طلب المال, وقتلوا من لم يصلح
للسبي,

(And they deflowered the virgins
and tortured the people with various types of torture in their quest
for money and killed those who
were unfit for captivity.)

و ذلك في المحرم سنة سبع عشرة وستمائة.   وكان ذلك في المحرم سنة سبع عشرة
وستمائة.

(And this [happened] in [the
month of] *Muḥarram* of the year
617.)[1]

(And this was in [the month of]
Muḥarram of the year 617.)[2]

1. Al-Nuwayrī, *Nihāyat al-arab fī funūn al-adab*, ed. Saʿīd ʿĀshūr (Cairo, 1985),
27:308–9 (Bokhara), 311 (Samarqand).
2. Ibn al-Athīr, *Al-kāmil fī al-taʾrīkh*, ed. Carl J. Tornberg (corrected edition) (Beirut,
1966[1851–1876]), 12:366–68.

APPENDIX SIX
THE JACQUERIE FROM
THE NOBLES' VIEWPOINT

JEAN LE BEL	JEAN FROISSART	RAOUL TAINGUY
Ainsy ces gens assamblez sans chief ardoient et roboient tout et murdrissoient gentilz hommes et nobles femmes, et leurs enfans, et violoient dames et puchielles sans misericorde quelconques.	Et ces mescheans gens assamblés, sans chiés et sans armeures, reuboient et ardoient tout, et occioient tous gentilz hommes que il trouvoient, et efforçoient toutes dames et pucelles, sans pité et sans merci, ensi comme chiens esragiés.	Et ces meschans gens, assemblez sans chief et sans nulles armeures, roboient et ardoient tout et tuoient et efforçoient et violoient toutes dames et damoiselles et toutes pucelles, sanz nulle pitié ne merci, ainsi comme chiens enrragiez et forsennez.
Certes entre les crestiens ne serrasins n'avint oncques rage si desordonée ni si dyablesse, car qui plus faisoit de maulx et de vilains faiz, telx maulx que seulement creature humaine ne les debvroit penser sans honte et vergongne, il estoit le	Certes, onques n'avint entre crestiiens ne Sarrasins tèle forsenerie que ces meschans gens faisoient; car qui plus faisoit de maus ou plus de villains fais, telz fais que creature humainne ne deveroit oser penser, aviser ne regarder,	Certes onques n'avint entre Juifs ne Sarrazins tèle rage ne forsennerie que ces gens faisoient, ne qui plus feissent de maulx et de plus villains et detestables faiz et inconvenables qu'ilz faisoient aux dames, damoiselles et pucelles. Et pour ce m'en tais-je,

plus grand maistre. Je n'oseroie escrire ne raconter les horribles faiz ne les inconveniens que faisoient aux dames.

cilz estoit li plusprisiés entre yaus et li plus grans mestres. Je n'oseroie escrire ne raconter les horribles fais et inconvignables que il faisoient as dames.

car j'auroie grant horreur du raconter; ne il n'est nul homme qui n'eust grant horreur et grant abhominacion de veoir les villains et detestables atouchemens qu'ilz faisoient sodomitement et desordoneement contre les dames et damoiselles. Et cellui qui le plus en faisoit entr'eulx, estoit le plus prisié et le plus grant maistre entre eulx.

mais, entre les aultres deshonnestes faiz, ilz tuerent ung chevalier et le mirent en haste et le rostirent, voyant la dame et les enfans.

Mès, entre les aultres ordenances et villains fais, il tuerent un chevalier et boutèrent en un hastier, et tournèrent au feu et le rostirent, voiant la dame et ses enfans.

Mais, entre les autres desordonnances et villains faiz qu'ilz firent, ilz tuèrent un autre chevalier que cellui dont j'ay ci devant parlé, et le mistrent en une broche, et puis le tournèrent au feu et le rostirent devant la dame et ses enfans,

Apres ce que X ou XII eurent enforcié la dame, il luy en voulurent faire mengier par force, pui ilz le firent morir de male mort.[1]

Apriès ce que dix ou douze eurent la dame efforcie et violée, il les en vorrent faire mengier par force, et puis les fisent morir de male mort.[2]

tout après ce que dix ou douze orent la dame sa femme violée et efforcée. Et puis après cestes mauvaises iniquitez, ils en vouldrent à la dame faire mengier par force, et aussi à ces douze villains tuffes qui la dicte dame avoient

efforciée, si comme j'ay
dit, pour eulx acharner
tousjours plus à tèles
cruaultez faire, mais ilz
n'en vouldrent onques
mangier; et pour ce les
autres villains tuffez et
guieliers les tuèrent et
firent mourir de vil-
laine mort.[3]

1. Jean le Bel, *Chroniques*, ed. Jules Viard and Eugène Déprez (Paris, 1895), 257.

2. Jean Froissart, *Chroniques* 1:413, ed. Siméon Luce (Paris, 1876), 5:100.

3. Cited in an appendix to Luce, *Histoire de la Jacquerie* (Paris, 1894), 338–42 (from University of Leiden, fonds Vossius, French manuscript no. 9, ff. 228–29).

GLOSSARY OF LATIN TERMS

atrocitas	brutality, savagery, atrocity
clementia	mercy, clemency
crudelis	cruel
crudelitas	cruelty
feritas	ferocity, brutality
furor	frenzy, madness
imhumanus	inhuman, barbarous
immanis	brutal, savage
ira	wrath, anger
justitia	justice
misericordia	pity, compassion, mercy
passio (pl. passiones)	passion, martyrdom (of a saint)
saevire	to be cruel
saevitia	savagery, cruelty
severitas	severity (in judgment)
tyrannus	tyrant

SELECTED BIBLIOGRAPHY

Algazi, Gadi. "The Social Use of Private War: Some Late Medieval Views Reviewed," *Tel Aviver Jahrbuch für deutsche Geschichte* 22 (1993): 253–73.

Anna, Luigi de. "Elogio della crudeltà. Aspetti della violenza nel mondo antico e medievale," in *Crudelitas: The Politics of Cruelty in the Ancient and Medieval World.* Edited by Toivo Viljamaa, Asko Timonen, and Christian Krötzl, 81–113. Krems, 1992.

Aron, Raymond. *Peace and War.* Translated by Richard Howard and Anette Baker Fox. London, 1966[1962].

Auerbach, Erich. *Literary Language and its Public in Late Latin Antiquity and in the Middle Ages.* Translated by Ralph Manheim. London, 1965[1958].

—. *Mimesis.* Translated by Willard R. Trask. Princeton, N.J., 1953[1946].

Al-Azmeh, Aziz. "Barbarians in Arab Eyes," *Past and Present* 134 (1992): 3–18.

Baker, Denise N. *Julian of Norwich's 'Showings.'* Princeton, N.J., 1994.

Bakhtin, Mikhail. *Rabelais and His World.* Translated by Hélène Iswolsky. Bloomington, Ind., 1984[1965].

Baraz, Daniel. "Seneca, Ethics, and the Body—The Treatment of Cruelty in Medieval Thought," *Journal of the History of Ideas* 59:2 (1998): 195–215.

Baraz, Michaël. *L'être et la connaissance selon Montaigne.* Paris, 1968.

Bartlett, Robert. *The Making of Europe.* Princeton, N.J., 1993.

Bisson, Thomas N. "The 'Feudal Revolution,'" *Past and Present* 142 (1994): 6–42.

—. *Tormented Voices.* Cambridge, Mass., 1998.

Blomme, Robert. *La doctrine du péché dans les écoles théologiques de la première moitié du XIIe siècle.* Louvain, 1958.

Bloomer, W. Martin. *Valerius Maximus & the Rhetoric of the New Nobility.* Chapel Hill, N.C., 1992.

Bloomfield, Morton W. *The Seven Deadly Sins.* East Lansing, Mich., 1952.

Bonnassie, Pierre. "Consommation d'aliments immondes et cannibalisme de survie dans l'Occident du Haut Moyen Age," *Annales E.S.C.* 44:5 (1989): 1035–56.

Boswell, John. *Christianity, Social Tolerance, and Homosexuality.* Chicago, 1980.

Bosworth, Joseph and Thomas N. Toller. *An Anglo-Saxon Dictionary.* London, 1898.

Bowersock, Glen W. *Martyrdom and Rome.* Cambridge, 1995.

Boyle, John A. "The Death of the Last Abbasid Caliph: A Contemporary Muslim Account," *Journal of Semitic Studies* 6 (1961): 145–61.

Brandt, William J. *The Shape of Medieval History*. New Haven, Conn., 1966.

Breisach, Ernst. *Historiography*. Chicago, 1983.

Brown, Peter. "Eastern and Western Christendom in Late Antiquity. Parting of the Ways," in *The Orthodox Churches and the West*. Edited by Derek Baker, 1–24. Oxford, 1976.

—. *The Body and Society*. New York, 1988.

Brundage, James A. *Law, Sex, and Christian Society in Medieval Europe*. Chicago, 1987.

Brunel, Clovis. "David d'Ashby auteur méconnu des *Faits des Tartares*," *Romania* 79 (1958): 39–46.

Budge, Ernest A. Wallis. Introduction to Bar Hebraeus, *Chronography*. Translated by E. A. Wallis Budge. Amsterdam, 1976[1932].

Burckhardt, Jacob. *The Civilization of the Renaissance in Italy*. Translated by S. G. C. Middlemore. New York, 1965.

Callu, Jean-Pierre. "Le jardin des supplices au Bas-Empire," in *Du châtiment dans la cité*, 315–55. Rome, 1984.

Carlton, Eric. *Massacres: An Historical Perspective*. Aldershot, 1994.

Cazelles, Raymond. "La Jacquerie fut-elle un mouvement paysan?," *Comptes rendus de l'Academie des Inscriptions et Belles-lettres* (1978): 654–66.

Certeau, Michel de. "Le lieu de l'autre. Montaigne: 'Des Cannibales,'" in *Le racisme: mythes et sciences*. Edited by Maurice Olender, 187–200. Brussels, 1981.

Chatman, Seymour. *Story and Discourse*. Ithaca, 1978.

Chazan, Robert. "The Deteriorating Image of the Jews—Twelfth and Thirteenth Centuries," in *Christendom and Its Discontents*. Edited by Scott L. Waugh and Peter D. Diehl, 220–33. Cambridge, 1996.

—. "Twelfth Century Perceptions of the Jews: A Case Study of Bernard of Clairvaux and Peter the Venerable," in *From Witness to Witchcraft: Jews and Judaism in Medieval Christian Thought*. Edited by Jeremy Cohen, 187–201. Wiesbaden, 1996.

Christys, Ann. *Christians in al-Andalus 711–c. 1000*. Richmond, Surrey, 2002.

Cockburn, J. S. "Patterns of Violence in English Society: Homicide in Kent 1560–1985," *Past and Present* 130 (1991): 70–106.

Cohen, Esther. "Towards a History of European Physical Sensibility: Pain in the Later Middle Ages," *Science in Context* 8:1 (1995): 47–74.

Cohen, Jeremy. "The Jews as the Killers of Christ in the Latin Tradition, from Augustine to the Friars," *Traditio* 39 (1983): 1–27.

Coleman, K. M. "Fatal Charades: Roman Executions Staged as Mythological Enactments," *Journal of Roman Studies* 80 (1990): 44–73.

Colin, Gérard. "Le Synaxaire Ethiopien: état actuel de la question," *Analecta Bollandiana* 106 (1988): 273–317.

Constable, Giles. "The Second Crusade as Seen by Contemporaries," *Traditio* 9 (1953): 213–79.

Coope, Jessica A. "Religious and Cultural Conversion to Islam in Ninth-Century Umayyad Córdoba," *Journal of World History* 4 (1993): 47–68.

—. *The Martyrs of Córdoba: Community and Family Conflict in an Age of Mass Conversion*. Lincoln, Neb., 1995.

Corbin, Alain. *Le village des cannibales*. Paris, 1990.

Cottingham, John. "Punishment and Respect for Persons," in *Law, Morality and Rights*. Edited by Michael A. Stewart, 423–31. Dordrecht, Holland, 1979.

Coupland, Simon. "The Rod of God's Wrath or the People of God's Wrath? The Carolingian Theology of the Viking Invasions," *Journal of Ecclesiastical History* 42:4 (1991): 535–54.

Crouzet, Denis. *Les guerriers de Dieu*. Paris, 1990.

Darnton, Robert. *The Great Cat Massacre and other Episodes in French Cultural History*. New York, 1984.

Davies, Brian. *The Thought of Thomas Aquinas*. Oxford, 1992.

Deferrari, Roy J. and James M. Campbell. *A Concordance of Prudentius*. Hildesheim, Germany, 1966.

Delehaye, Hippolyte. "S. Romain martyr d'Antioche," *Analecta Bollandiana* 50 (1932): 241–83.

—. *Les passions des martyres et les genres littéraires*. Brussels, 1966[1921].

Donaldson, Ian. *The Rapes of Lucretia*. Oxford, 1982.

Dossat, Yves. "La croisade vue par les chroniqueurs," *Cahiers de Fanjeaux* 4 (1969): 221–59.

Drees, Clayton J. "Sainthood and Suicide: The Motives of the Martyrs of Córdoba, A.D. 850–859," *Journal of Medieval and Renaissance Studies* 20:1 (1990): 59–89.

Dubois, Jacques. *Les martyrologes du Moyen Age latin*. Turnhout, Belgium, 1978.

Duggan, Anne. *Thomas Becket: A Textual History of His Letters*. Oxford, 1980.

Edgerton, Samuel Y. Jr. *Pictures and Punishment*. Ithaca, 1985.

Effros, Bonnie. "Usuard's Journey to Spain and Its Influence on the Dissemination of the Cult of the Cordovan Martyrs," *Comitatus* 21 (1990): 21–37.

Einarsson, Bjarni. "*De Normannorum atrocitate*, or on the Execution of Royalty by the Aquiline Method," *Saga-Book* 22:1 (1986): 79–82.

Einarsson, Bjarni and Roberta Frank. "The Blood-Eagle Once More: Two Notes," *Saga-Book* 23:1 (1990): 80–83.

Elias, Norbert. *The Civilizing Process*. Translated by Edmund Jephcott. New York, 1978[1939].

Enders, Jody. *The Medieval Theater of Cruelty: Rhetoric, Memory, Violence*. Ithaca, 1999.

Evans, Gillian R. *Bernard of Clairvaux*. Oxford, 2000.

—. *Augustine on Evil*. Cambridge, 1991[1982].

Febvre, Lucien P. "La sensibilité et l'histoire: comment reconstituer la vie affective d'autrefois," *Annales d'histoire sociale* 3 (1941): 5–20.

Finke, Laurie A. and Martin B. Shichtman, eds. *Medieval Texts and Contemporary Readers*. Ithaca, 1987.

Fiorelli, Piero. *La tortura giudiziaria nel diritto comune*. Milan, 1953–54.

Foot, Sarah. "Violence against Christians? The Vikings and the Church in Ninth-Century England," *Medieval History* 1:3 (1991): 3–16.

Foucault, Michel. *Moi, Pierre Rivière, ayant égorgé ma mère, ma soeur et mon frère . . .* Paris, 1973.

—. *Surveiller et punir.* Paris, 1975.

Fouracre, Paul. "Merovingian History and Merovingian Hagiography," *Past and Present* 127 (1990): 3–38.

Fox, Michael. "'Animal Liberation': A Critique," *Ethics* 88 (1978): 106–18.

Frank, Roberta. "Viking Atrocity and Skaldic Verse: The Rite of the Blood-Eagle," *English Historical Review* 99 (1984): 332–43.

—. "The Blood-Eagle Again," *Saga-Book* 22:5 (1988): 287–89.

Freedman, Paul. "The Evolution of Servile Peasants in Hungary and in Catalonia: A Comparison," *Anuario de Estudios Medievales* 26 (1996): 909–32.

—. *Images of the Medieval Peasant.* Stanford, Calif., 1999.

—. "The Medieval 'Other': The Middle Ages as 'Other,'" in *Marvels, Monsters, and Miracles: Studies in the Medieval and Early Modern Imagination.* Edited by Timothy S. Jones and David A. Sprunger, 1–24. Kalamazoo, Mich., 1999.

—. *The Origins of the Peasant Servitude in Medieval Catalonia.* Cambridge, 1991.

—. "Peasant Anger in the Late Middle Ages," in *Anger's Past: The Social Uses of an Emotion in the Middle Ages.* Edited by Barbara H. Rosenwein, 171–88. Ithaca, 1998.

Freeman, Michael D. A. "Retributivism and the Death Sentence," in *Law, Morality and Rights.* Edited by Michael A. Stewart, 405–22. Dordrecht, Holland, 1979.

Frend, William H. C. *The Rise of Christianity.* London, 1984.

Freud, Sigmund. "Thoughts for the Times on War and Death," in *The Standard Edition of the Complete Psychological Works of Sigmund Freud.* Vol. 14. Translated by James Strachey, 275–300. London, 1957[1915].

—. "Three Essays on the Theory of Sexuality," in *The Standard Edition of the Complete Psychological Works of Sigmund Freud.* Vol. 7. Translated by James Strachey, 123–243. London, 1953[1905,1920].

Friedrich, Hugo. *Montaigne.* Translated by Dawn Eng. Berkeley, Calif., 1991 [1967,1949].

Geertz, Clifford. *The Interpretation of Cultures.* New York, 1973.

—. *Local Knowledge.* New York, 1983.

Genette, Gerard. *Narrative Discourse.* Ithaca, 1980[1972].

Gerstein, Robert S. "Capital Punishment—'Cruel and Unusual'?: A Retributivist Response," *Ethics* 85 (1974): 75–79.

Gilson, Etienne. *The Philosophy of St. Thomas Aquinas.* Translated by Edward Bullough. New York, 1929[1924].

—. *The History of Christian Philosophy in the Middle Ages.* New York, 1955.

Goffart, Walter. *The Narrators of Barbarian History.* Princeton, N.J., 1988.

Goitein, Shlomo D. "Glimpses from the Cairo Geniza on Naval Warfare in the Mediterranean and on the Mongol Invasion," in *Studi orientalistici in onore di Giorgio Levi Della Vida.* Vol. 1, 393–408. Rome, 1956.

Gow, Andrew C. *The Red Jews.* Leiden, 1995.

Gradval, Kathryn. "Chrétien de Troyes, Gratian, and the Medieval Romance of Sexual Violence," *Signs* 17:3 (1992): 558–85.

Griffin, Miriam T. *Seneca—A Philosopher in Politics*. Oxford, 1976.

Gurevich, Aron I. *Medieval Popular Culture*. Cambridge, 1988[1981].

Guzman, Gregory G. "Reports of Mongol Cannibalism in the Thirteenth-Century Latin Sources: Oriental Fact or Western Fiction?" in *Discovering New Worlds*. Edited by Scott D. Westrem, 31–68. New York, 1991.

Hacking, Ian. *The Emergence of Probability*. Cambridge, 1975.

—. "From the Emergence of Probability to the Erosion of Determinism," in *Probabilistic Thinking, Thermodynamics and the Interaction of the History and Philosophy of Science*. Vol. 2. Edited by Jaakko Hintikka, David C. Gruender, and Evandro Agazzi, 105–23. Dordrecht, Holland, 1981.

Hald, Anders. *A History of Probability and Statistics and Their Applications before 1750*. New York, 1990.

Halkin, Leon-Ernest. "Hagiographie protestante," *Analecta Bollandiana* 68 (1950): 453–63.

Hallie, Philip P. *The Paradox of Cruelty*. Middletown, Conn., 1969.

Halperin, Charles J. *The Tatar Yoke*. Columbus, Ohio, 1985.

Halsall, Guy. "Playing by Whose Rules? A Further Look at Viking Atrocity in the Ninth Century," *Medieval History* 2:2 (1992): 2–12.

Hartog, François. *The Mirror of Herodotus: The Representation of the Other in the Writing of History*. Translated by Janet Lloyd. Berkeley, Calif., 1988[1980].

Hay, Denys. *Annalists and Historians*. London, 1977.

Helmholz, Richard H. *Marriage Litigation in Medieval England*. Cambridge, 1974.

Hogg, Michael and Dominic Abrams. *Social Identifications*. London, 1988.

Hornstein, Harvey A. *Cruelty and Kindness—A New Look at Aggression and Altruism*. Englewood Cliffs, N.J., 1976.

Horowitz, Maryanne C. *Seeds of Virtue and Knowledge*. Princeton, N.J., 1998.

Hsia, Ronnie Po-Chia. *The Myth of Ritual Murder*. New Haven, Conn., 1988.

—. *Trent 1475*. New Haven, Conn., 1992.

Huizinga, Johan. *The Autumn of the Middle Ages*. Translated by Rodney J. Payton and Ulrich Mammitzsch. Chicago, 1996[1924].

Irving, Thomas B. "Peter the Cruel and Ibn Khaldun," *Islamic Literature* 11 (1959): 5–17.

Iser, Wolfgang. *The Implied Reader*. Baltimore, 1974[1972].

Islam, Syed M. "Marco Polo: Order/Disorder in the Discourse of the Other," *Literature and History* 2:1 (1993): 1–22.

Jauss, Hans R. *Toward an Aesthetic of Reception*. Minneapolis, 1982[1970].

Kagay, Donald J. and L. J. Andrew Villalon, eds. *The Final Argument: The Imprint of Violence on Society in Medieval and Early Modern Europe*. Rochester, N.Y., 1998.

Kappler, Claude C. "L'image des Mongols dans le *Speculum historiale* de Vincent de Beauvais," in *Vincent de Beauvais: intentions et réceptions d'une oeuvre encyclopédique au Moyen Age*. Edited by Monique Paulmier-Foucart, Serge Lusignan, and Alain Nadeau, 219–40. Paris, 1990.

Kedar, Benjamin Z. *Crusade and Mission*. Princeton, N.J., 1984.

Kellert, Stephen R. and Alan R. Felthous. "Childhood Cruelty toward Animals among Criminals and Noncriminals," *Human Relations* 38:12 (1985): 1113–29.

Kelly, Henry A. *Ideas and Forms of Tragedy from Aristotle to the Middle Ages*. Cambridge, 1993.

—. "Meanings and Uses of *Raptus* in Chaucer's Time," *Studies in the Age of Chaucer* 20 (1998): 101–65.

Kenny, Anthony. *Aquinas on Mind*. London, 1993.

Kraemer, Joel L. "Apostates, Rebels, and Brigands," *Israel Oriental Studies* 10 (1980): 34–73.

Langmuir, Gavin I. "The Tortures of the Body of Christ," in *Christendom and Its Discontents*. Edited by Scott L. Waugh and Peter D. Diehl, 287–309. Cambridge, 1996.

—. *Towards a Definition of Antisemitism*. Berkeley, Calif., 1990.

Lindkvist, Thomas. "The Politics of Violence and the Transition from Viking Age to Medieval Scandinavia," in *Crudelitas: The Politics of Cruelty in the Ancient and Medieval World*. Edited by Toivo Viljamaa, Asko Timonen, and Christian Krötzl, 139–47. Krems, 1992.

Lintott, Andrew. "Cruelty in the Political Life of the Ancient World," in *Crudelitas: The Politics of Cruelty in the Ancient and Medieval World*. Edited by Toivo Viljamaa, Asko Timonen, and Christian Krötzl, 9–27. Krems, 1992.

Loades, David. "John Foxe and the Traitors: The Politics of the Marian Persecution," in *Martyrs and Martyrologies*. Edited by Diana Wood, 231–44. Oxford, 1993.

Long, Thomas A. "Capital Punishment—'Cruel and Unusual'?," *Ethics* 83:3 (1973): 214–23.

Luce, Siméon. *Histoire de la Jacquerie*. Paris, 1894.

Marsden, John. *The Fury of the Normans*. New York, 1993.

Martellotti, Guido. "La questione dei due Seneca da Petrarca a Benvenuto," *Italia medioevale e umanistica* 15 (1972): 149–69.

Martens, Francis. "Le miroir du meurtre ou la synagogue dévoilée," in *Le racisme— mythes et sciences*. Edited by Maurice Olender and Pierre Birnbaum, 61–73. Brussels, 1981.

McCulloh, John M. "Jewish Ritual Murder: William of Norwich, Thomas of Monmouth, and the Early Dissemination of the Myth," *Speculum* 72:3 (1997): 698–740.

McKeon, Peter R. *Hincmar of Laon and Carolingian Politics*. Urbana, Ill., 1978.

McKinnon, Christine. "Ways of Wrong-Doing, the Vices, and Cruelty," *Journal of Value Inquiry* 23 (1989): 319–35.

Medeiros, Marie-Thérèse de. *Jacques et chroniqueurs*. Paris, 1979.

Mellinkoff, Ruth. *Oucasts: Signs of Otherness in Northern European Art of the Late Middle Ages*. Berkeley, Calif., 1993.

Meyuhas-Ginio, Alisa. "'The Fortress of Faith' at the End of the West: Alonso de Espina and his *Fortalitium Fidei*," in *Proceedings of the Tenth World Congress of Jewish Studies*, Division B. Vol. 1, 101–8 (in Hebrew). Jerusalem, 1989.

—. "The Expulsion of the Jews from the Kingdom of France in the Fourteenth Century and its Significance as Viewed by Alonso (Alfonso) de Espina, Author of *Fortalitium fidei*" (in Hebrew), *Michael* 12 (1991): 67–82.

Miller, William Ian. *Humiliation*. Ithaca, 1993.

Miola, Robert S. *Shakespeare and Classical Tragedy*. Oxford, 1992.

Moore, Robert Ian. *The Formation of a Persecuting Society*. Oxford, 1987.

—. "Anti-Semitism and the Birth of Europe," in *Christianity and Judaism*. Edited by Diana Wood, 33–57. Oxford, 1992.

Murphy, Jeffrie G. "Cruel and Unusual Punishments," in *Law, Morality and Rights*. Edited by Michael A. Stewart, 373–404. Dordrecht, Holland, 1979.

Münster, Sebastian. *Cosmographia*. Basel, 1550.

Nersessian, Sirarpie Der. "The Armenian Chronicle of the Constable Smpad or of the 'Royal Historian,'" *Dumbarton Oaks Papers* 13 (1959): 141–68.

Ocker, Christopher. "Ritual Murder and the Subjectivity of Christ: A Choice in Medieval Christianity," *Harvard Theological Review* 91:2 (1998): 153–92.

Olsen, Birger Munk. *L'étude des auteurs classiques latins aux XIe et XIIe siècles*. Paris, 1985.

Paden, William D. "Rape in the Pastourelle," *Romanic Review* 80:3 (1989): 331–49.

Page, Raymod I. "'A Most Vile People': Early English Historians on the Vikings." Dorothea Coke Memorial Lecture in Northern Studies, 19 March 1986. London, 1987.

Palmer, John J. N. Introduction to *Froissart: Historian*. Edited by John J. N. Palmer. Woodbridge, Suffolk, 1981.

Passmore, John. "The Treatment of Animals," *Journal of the History of Ideas* 36 (1975): 195–218.

Perrens, François T. *Étienne Marcel*. Paris, 1874.

Peters, Edward M. "*Crimen exceptum:* The History of an Idea," in *Proceedings of the Tenth International Congress of Medieval Canon Law*, 137–94. Vatican City, 2001.

—. *Torture*. New York, 1985.

Petroff, Elizabeth A. "Eloquence and Heroic Virginity in Hrotsvit's Verse Legends," in *Hrotsvit of Gandersheim: Rara Avis in Saxonia*. Edited by Katharina M. Wilson. Ann Arbor, Mich., 1987.

Primoratz, Igor. *Justifying Legal Punishment*. Atlantic Highlands, N.J., 1989.

Quentin, Henry. *Les martyrologes historiques du moyen âge*. Paris, 1908.

Regan, Tom. "Cruelty, Kindness, and Unnecessary Suffering," *Philosophy* 55 (1980): 532–41.

Reynolds, Leighton D. "The Medieval Tradition of Seneca's *Dialogues*," *Classical Quarterly* 18:2 (1968): 355–72.

Riley-Smith, Jonathan. *The First Crusade and the Idea of Crusading*. London, 1986.

Rimmon-Kenan, Shlomith. *Narrative Fiction*. London, 1983.

Roccas, Sonia and Shalom H. Schwartz. "Effects of Intergroup Similarity on Intergroup Relations," *European Journal of Social Psychology* 23 (1993): 581–95.

Rodriguez-Monino, Antonio, ed. *Las fuentes del Romancero General*. Madrid, 1957.

Rosen, Carol C. "The Language of Cruelty in Ford's *'Tis Pity She's a Whore*," in *Drama in the Renaissance*. Edited by Clifford Davidson, C. J. Gianakaris, and John H. Stroupe, 315–27. New York, 1986.

Rouse, Richard H. "The *A* Text of Seneca's Tragedies in the Thirteenth Century," *Revue d'histoire des textes* 1 (1971): 93–121.

—. "New Light on the Circulation of the *A* Text of Seneca's Tragedies," *Journal of the Warburg and Courtauld Institute* 40 (1977): 283–86.

Rubin, Miri. *Gentile Tales: The Narrative Assault on Late Medieval Jews*. New Haven, Conn., 1999.

—. "Desecration of the Host: The Birth of an Accusation," in *Christianity and Judaism*. Edited by Diana Wood, 169–85. Oxford, 1992.

Ruiz, Teofilo F. "Violence in Late Medieval Castile: The Case of the Rioja," *Revista de História* 133 (1995): 15–36.

Sawyer, Peter H. *The Age of the Vikings*. London, 1962.

—. *Kings and Vikings: Scandinavia and Europe A.D. 700–1100*. London, 1982.

Seager, Robin. *Ammianus Marcellinus*. Columbia, Mo., 1986.

Shapiro, Barbara J. *Probability and Certainty in Seventeenth-Century England*. Princeton, N.J., 1983.

Shaw, Brent D. "'Eaters of Flesh, Drinkers of Milk': The Ancient Mediterranean Ideology of the Pastoral Nomad," *Ancient Society* 12 (1982): 5–31.

—. "The Passion of Perpetua," *Past and Present* 139 (1993): 3–45.

Shklar, Judith N. *Ordinary Vices*. Cambridge, Mass., 1984.

Siberry, Elizabeth. *Criticism of Crusading 1095–1274*. Oxford, 1985.

Steintrager, James A. "Perfectly Inhuman: Moral Monstrosity in Eighteenth-Century Discourse," *Eighteenth-Century Life* 21.2 (1997) 114–32.

Stroumsa, Guy G. *Savoir et salut*. Paris, 1992.

Stull, William L. "'This Metamorphosde Tragoedie': Thomas Kyd, Cyril Tourneur, and the Jacobean Theatre of Cruelty," *Ariel* 14 (1983): 35–49.

Sweeney, James R. "Thomas of Spalato and the Mongols: A Thirteenth-Century Dalmatian View of Mongol Customs," *Florilegium* 4 (1982): 156–83.

Tajfel, Henri. "Social Identity and Intergroup Behaviour," *Social Science Information* 13 (1974): 65–93.

Tambiah, Stanley J. *Buddhism Betrayed*. Chicago, 1992.

Tattersall, Jill. "Anthropofagi and Eaters of Raw Flesh in French Literature of the Crusade Period: Myth, Tradition, and Reality," *Medium Aevum* 57:2 (1988): 240–53.

Timonen, Asko. "Saint Olaf's 'cruelty': Violence by the Scandinavian King Interpreted over the Centuries," *Journal of Medieval History* 22 (1996): 285–96.

Vauchez, André. *La sainteté en Occident aux derniers siècles du Moyen Age*. Rome, 1988.

Wabuda, Susan. "Henry Bull, Miles Coverdale, and the Making of Foxe's *Book of Martyrs*," in *Martyrs and Martyrologies*. Edited by Diana Wood, 245–58. Oxford, 1993.

Wallace-Hadrill, John M. *The Vikings in Francia*. Reading, 1975.

Watling, E. F. "Introduction" to *Seneca - Four Tragedies and Octavia*. Harmondsworth, 1966.

Wetzel, James. *Augustine and the Limits of Virtue*. Cambridge, 1992.

Wilson, Katharina M. *Hrotsvit of Gandersheim: The Ethics of Authorial Stance*. Leiden, 1988.

Wolf, Kenneth B. *Christian Martyrs in Muslim Spain*. Cambridge, 1988.

Wolfthal, Diane B. "'A Hue and Cry': Medieval Rape Imagery and its Transformation," *Art Bulletin* 75:1 (1993): 39–64.

Wright, Quincy. *A Study of War*. Chicago, 1942.

Yuval, Israel J. "Vengeance and Damnation, Blood and Defamation: From Jewish Martyrdom to Blood Libel Accusations" (in Hebrew), *Zion* 58:1 (1993): 33–90.

Zwierlein, Otto. "Spuren der Tragoedien Senecas bei Bernardus Silvestris, Petrus Pictor und Marbod von Rennes," *Mittellateinisches Jahrbuch* 22 for 1987(1989): 171–96.

INDEX

Ibn al-Athīr, 106–7, 108, 109, 111, 112, 114, 117
Ibn Khaldūn, 114, 133
imitatio Christi, 78, 140. *See also* mysticism
implied audience. *See* reader-response criticism
Indians (native population of the New World), 12, 143, 145, 157, 168–72
Inquisition, 27, 101, 176
intentions. *See* ethics
Irenaeus, martyr, 37
Ivo of Narbonne, 96, 98

Jacquerie, 124–31, 136, 142
Jean le Bel, 127–30 passim
Jerome, 2–3, 15, 17–18, 19, 24, 27, 35, 74, 178
Jews, 16, 24, 76, 81, 83, 84, 85, 89, 96, 97, 98, 113, 116, 121, 125, 128, 136, 140, 167, 175. *See also* blood libel accusations
John of Plano Carpini, 94, 99, 103, 108
John of Salisbury, 81–83 passim, 124
Julian of Norwich, 124, 137–40 passim
Juvaini, 106–10, 112, 113, 114, 118
Al-Jūzjānī, 109, 110, 112, 113, 116

Kempe, Margery, 140
Kirakos of Gandzak, 116, 119
Kyd, Thomas, 156

Lactantius, 33
Laib, Conrad, 175
Laurent de Premierfait, 153–54
Laurent, Frère, 75
Léry, Jean de, 12, 145, 167–74
Leudegar, Saint, bishop of Autun, 51–52, 57
Lindisfarne, Viking attack on, 64
Livre des vices et des vertus. See Laurent, Frère
López de Ayala, Pedro, 132–34
Lothar I, Frankish king, 49
Lucretia, 34, 35, 45
Lydgate, John, 144, 153–55

Al-Maqrīzī, 108, 113
Marcel, Étienne, provost of Paris merchants, 129–30, 143
martyrdom, 5, 11, 17–18, 29–30, 32, 34–46, 47, 48–59, 62, 68–72, 74, 76, 78–85, 117, 121, 123, 136–40, 144, 145–49, 152, 154, 158–67, 176, 178
martyrologies, 46, 48, 52, 55–58, 71, 117, 137, 144–45, 158–67, 176
Massacre of the Innocents, 175
Master Roger, 90, 92–93, 95, 101
Matthew Paris, 66–68, 73, 80, 91, 94, 96, 98–100, 102, 104, 111, 150, 171
Maxentius, Roman emperor, 44
Maximin, Roman emperor, 44
Meditationes vitae Christi. See pseudo-Bonaventure
Mongols, 3, 10–11, 41, 76, 89, 90–122, 123, 125, 126, 127, 128, 129, 131, 136, 146, 148, 150, 151, 152, 171, 175, 178, 179, 180
Montaigne, Michel Eyquem de, 7, 11, 13, 24–26, 28, 167–68, 169, 171, 173–74
Morellet, André, 27
Münster, Sebastian, 102, 144, 148, 150–52
Muslims, 3, 7, 11, 47, 48, 53–59, 60, 61, 62, 70, 71, 74, 76, 77, 81, 85, 86, 90, 91, 98, 103, 105–15, 116–20 passim, 123, 125, 132, 133, 134, 136, 164, 178, 180
Mussato, Albertino, 156
mysticism, 124, 136–42, 148, 179

narrative techniques, 38–39, 45, 73, 101, 110, 113, 117, 129, 137, 146–47, 152, 158, 160, 166
telling vs. *showing*, 44, 49, 50, 71, 72–73, 87, 136, 141, 150, 165
Natural Born Killers, 127
Nero, 14, 29, 30, 129, 153–54
Njal's Saga, 73
Notker the Stammerer (*Balbulus*), 56
Al-Nuwayrī, 106, 111–12

Oecolampadius, Johannes, 161
Orwell, George, 9
Osbern of Canterbury, 72
"other," 4, 5, 9, 11, 14, 29–35 passim, 41,
    46, 59–65 passim, 68–71 passim,
    74, 76, 77, 78, 81, 83–86, 90, 97,
    100, 102–5, 110, 114, 119, 121–22,
    123–26, 128, 130, 133, 136, 142,
    148, 150, 158, 161–64, 171, 175,
    176, 178–80. *See also* barbarians
Ovid, 11, 32, 45, 96, 121, 127, 175,
    177

passion of Christ, 5, 71, 78, 82–83, 121,
    124, 136–42, 144, 146, 148, 179.
    See also mysticism
Pedro I, king of Castile ("the Cruel"),
    12, 124, 132–36, 142
Pelagius, martyr, 58–59, 62
Peña, Francisco, 27
Peristephanon. See Prudentius, Aurelius
    Clemens
Perpetua, martyr, 35, 36, 38, 160
Peter Damian, 19
Peter of Vaux-de-Cernay, 1, 3, 8, 86–89,
    177, 180
Peter, Russian archbishop, 99, 100, 103
Petrarch, Franceso, 155
Phalaris, 14, 15, 19, 129
Phileas, martyr, 36, 37, 57, 129, 160
Philomela, 32, 156
Pietro Aretino, 144, 152
Pionius, martyr, 38
Plato, 9, 16, 22
Polycarp, martyr, 36
Ponce de Aubon, 96
Privity of the Passion, 137–38
probability, 173
Procne, 32, 127, 156
Prudentius, Aurelius Clemens, 40–42,
    47, 51, 59
pseudo-Bonaventure, 137, 139, 140

quantification, 167, 174–75

Rabanus Maurus, 52, 56–57
Raoul Tainguy, 127–28, 129, 151
rape. *See* sexual cruelty

Rashīd al-Dīn, 106, 109
reader-response criticism, 8, 38–39
Richard Rolle, 138
Romancero General, 135
Romanus, martyr, 51–52
Rufinus of Aquileia, 43–46, 57, 120

Sade, marquis de, 12
Schedel, Hartmann, 148–49
Scriptures, 4–5, 38, 42, 63, 65, 91, 105,
    119
Scythians, 5, 14, 30–31, 69, 72, 74, 97,
    121, 151–52, 165
Seneca, 7, 11, 13, 14, 16, 19, 21, 22, 23,
    24, 25, 26, 28, 29, 30, 32, 35, 44,
    153, 155–56, 177, 179
    De clementia, 14–15, 21, 25, 26, 75
    tragedies, 21, 26, 32, 96, 121, 127,
    155–56, 175, 177
sexual cruelty, 3, 12, 33, 35, 44–45, 46,
    58–59, 65, 68, 76, 94, 95–96,
    100–102 passim, 109, 122, 126–28,
    144, 153, 154, 156, 176
Shakespeare, William, 139, 153
Shlomo bar Shimshon, 77
showing. See narrative techniques
Sigebert of Gembloux, 62
Sigusmund, king of Burgundy, 48–49
Silence of the Lambs, 176
Simeon of Durham, 64–65, 70. *See also*
    Historia regum
Simon of Monfort, 1, 8, 86, 89, 177,
    180
Simon of St. Quentin, 94, 99, 100, 102,
    104, 115, 117, 118
Simon of Trent, 144, 145–49, 151, 167
Sixtus IV, pope, 148
Smpad, Armenian chronicler, 116, 119
Sophronia, 44–45
Stone, Oliver. *See Natural Born Killers*
style. *See* narrative techniques
Suetonius, 30
Synaxary, Coptic, 117

Tacitus, 30, 102, 178
telling. See narrative techniques
Tereus, king of Thracia, 32, 156
Tertullian, 17, 45

theodicy, 38, 141
Theudebert, son of Chilperic I, 50
Thomas Aquinas, 7, 13, 20–23, 24, 25,
  28, 103, 104, 124, 178
Thomas Becket, 76, 81–85, 179
Thomas of Monmouth, 79–80
Thomas of Spalato, 93–94, 101
Thyestes, 32, 96, 127
Tiberino, Giovanni Mattia, 144,
  146–49, 150, 167
Tractatus de indiciis & tortura, 27, 166
Tractatus de tormentis, 27, 166
Turks, 12, 89, 123, 145, 159–61, 162–64
  passim, 164–65, 166, 168, 169–70,
  172
tyranny, 10, 12, 15, 24, 29, 31, 32, 33,
  34, 35, 36, 42, 44–46 passim, 51,
  69, 70, 74, 75, 82, 87–88, 124,
  132–36, 142, 153–54, 156, 159,
  162–63, 167, 169, 171, 179

U.S. Constitution, 7
Usuard, 48, 54, 55–58 passim

Valerius Maximus, 30–32 passim, 41, 178
Vandals, 3, 33–34, 52, 60, 63, 65, 76, 90
Victor of Vita, 33–34, 39, 47, 57, 60, 65
Vikings, 3, 7, 11, 47, 48, 59–74, 76, 77,
  92, 95, 97, 113, 114, 117, 119, 123,
  127, 129, 131, 150, 178
vilain, 125, 127, 128
Vincent of Beauvais, 99, 104, 114, 137
Vulgata. See Scriptures

wars of religion, 24, 143, 144, 156–75,
  180
William FitzStephen, 83, 84
William of Norwich, 76, 78–80, 81, 121,
  144
William of Rubruck, 94, 66, 103
William of Tyre, 78